ID0875474

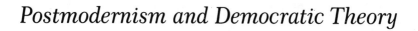

Postmodernism and Democratic Theory

Postmodernism
and
Democratic
Theory · ARYEH
BOTWINICK

T · TEMPLE UNIVERSITY PRESS   *Philadelphia*

Temple University Press, Philadelphia 19122
Copyright © 1993 by Temple University. All rights reserved
Published 1993
Printed in the United States of America

The paper used in this publication meets the minimum requirements of American
National Standard for Information Sciences—Permanence of Paper for Printed Library
Materials, ANSI Z39.48–1984 ⊗

Library of Congress Cataloging-in-Publication Data
Botwinick, Aryeh.
   Postmodernism and democratic theory / Aryeh Botwinick.
    p. cm.
   Includes bibliographical references and index.
   ISBN 0-87722-997-X (cloth : alk. paper)
   1. Postmodernism. 2. Skepticism. 3. Political science—
Philosophy. 4. Democracy. I. Title.
B831.2.B688 1993
320′.01—dc20   92-15679

Wittgenstein excerpts are reprinted with the permission of Macmillan Publishing Company from *Philosophical Investigations* by Wittgenstein. Copyright © 1953 by Macmillan
Publishing Company.

For Sheldon Wolin
—In Celebration of His Seventieth Birthday

Where can legitimacy reside after the metanarratives?
JEAN-FRANÇOIS LYOTARD

Contents

P A R T   T W O
BETWEEN HOBBES AND PLATO:
ENVISIONING THE TRANSITION BETWEEN
MODERNIST AND POSTMODERNIST
DEMOCRATIC SOCIETY

•

Preface

The term "postmodernism" has important political-economic and epistemological-metaphysical dimensions. In a political-economic sense,
postmodernism evokes the image of a society of diminishing economic
growth (with emphasis being shifted to service and information sectors) in which rising budget and trade deficits are not ameliorable by
the classic economic remedies of the right, left, or center. From an
epistemological-metaphysical perspective, postmodernism suggests a
systematic exposure of the sources of our uncertainty and the consequent restructuring of the intellectual life in order to integrate properly
what the absence of secure intellectual markers means. This restructuring will emphasize relational and contextual factors as central to both
our knowledge claims and ethical beliefs. The first part of this book
addresses some key epistemological-metaphysical dilemmas of postmodernism; the second half considers its political-economic prospects
from the perspective of some of the dominant categories of Western
political thought. The negative (in the sense of negative theology) patterns of reasoning explored in the first half of the book constitute
an implicit basis for a rearticulated version of democratic legitimacy
appropriate to the society of diminished growth considered in the second half. Just as negative theology leads to a perpetual disowning of
all imputations of worldly attributes to God, so democratic politics in
a postmodern age will likely be characterized by continual deferral of
both the location of sovereignty and the content of supreme value.
Postmodern democratic societies might learn to look at themselves in
such a way that the nature of the past is rearticulated by successive
presents—and the content of the present is deferred to successive
futures.

    Postmodernism and Democratic Theory continues and expands upon
the argument of my earlier book, *Skepticism and Political Participation*.
Whereas that work explored five strategies for rendering formulations
of skepticism consistent and considered the political implications and

applications of each approach, this book argues more concertedly in defense of a generalized agnosticism as the most coherent way to construe these five strategies and thus to come to grips with the problematics unleashed by formulations of skepticism and relativism. As a participatory society emerges in the first part of the book as the closest sociological analogue to a generalized agnosticism, participation is also seen in the second part of the book as the most fitting political complement to a society of limited growth.

Skepticism is a self-referentially unsustainable philosophical thesis, since to be consistently skeptical requires one to be skeptical of skepticism itself, as well of all competing and alternative philosophical theses. The presuppositions of the skeptic's argument are in tension with her explicit formulations. In formulating her argument the extreme skeptic is presupposing that it is possible to doubt everything, whereas in order to render consistent the individual statements that go to compose her argument the skeptic is required to be skeptical of her own skepticism and thus to withdraw from the extreme position that she set out to formulate. This book is replete with examples of this dilemma concerning the reconciliation of presuppositions with explicit statements of argument occurring in diverse regions of thought. Thus the problematic of the skeptic might be generalized as the Thinker's Dilemma. Given the pervasiveness and deep-rootedness of this dilemma highlighted in the case of the skeptic, it becomes apparent that what is at stake in the analysis is not just a matter of false dichotomizations and distortions of the appropriate alternatives of diverse arguments; it is a revised understanding of what is involved in thinking. The most parsimonious way to proceed is to acknowledge that paradox needs to be converted into platitude—with the gap between presupposition and explicit statement of argument closed by a receptivity to multivalued logics. The argument of the skeptic—as well as the parallels and analogues to it discussed in the text—needs to be moved in the direction of a generalized agnosticism. This stance posits that our knowledge of objective reality remains incomplete and holds that a multivalued logic—one that maps the suspension of the law of excluded middle[1]—might encode reality more accurately than the traditional Aristotelian logic does. Our alternatives are thereby increased beyond A and not-A, and formulations of skepticism can legitimately be skeptical of everything but their own tenets.

There is a connection between the epistemological issues explored in Part One of the book and issues of democratic theory concerning representation and participation discussed in Part Two. A confident deployment of reason that avoids confrontation with its self-stultifying effects grouped under the term "issues of self-referentialism" is associated with representation and democratic elitism. A mobilization of critical reason preoccupied with issues of self-referentialism, on the other hand, is linked with participation. In a manifestation of confident reason that remains aloof from issues of self-referentialism, activities of mind generalize and stabilize the individual reasoning moves that one makes into full-dress rational positions that presumably become transparently appealing to other minds. Before political representation becomes an outward mechanism for generalizing and stabilizing opinion, the routine operations of mind undistracted by self-referentialist concerns provide it with an internal model of a faculty that processes thought into conveniently mutually intertranslatable form. With the postulation of mind capable of evolving stable counters of thought, the temporal character of thinking—its jerkiness and constant movement to and fro—becomes spatialized as the concrete thought.

In acts of critical thinking focused on issues of self-referentialism, there is movement in a reverse direction. The spatialized unit of thought becomes temporalized again. Issues of self-referentialism render the grouping and abstracting faculties of reason problematic. Generalization and the conceptual stability that results become precarious. Directing back toward the questioning and skeptical operations of thinking the same critical canons that are originally directed toward the objects of thought fragments the units of thought and disbars thought from properly individuating and characterizing what it is about. An inexorable process of deferral sets in—which depends upon later acts of conceptualization and crystallization to complete what in fact usually turns out to be an uncompletable process. Mind, from the perspective of self-referentialist concerns, does not represent in the guise of finished intellectual products; it asserts in ways that guarantee that solid anchorage cannot be established anywhere. The protocols of thinking continually get in the way of the content of thought—so that thought works to unmask itself before it can effectively unmask any object of thought.

The appropriate political analogue to the radical self-questioning process aroused by concentration on issues of self-referentialism is democratic participation—where individual political involvement and assertion cannot be delegated or raised to a higher level of smoothness

and generality by being entrusted to a cadre of professional represen-
tatives, and where the democratic character of the polity insures the
institutionalization of the intrinsically unfinished character of participation through the proliferation of participatory democratic forums,
which enables citizens to endlessly qualify and clarify an originary
participatory moment that never quite comes into focus. In Part Two
I uncover and analyze participatory undercurrents in the thought of
Hobbes and Plato, and try to plot on the basis of their work the transition between modernist and postmodernist democratic society.

This book was begun in Philadelphia and New York and completed under the auspices of a Temple University research leave for
1991–1992, while I was a Lady Davis Visiting Professor at the Hebrew
University of Jerusalem during the spring semester of 1992. I am grateful to the Lady Davis Fellowship Trust—and to its very gracious and
helpful executive secretary, Tova Wilk—for the opportunity they gave
me to think through the argument of the book in an atmosphere
charged with the "pursuit of interconnections." My contemplation of
the relationship between the modern and the postmodern seemed to
be thoroughly normalized against the background of constant reshuf-
fling of unfinished pasts, presents, and futures characteristic of the
city of Jerusalem. Yaron Ezrahi of the Hebrew University was an un-
surpassed conversation partner. We shared enough in terms of our
starting points and organizing perspectives so that his comments on
my work were of the most helpful, illuminating, "internalist" sort. I
learned a great deal from Zev Harvey of the Hebrew University concerning Maimonides and his rabbinic and philosophical antecedents
and successors. I am also grateful to Zev Harvey and to Josef Stern
for their comments on the Strauss-Maimonides chapter. My conver-
sations with Erik Cohen helped me to gain a firmer grasp of the inclinations and tendencies of my own argument. Joseph Margolis and
David Shatz helped to clarify for me the role of the suspension of the
law of excluded middle in the argument.

Over the years that I have been at Temple University, Peter Bachrach has been a constant source of enlightenment and encouragement,
helping me to perceive and respond to participation as a central theme
in Western political thought and to its philosophical ramifications.

Bruce Jennings, the executive director of the Hastings Center,
with his immense learning and acute critical sense, has, as always,
helped to illuminate dark passages of exposition and argument.

I am indebted to Jane Cullen, my editor at Temple University

Press, whose patience and encouragement have enabled the book to come to fruition. Joan Vidal and Frank Austin, my production and copy editors, respectively, at Temple University Press have contributed tremendously in shepherding the book through the publication process. I have benefited greatly from the comments of the two anonymous readers for the Press. I am heavily indebted to Gloria Basmajian for her skill and patience in typing and retyping the manuscript, and to Kathy Lambert for compiling the index and the bibliography.

Needless to say, I alone am responsible for any errors and shortcomings that remain.

Postmodernism and Democratic Theory

1 • *Introduction*

This book grows out of a sense of convergence between history and theory in the shaping of postmodern civilization. Philosophers of the postmodern have displayed a certain playfulness and even abandon with regard to the constraining and ordering categories of traditional logic. They have argued in skeptical and relativist fashion about a host of metaphysical and political issues while vehemently resisting the need to justify their skepticism and relativism, and at the same time proclaimed their very "liberation" from traditional logical constraints as a primary identifying mark of their postmodernism. It seems to me that the best way to make sense of the postmodernist impulse is to regard it as a decoding of the implications of the impasses reached in the pursuit of skeptical and relativist arguments themselves. To be consistently skeptical and relativist requires one to be skeptical of one's skepticism and relativist about one's relativism. This means that the conclusions of straightforwardly skeptical and relativist arguments cannot be logically supported by the unamplified premises of those arguments. Protocols of self-referentialism—invoking against one's own premises the same critical canons that are deployed against external targets—limit the efficacy of skeptical and relativist arguments to a position of what we might call a generalized agnosticism. To be consistently skeptical and relativistic means that at any given moment in historical time one has to countenance the possible severance of one's theoretical formulations from reality. If our denials are as epistemologically precarious as our affirmations, then we need to acknowledge the possibility of an unbridgeable distance between theory and reality. In Thomas Nagel's phrase, we confront only "the incompleteness of objective reality."[1] This compels us continually to reexamine the multiple metatheoretical schemata and categories by which we generally classify our statements in accordance with their nearness to and distance from some putatively given reality.

Some of the dominant political events of the 1990s seem tacitly to corroborate some of the salient tendencies of postmodernist thought. Democracy appears to be "catching on" across the world, proving virtually irresistible in regions as diverse as central and eastern Europe and the Far East. As we shall shortly see in this Introduction in brief discussions of the work of Claude Lefort and Ernesto Laclau—and as emerges more fully in the body of the book in analyses of hidden convergences between contemporary liberal and communitarian thinking, and of the work of Jürgen Habermas, Leo Strauss, and Robert Dahl—it is the reading of democracy as the institutionalization of a generalized agnosticism that serves as the key factor in disclosing convergence and maximizing coherence in the thinkers mentioned. History in the 1990s seems to be keeping pace with and embodying the latest insights of theory, so that what might appear as abstract philosophical argument in the pages that follow has its "payoffs" in the current shape of political reality.

What the world witnessed in 1989 in central and eastern Europe was the conversion of Lockean normative political theory concerning an appeal to heaven into descriptive sociology: given governments' inability to cope with vast economic and administrative problems, power simply devolved back unto the people. The first phases of the revolutions of 1989 could be described as democracy by default. Totalitarianism, as theorists like Hannah Arendt and J. L. Talmon have reminded us,[2] had always coexisted with—indeed required—the active involvement of the democratic mass in order to function. In 1989, when the totalitarian state machinery of one country after another in the former Soviet bloc withered away in the face of insuperable agendas of problems, what was left was the still-activated democratic mass.

One of the astounding results of the revolutions of 1989 was the emergence of democracy as a tradition—one is tempted to say the monolithic political tradition of modernity—in contrast to the traditionalistic status it previously enjoyed in relation to such other modernistic political traditionalisms as communism. The distinction between tradition and traditionalism is central to Joseph Levenson's great trilogy, *Confucian China and Its Modern Fate*.[3] "Tradition" for Levenson is coterminous with an unself-conscious acceptance of a way of life, with only a dim (or an unactivated) awareness of alternatives to it. "Traditionalism," by contrast, involves the self-conscious affirmation of tradition in the face of competing alternatives.[4] The rise of modernity, which was marked by a heightened self-consciousness—a preoccupation with method and the emergence of a methodologically purged, instrumentalized, and (in the words of Charles Taylor) punctual self[5]—has generally been seen as sounding the death knell for tradition and facilitating the emergence of multiple traditionalisms. The political events of 1989 compel us to reassess this reading (and the presumed legacy) of modernity—and also to reconceive the relationship between modernity and postmodernity.

The resurgence of democratic tradition is taking place simultaneously with a recrudescence of nationalism in areas such as eastern and central Europe—and the former Soviet Union—where democracy seemed to emerge with such alacrity and exuberance from 1989 through 1991. Seyla Benhabib[6] (following in the footsteps of an analysis by Claus Offe)[7] traces the sources of the tension between democratic eruption and nationalist revival to the following three factors:

First, heightened nationalist expression serves as an escape valve for the intense frustration that newly liberated democratic mass constituencies feel in confronting the asymmetries between capitalism and democracy. Instituting the rudiments of a capitalist political economy in the wake of democratic revolution to solve economic woes initially results in grave economic and social dislocations for masses of the citizenry—usually those strata of the population that were instrumental in the fashioning of democratic revolution. The difficulties experienced in grafting principles of political equality that were central in motivating the revolutions onto the structure of capitalist economy provoke newly liberated democratic masses into nationalist overreaction.

A major strategy for coping with the tensions subsisting between democracy and capitalism is the designing of a democratic political economy focusing on decision-making power for the worker; this extends in the course of time to encompass a participatory reshaping of all significant arenas of decision making within society. To achieve an alternative to a political system that is skewed in all sorts of overt and subtle ways by the lurking inequalities present in the economic system (as is the case in most currently existing liberal democracies), democrats on a worldwide scale should mobilize their energies to restructure economic decision making so that it reflects the principles of equality officially enshrined in a democratic political system. Peter Bachrach and I propose this approach in our book *Power and Empowerment: A Radical Theory of Participatory Democracy*.[8]

A second factor that might help account for the rapid devolution of democratic outpouring into nationalist outbursts in eastern and central Europe and the states of the former Soviet Union is the Tocquevillian one: In order to sustain itself, political democracy requires an ethos of "civic, cultural, and associational democracy." Here again a re-envisioning of democracy along participatory lines would have the tremendous incidental benefit of nurturing the larger social context that makes political democracy in its narrower sense possible.

Third, the ferocious re-emergence of the "nationalities" question after fifty years of Soviet rule accentuates the elements of political congestion affecting those countries that have recently experienced democratic revolution. Offe observes that "the very simultaneity of the three transformations (the economic one; the political one; and the resurfacing of the 'nationalities' question) generates decision loads of unprecedented magnitude. Unlike the situation in the Western democracies, there is no time for slow maturation, experience, and learning along the evolutionary scale of nation-building, constitution-making, and the politics of allocation and distribution. . . . As a consequence the decisions made on all three of these levels may easily turn out to be incompatible so as to obstruct each other rather than forming a coherent whole."[9] To the extent that the "nationalities" question is taken seriously as a substantive political issue and is not viewed simply as symptomatic of graver and more deep-seated political dislocations and anxieties, it serves to highlight the element of formal intractability introduced by the confluence of economics, politics, and nationality.

If, as Offe suggests, the challenges confronting the nations of eastern and central Europe—and of the former Soviet Union—are emerging in a bewilderingly simultaneous, non-evolutionary way, then perhaps the best way to confront them is in a correspondingly headlong, self-conscious manner: through the reinforcement of workplace democracy, driven by the desire to enhance equality of decision-making power by workers. With regard to the nationalities issue taken at face value,[10] conceiving of both postmodernism and democracy in generalized agnostic terms means that endless deferral and displacement constitute our enduring metaphysical condition and provide a theoretical hedge against newly released explosive nationalisms wantonly treading on vulnerable minorities within their own midst.

In order to achieve the true globalization of democracy, what might be required, as Stanley Hoffmann has recently suggested,[11] is a further loosening of the distinction between domestic affairs and relations among states beyond what has been accomplished by a rapidly advancing and homogenizing technology. This would enable the United Nations Security Council to respond immediately in the face of impending civil war that threatened to have disastrous external consequences or to involve extensive violations of human rights. The Security Council could "assimilate such a case to the threats to peace and security among states covered by Chapter VII of the Charter and not delay for months as was the case in Yugoslavia."[12]

Robert Reich has argued that with the corporatist internationalization of the economy—with the emergence of what Benjamin Barber has called "McWorld"—a counterveiling need for expressions of localism and cultural distinctiveness, for what Barber calls "Jihad," becomes especially acute.[13] "In the face of the brutal realities of Jihad and the dull realities of McWorld," Barber argues that the most attractive democratic ideal "will be a confederal union of semi-autonomous communities smaller than nation-states, tied together into regional economic associations and markets larger than nation-states—participatory and self-determining in local matters at the bottom, representative and accountable at the top. The nation-state would play a diminished role, and sovereignty would lose some of its political potency. The Green movement adage 'Think globally, act locally' would actually come to describe the conduct of politics."[14]

Our contemporary political situation thus seems to require equal emphasis on the participatory and procedural dimensions of democracy. Masses of people worldwide feel the need to enact politically a richly textured, culturally and ethnically rooted self at the same time that they need to be reminded of the enduring process character of democratic politics—of how resolutions of majority rule versus minority rights dilemmas remain irredeemably "proximate" in character. The generalized agnostic conception of democracy developed in this book serves as a theoretical backdrop that enables me to make sense of both the participatory and procedural aspects of democracy.

A democratic "tradition"—a term that the important post-Marxist theorist Ernesto Laclau also favors precisely because of what appear to him as its humanly centered, voluntarist connotations[15]—suggests continuities and commonalities between the events and the emerging politics of at least some of the countries of central and eastern Europe (e.g., Czechoslovakia, Germany, Hungary) and those of the United States. What are some of these continuities and commonalities?

1. The rehabilitation of tradition, paradoxically, goes hand in hand with the rise of postmodernist sensibility. A cyclical movement appears to be present within modernity itself poising it toward a recapturing of tradition. When we begin to ponder the nature of democratic tradition, the vocabulary of postmodernism becomes helpful and illuminating.

Postmodernism in nearly all of its guises—whether deriving from Jacques Derrida, Richard Rorty, Jean-François Lyotard, or in the form that I shall be advocating of a generalized agnosticism—is characterized by a preoccupation with the middle. As Richard Bernstein observes, with postmodernism we are always "in medias res."[16] Whether because the unending play of signifiers continually defers the fixity of meaning; or because the critique of foundationalism shifts the center of gravity of all arguments to the middle, to their immediate implications and the argumentative moves and practical consequences that they facilitate; or because the "suspicion of metanarrativity" concentrates philosophical attention on atomized argumentative moves and resists the temptation to agglomerate them into metaphysical postulates and positions of all sorts—the backing away from ultimate questions and ultimate positions transforms us into people who act as if we shared a common tradition, a common world. The negative effects of postmodernism are to catapult us back into a traditional world where large (external) questions are bracketed off for the sake of an enhanced preoccupation with the intermediate level—internal questions that assume prominence when the large questions have either been taken to be answered (tradition) or to be incapable of being respectably formulated and answered (postmodernism). On a phenomenological level, in a certain sense, we might say that with postmodernism we are back in the world of tradition.

2. Postmodernism, with its rampant skepticism and relativism (and its search for continually more elegant and refined strategies for being able to negotiate an avoidance of its avoidance of those issues in its theorizing), hits up implacably against problems of self-

referentialism. To be consistently skeptical requires one to be skeptical of one's own skepticism, and to be consistently relativistic requires one to be relativistic about one's own relativism, in order to prevent the skepticism and relativism from becoming self-refuting. In the epistemological model for postmodernism outlined in Chapter 2, I discuss five strategies for rescuing skepticism and relativism from charges of self-refutation. The first is to acknowledge that skepticism cannot be stated; it can only be enacted or dramatized in the form of collective participation in which individual members of society contribute in shaping a collective rationality. A second approach consists in subsuming skepticism and relativism under a tacit-knowledge epistemological paradigm which suggests that the inability to fully rationalize the tenets of skepticism and relativism conforms to the norm of our knowledge statements and claims, rather than constituting a deviation from them. A third strategy for making sense of skepticism and relativism invokes Antonio Gramsci's notion of "dialectical historicism," which stresses the historical rootedness of even our most abstract ideas and their eventual supersession in the course of the class and power struggles that typify our existence in historical time. A fourth approach for resolving issues of skeptical and relativist consistency points to an intuitionistic logic as one example of a multivalued logic that maps the suspension of the law of excluded middle as a means of encoding the legitimation of the "inconsistency" attendant to formulations of skepticism and relativism. An intuitionistic logic is conjoined in this approach with reverse causation as a strategy for remedying the inconsistency that the tenets of intuitionism cannot themselves be interpreted intuitionistically. (They cannot themselves be suspended.) A fifth approach for grappling with the logical dilemmas surrounding formulations of skepticism and relativism consists in marshaling Lyotard's version of postmodernism as "suspicion of metanarrativity," which nudges us to engage in radical acts of atomization in severing the tenets of skepticism and relativism from their presuppositions and implications.

There are three dimensions of the issue of self-referentialism present in each of the five approaches I have just outlined. The first has to do with these formulations exceeding their own epistemological warrant—being committed to more than what they are officially allowing in their own conceptual formulations in order for their concepts to be formulable altogether. A second self-referentialist dilemma is that the five approaches' ostensible monopolizing of their disparate explanatory fields to themselves is predicated upon the simultaneous coexistence of countervailing approaches to themselves that they reject in order for their formulations to wield explanatory force. Otherwise, each approach would be merely tautologous. A third dimension of the issue of self-referentialism is that *the drawing of the distinction* between each of these approaches and their opposite numbers is not itself derivable from the content of either group.

Strategies for Rescuing Skepticism and Relativism from Charges of Self-Refutation	*Dimensions of Self-Refutation Common to the Strategies*
a. Skepticism cannot be stated; it can only be enacted through collective participation.	a. Do the formulations exceed their epistemological warrant? Are they committed to more than they allow in their own conceptual frameworks in order for their concepts to be formulable? Does formulating them violate their own tenets?
b. As tacit knowledge, skepticism and relativism can never be fully rationalized.	
c. From Gramsci's "dialectical historicism": Since skepticism and relativism are rooted in history, they will be superseded or transformed during class and power struggles.	
d. Multivalued logic (e.g., intuitionism), by suspending the law of excluded middle, renders the "inconsistency" of skepticism about skepticism and of relativism about relativism moot. (Intuitionistic logic combined with reverse causation remedies the problem of intuiting intuitionism.)	b. The concepts seem to monopolize their own explanatory fields. This depends on the existence of competing approaches that they reject for their explanations to have force.
e. From Lyotard's "suspicion of metanarrativity": The tenets of skepticism and relativism are separate from their presuppositions and implications.	c. The drawing of distinctions between these and competing approaches cannot be derived from the content of either group.

Of the five strategies outlined for accommodating dilemmas of self-referentialism in the formulation of skepticism and relativism, one, the tacit-knowledge approach, seems to fall under the rubric of realism, while the others appear to manifest antirealist tendencies or to come under the heading of nominalism. The three dimensions of the issue of self-referentialism discerned in all the formulations also appear to be present with regard to the nominalism-realism dispute. Our continual disclosing of dilemmas of self-referentialism suggests the need of a generalized-agnostic construal of our theoretical formulations in order to ward off an infinite regress—in the sense that each new layer of argument adduced to cope with dilemmas of self-referentialism itself manifests those dilemmas when its tenets are construed outside the ambit of a generalized agnosticism. "Self-referentialism" emerges as an issue only if the law of excluded middle is presumed to hold. Under the constraints of this law, our alternatives are restricted to A and not-A. We cannot uphold skepticism and relativism in relation to their targets while disowning them in relation to themselves. However, if we adhere to a generalized agnosticism—claiming that we have only "incomplete knowledge of objective reality," so that all possibilities remain open—then perhaps a multivalued logic such as intuitionism (itself intuitionistically interpreted) that maps the suspension of the law of excluded middle encodes reality more faithfully than the classic Aristotelian law. In this case, our alternatives are increased beyond A and not-A. In this way we can affirm skepticism and relativism in all cases except the theories formulating their tenets themselves.

The price of such an approach is the possible severance at any given moment of historical time of our theoretical statements from reality. Theorizing from the perspective of a generalized agnosticism has to be viewed as a thoroughly naturalized activity—as being constitutionally unable to certify to its connectedness to any of its objects. The prospect of an irretrievably disparate distribution of theorizing to one domain and its objects to other domains could have highly beneficial consequences morally. Casting theorizing adrift from its objects means that perhaps the last of the bulwarks protecting us against our own uncertainties—a theoretical delineation of particular terrains and regions of experience—has been removed, so that we have nothing but our own continually reactivated moral intuitions and alarm systems, however inchoately and inscrutably formed, to rely on (which is all we generally have anyway, but now the scales have been removed from our eyes) in resisting morally oppressive pronouncements and behavior.

The primacy of lived experience over theory that a generalized-agnostic reading of postmodernism affords again leads to a negative rehabilitation of tradition.

3. Claude Lefort's theorizing of democracy in *Democracy and Political Theory* comports with the generalized-agnostic construal of postmodernism that I have been advancing. "The important point," he writes, "is that democracy is instituted and sustained by the dissolution of the markers of certainty. It inaugurates a history in which people experience a fundamental indeterminacy as to the basis of power, law and knowledge, and as to the basis of relations between self and other, at every level of social life." [17] "The dissolution of the markers of certainty" is presumably broad and deep enough to encompass skeptical and relativist critiques of knowledge and of value and thus to eventuate in a generalized agnosticism. The institutional manifestation of this attitude in democratic society according to Lefort is in the unlocatability of sovereignty. The people in his theorizing emerge as an "absent presence," or, in Fred Dallmayr's paraphrase, "neither as a compact body nor as a nullity." [18] The organizing principles of a democratic polity are dispersal and deferral—without succumbing to the temptation of therefore assuming (or postulating) nonexistence. The legitimating apparatus of sovereignty is in the process of being continually built up in Lefort's theorizing of the democratic polity— with images of the present and past getting continually rearticulated in the light of future contingencies. Lefort thus projects an image of the democratic state carved out of the theoretical materials of a generalized agnosticism—where the categories of value, truth, and democratic legitimacy retain their hold upon people, even though no part of the content of these categories locks securely and completely into place. Lefort has his own vocabulary for registering this dynamic. "We must recognize," he says, that "any move towards immanence is also a move towards transcendence." [19] Under a generalized-agnostic dispensation, we notice (or confer) value without ever leaving the plane of a continually expanding present.

4. "The cause of America is in a great measure the cause of all mankind," Tom Paine proudly and daringly announced in his pref-

ace to *Common Sense* in 1776. Since 1989, we have all had vicarious opportunity to experience the triumphal sense in which this statement remains true. Charles Taylor has reminded us of a common legacy of problems uniting socialist and liberal-democratic societies. "The uncontrolled drive to growth, concentration, mobility; the exaltation of instrumental reason over history and community; these," Taylor writes, "have been features of most hitherto attempted models of socialism."[20] They are not just contradictions of capitalism. What is becoming abundantly clear since the revolutionary events themselves is an additional ironic sense in which Tom Paine's statement holds sway. American democracy has been in continuing crisis since the middle 1970s because some key economic preconditions of its survival and flourishing have been seriously threatened. Because of diminished economic growth, Mickey Kaus wrote in an influential article in the *New Republic* in 1990, "none of the suggested methods for restoring America's former level of inequality is very plausible."[21]

A tacit premise of abundance underlies the establishment and subsequent history of American constitutionalism. Such doctrines as separation of powers and checks and balances, which officially aim at inhibiting the fund of governmental power, have seemed plausible in governing a republic as vast and heterogeneous as the United States only because of the abundance of resources available for cultivation; governmental authority did not have to be immediately invoked to mitigate conflict and regulate distribution. Disadvantaged parties could strive to rectify the balance on their own by seeking out new opportunities. Also because of the abundance of resources, when government has had to step in to regulate it has been able to preserve a façade of neutrality. The economy was rich enough to sustain the entrenched positions of the powerful, as well as to grant some demands of the less powerful for an institutional stake in the game.

In the current climate of diminished economic growth, these ground rules are in danger. A participatory restructuring of American society—encompassing all levels of human organization, from educational and social networks to the workplace and government—furnishes a most promising strategy for ensuring the survival of liberal-individualist values in a social and economic setting that, on the surface, appears grossly inhospitable to them. If the cultivation of individuality, diversity, and freedom of expression can no longer be supported even in a partial and distorted way by a shrinking resource base of society, they can perhaps be nurtured by a participatory praxis that teaches human beings the value of these notions through doing—by actualizing them in a participatory framework and thereby developing allegiance toward them.[22] The result would be in some sense the emergence of a true liberalism after the historical era of liberalism was over.

What *currently* links American democracy to the rest of the world therefore is the need to have recourse to participatory democracy—the cultivation of a nationwide democratic praxis in as many of its senses as possible—as a means of fostering and cementing allegiance to liberal-democratic values during an era of diminished economic growth, when the economic payoffs for such allegiance are eroding. In the countries of the former Soviet bloc as well (given their economic woes and the dim prospects for economic flourishing in the short term), a participatory-democratic strategy pursued steadfastly on a broad societal basis might help to institutionalize the development of democracy and stave off the appeal of fascism and varieties of exacerbated nationalism.

5. Redefining and resituating a radical politics poses a common challenge and invites common responses in the United States and in central and eastern Europe. "All social order," Ernesto Laclau observes, "can only affirm itself insofar as it represses a 'constitutive outside' which negates it—which amounts to saying that social order never succeeds in entirely constituting itself as an objective order."[23] The notion of "constitutive outside" represents a transposition to political theory of Jacques Derrida's central notion of *différance*—his idea that the play of signifiers is grouped to yield significant meaning only in relation to receding contexts of what is other than itself, so that meaning and, *a fortiori*, objectivity are endlessly displaced and deferred. Analogously, all principles of social organization, no matter how seemingly egalitarian and just, are constituted as such—are endowed with a determinate identity—through contrast with unstable constellations of "others," of what differs from themselves. This introduces an irremediable element of arbitrariness in all social orders, no matter how large the aspirations toward and the achievement of justice. According to Laclau, this Derridaean insight into the moral and epistemological fragility of political order sets the stage for a new slant in our vision of democracy—if not for a new definition: democracy as the affirmation (if not the constantly renewed institutionalization) of the "constitutive outside." Invoking an idiom that is reminiscent of Hannah Arendt and Sheldon Wolin, as well as of Gramsci,

Laclau also speaks of postmodernity as involving a "continual withering away of the 'social'" and "the concurrent expansion of the realm
of political strategies and argumentation."[24] The antidote to the arbitrariness manifested by the constitutive role played by the other is a
reinvigorated assertion of will expressed by the political. The crucial
category for Laclau at this juncture is a rearticulated version of Grams-
cian "hegemony." In Gramsci's thought, "hegemony" is coextensive
with the notion of "historical bloc," which in turn "replaces the base/
superstructure duality [and] is entirely grounded on pragmatic and
contingent hegemonic articulations."[25] The "constitutive outside," the
skewed arbitrariness, of all social orders and all social formations periodically—contingently—prods different groups to call the social order
into question and to detach it from the particular "constitutive outside" that previously defined it. In this way, continual waves of equalization mark democratic society. "The democratic logic of equality,"
Laclau maintains, "in not adhering to any concrete content, tends to
become a pure logic of the circulation of signifiers. This logic of the
signifier—to use the Lacanian expression—is closely related to the
growing politicization of the social, which is the most remarkable feature of democratic societies."[26] The point of the participatory politics
discussed earlier as a salient means for ensuring the survivability of
liberal-democratic values in economic climates in central and eastern
Europe and in the United States that are grossly inhospitable to them
is also equally to ensure the continual diffusion of power in an endless
reenactment of the dialectic of hegemony-counterhegemony.

6. The upshot of this analysis for an image of human beings appropriate to our postmodern age is very well put by Laclau: "True
liberation does not therefore consist in projecting oneself towards a
moment that would represent the fullness of time, but, on the contrary,
in showing the temporal—and consequently transient—character of
all fullness."[27] This partial, segmentary character of redemption, in
turn, leads to a renewed preoccupation with the present as the appropriate temporal focus for the achievement of human redemption.
In the words of Michael Oakeshott in one of his last letters: "What I
would like to write is a new version of Anselm's *Cur Deus Homo*—in
which (amongst much else) 'salvation,' 'being saved,' is recognized as
[having] nothing whatever to do with the *future*."[28]

In Part One of the book, I conceptually refine and explore the
ramifications of a generalized agnosticism in relation to theorists and

philosophers ranging from Jean-Jacques Rousseau to John Rawls. A generalized agnosticism functions both as a critical vantage point from which to assess the limitations and deficiencies of the theorists addressed and as a hermeneutical strategy that helps to augment the coherence of those thinkers. A generalized agnosticism serves both to highlight where a theory has gone astray and to indicate how it might be reconstituted at a higher level of coherence.

In Part Two of the book, I use the writings of Plato and Thomas Hobbes as a theoretical prism by which to plot the transformation of the key metaphysical conceptions and institutional mechanisms of modernist political society into those of postmodernist political society. Diminished economic growth and the emergence of prefigurations of a stationary society appear to be propelling modernist culture in a postmodernist direction—away from being mesmerized by an ideology of growth and toward preoccupation with some of the ostensibly built-in and recurring limitations of the human condition suggested by my term "a generalized agnosticism."

PART ONE ·

FIXING THE THEORETICAL AND INTELLECTUAL-HISTORICAL CONTOURS OF A GENERALIZED AGNOSTICISM

2 • An Epistemological Model for Postmodernism

Engaging in a thought experiment and pursuing a nominalist impulse—taking as little as possible for granted concerning the nature of man and the world—how can we deploy philosophical argument so as to yet yield our familiar world? The most reduced premise we can opt for is that of extreme skepticism. How viable are its tenets?

The logical form of the problem of expressing a consistent skepticism is a special case of the broader conundrum known as the Liar paradox. Epimenides the Cretan said that all Cretans were liars; "If he spoke the truth, he was a liar."[1] Benson Mates cites a later formulation attributed to the Aristotelian commentator Alexander of Aphrodisias: "The man who says 'I am lying' is both lying and telling the truth."[2] Similarly, the argument of the persistent skeptic founders on the paradox that if skepticism is correct (that it is justifiable to doubt everything) then it too becomes a valid subject of doubt, so that skepticism gets aborted even before it can get formulated. The reduction to language of a persistently skeptical position seems to self-destruct before the targets of skepticism can be negotiated.

I shall deploy several strategies for grappling with this paradox. One consists in drawing an explicit connection between skepticism and political participation. If people intuitively feel or act as if skepticism were correct, but it cannot even get consistently formulated, then the appropriate move is to acknowledge that skepticism cannot be coherently stated: It can only be enacted. By multiplying participatory networks across society—from informal social settings to the workplace to official governmental contexts of decision making—we

enact skepticism by affording people an equal opportunity to participate in decisions that shape their lives, without having to shoulder
the burden of stating skepticism.

When I speak of a participatory political praxis as an enactment
of skepticism, "enactment" has a ground that, in a pragmatist sense,
is sufficiently checkable against the real world. It is not just the ongoing development of technology that is relevant for an adequate and
sustainable pragmatism but the whole edifice of science, our multiple
interim reports on knowledge. From a pragmatist perspective, "enactment" would be uncheckable only against some stable and enduring
version of the real world—which pragmatism would be theoretically
unable to locate and to validate. "Enactment" would, however, be
correlative to scientific communities' interim and evolving versions of
reality, which a consistent pragmatism is able to uphold.

An "enactment" resolution of the self-referential dilemma haunting formulations of extreme skepticism is evocative of a traditional
construal of Aristotle's practical syllogism. When Aristotle declares in
explicating this syllogism "and the conclusion is an action," John M.
Cooper argues that the practical syllogism as a whole is most usefully seen as a kind of mental representation of the stages through
which the agent passes in "generating action" and "ought not to be
regarded as part of practical reasoning at all."[3] Alasdair MacIntyre, in
contrast to Cooper affirming the more literal, traditional view, argues
that when Aristotle says that the conclusion is an action he is really
committed to the view of action as utterance, and that "what such
an action as utterance affirms in concluding a practical syllogism is
that that selfsame action, answering as it does to the description of
what is to be done furnished by the initial premise, is to be done."[4]
Analogously, in the case of skepticism, the conclusion to an argument
setting forth the premises of skepticism is an action—participation in
collective decision making.[5]

This approach is problematic, because the enactment of skepticism through participation is not the only recourse available to us
in the face of the unstatability of skepticism. If we are locked into a
doubly solipsistic universe, where we not only consider skepticism
to be the most defensible philosophical position but feel that the resources of language defeat the very possibility of coherently stating
this, then self-destructive, suicidal withdrawal seems as inherently
plausible an option as fashioning expanding networks for political
participation. There appear to be intervening layers of decision and

argument between recognizing the paradox attending formulations of skepticism and attaching primacy to participation. The preference for participation, therefore, can only be defended rhetorically, not rigorously established by logic.

A second approach to grappling with the problem of formulating a consistent version of skepticism invokes Michael Polanyi's concept of tacit knowledge. This view suggests that all of our knowledge statements are more "knowing" than what they can state or justify. Skepticism is qualitatively no different in this regard from the experience highlighted by Gestalt psychologists of being able to recognize a face without being able to set forth the indicators that enable us to discern it. Skeptical statements can most judiciously be construed as suppressed action statements that, while registering a limit of thought, covertly point to the transcendence of that limit through leaps into action that cannot be justified rationally. From the perspective of "tacit knowledge," statements of skepticism constitute a more heightened expression of the "justification gap" affecting even our ordinary statements in the world.

A third strategy expands upon Gramsci's "dialectically historical" notion of hegemony. "Hegemony" calls attention to the interrelatedness of the cultural products of an age and to the utter historical rootedness of even the most abstract philosophical speculations of an epoch. From this perspective, skepticism, with its attendant paradoxes, becomes a "self-consuming artifact"[6]—a mode of discourse, a style of self-understanding, whose very ground rules of intelligibility will be transformed as the proliferation of "organic intellectuals," an "intellectualized proletariat," articulates new rational canons more in conformity with its ethos of continual deconstruction of class-biased concentrations of power.

A fourth approach in formulating a consistent version of skepticism focuses on an intuitionistic logic, which maps the suspension of the law of excluded middle, combined with a concept of reverse causation.

A fifth approach toward resolving the problem of consistency argues in defense of postmodernism that the requirement of "metanarrativity," the fashioning of justificatory background narratives, is metaphysically dispensable, and that this dispensability constitutes the most effective purchase on the problem of stating skepticism consistently.

There are three dimensions to the problem of reflexivity, or self-referentialism, that one might want to say affect the five philosophical strategies I have summarized. I will present these three dimensions of reflexivity first in relation to a "tacit knowledge" approach for dealing with skepticism and then show how versions of them are present in relation to the four other philosophical strategies adopted for coping with skepticism.

One might argue that "tacit knowledge" leaves the problem of reflexivity unresolved. If tacit knowledge predicates that some dimensions of knowledge must remain implicit and suppressed, then to theorize what those dimensions are, to render them explicit, is already to be violating the tenets of tacit knowledge. The theorist of tacit knowledge is thus engulfed in a position where she or he needs to affirm that our knowledge statements have a preponderantly tacit character, except for the reflexive formulation of the tenets of "tacit knowledge" themselves. These, given the nature of theorizing, have an inexpugnably explicit character.

In response, one might say that this criticism conflates "tacit knowledge" as an epistemological doctrine with the linguistic apparatus through which it gets expressed. As an abstract, linguistically denuded epistemological doctrine, "tacit knowledge" *appears* to be inconsistent with its own premises. (If our knowledge statements harbor elements that remain partially tacit, contextual, and submerged, how can the theorist of tacit knowledge hope to disclose the content of whatever it is that remains tacit, contextual, and submerged?) However, from the perspective of the linguistic mechanics whereby the content of "tacit knowledge" is expressed, the theorist can validly and consistently say that in conformity with its premises the tenets of "tacit knowledge" too can only be incompletely stated—that they are not susceptible of receiving a fully explicit treatment. In this way, the formulation of the tenets of "tacit knowledge" can remain faithful to the protocols of statability enshrined in its theory.

A second dimension to the problem of reflexivity in relation to the theory of tacit knowledge is that the theorist of tacit knowledge has to concede intellectual space to what we might call a countervailing theory of explicit knowledge—that all of our knowledge statements and claims can be thoroughly, explicitly rationalized and justified—in order for the theory of tacit knowledge to have explanatory force. If all human utterance and written expression is conceptualized as communicable only through the machinery of "tacit knowledge," then the position constitutes a gigantic tautology. In order for "tacit knowledge" to retain its explanatory force and for invocations of the concept to constitute more than tautologies, the theoretical approaches to utterance and writing that it rejects must somehow continue to exist even after the theorist of tacit knowledge has postulated that no statement that we make can ever be fully rationalized. The explanatory force of "tacit knowledge" is parasitic upon the continued existence of contrasting theoretical understandings concerning the ever-expanding character of explicit knowledge that the theory of tacit knowledge was designed to displace.

There is a third dimension to the problem of reflexivity that one might claim haunts a tacit-knowledge approach to the issue of formulating a consistent version of extreme skepticism. This problem is patterned after Fred Dallmayr's identification of an analogous question in the work of Jürgen Habermas.[7] With regard to the broad distinction between instrumental and communicative rationality in Habermas, Dallmayr writes, "As in the previous distinction between form and content, one can ask what mode of reasoning or rationality informs this differentiation itself—since it is clearly not covered by either the instrumental or the purely communicative type."[8] From Habermas's particular perspective, instrumental and communicative rationality, as well as the distinction between form and content, are supposed to be two sets of mutually exclusive, exhaustive categories. Yet the *distinction* between instrumental and communicative rationality derives neither from the instrumental nor the communicative half of the content introduced by the distinction, and the *distinction* between form and substance transcends the content of both categories introduced by the distinction. Analogously, one might want to say that the *distinction* between tacit knowledge and explicit knowledge moves beyond the content of the categories of both tacit and explicit knowledge and therefore encounters difficulties in being reflexively sustained.[9]

I do not believe that Richard Bernstein's defense of Habermas against Dallmayr's criticism works.[10] Bernstein says that Dallmayr, in pushing the argument concerning reflexivity, is still a captive of a foundationalist paradigm for doing philosophy, whereas Habermas is doing philosophy nonfoundationalistically. "Philosophy does not rest," Bernstein says,

> on any ultimate foundations. It always begins in medias res, in response to problems, crises and conflicts. It is a hermeneutical enterprise that seeks to enlarge our critical understanding. This

is the procedure that Habermas has followed in seeking to clarify the character and interrelations between cognitive-instrumental and communicative reason. It is Dallmayr (not Habermas) who still seems to harbor a nostalgia for foundational projects when he constantly pursues self-referential arguments—asking what is the mode of reasoning that is presupposed when we differentiate instrumental and communicative rationality. . . . Of course when Habermas makes these distinctions he is advancing claims that are themselves subject to modification and revision by further argumentative inquiry.[11]

The argument that Bernstein makes in defense of Habermas can be converted into an argument against Bernstein himself. Does not his rejection of self-referential arguments constitute a lingering foundationalism? Is not Bernstein, in rejecting these sorts of arguments, to some extent presupposing them—or at least giving them enough intellectual space so that his rejection has a conceptual target to latch on to? His argument fails to meet the test of self-referentialism—of reflexivity—and he cannot prejudge whether this test has to be met at all without his argument becoming viciously circular, assuming the very thing it is trying to prove. Bernstein is presupposing precisely that which he is supposed to be establishing argumentatively.

On the basis of logic, one can neither affirm nor reject the role of self-referential arguments in philosophy. To invoke the requirement of reflexivity—to stress the need that arguments be self-referentially sound—is an extension of the requirement of consistency in the formulation of arguments generally. There is no higher order of justification of consistency beyond saying that this is the way we (certain cultures or certain groups within cultures) do things. This is the way we make our case in support of particular positions.

The all-important question therefore becomes the use(s) to which rejecting (or affirming) self-referential arguments can be put. In order for this overarching perspective of pragmatism to emerge as virtuously rather than as viciously circular—to itself conform to the requirements of consistency—any kind of ultimate linkage between pragmatism and reality would have to be denied, because otherwise pragmatism as an explanatory philosophical theory would fail the test of reflexivity. It would be privileging itself in relation to the theories that it criticizes. *They* all lack a realistic foundation and are merely pragmatically grounded, whereas pragmatism itself is responsive to the order of reality. For pragmatism to emerge as consistent, the concepts of "use" and of "reality" have to be dissociated to such an extent that it can be viewed as one possible ordering principle among many. That is to say, the so-called reality that pragmatism captures and whose exigencies constitute the ultimate determinative factors in our theoretical and practical constructions and construals is itself one of many possible realities, whose particular configurations of exigencies (or some other alternative, or counterpart, notational term) could have been registered by sets of notational principles aside from pragmatism.

A consistent pragmatism—or what I am also calling a generalized agnosticism—offers us the opportunity to formulate a more global response to the first dimension of the problem of reflexivity in relation to "tacit knowledge" than does the one sketched out above. The linguistic response elaborated earlier is more local to the tenets of tacit knowledge, which is, after all, at least partially a theory about language and its radical incompleteness. From a more global perspective, however, one might say that the statement "You can't theorize the tenets of tacit knowledge without violating the tenets of tacit knowledge" is true only if one holds that linguistic utterances make an unreserved claim concerning what the world is like. But if linguistic utterances are construed in a consistently pragmatic way, then they harbor no commitments concerning the nature of the world; it could be that a multivalued logic that maps the suspension of the law of excluded middle accurately reflects what the world is like. With our alternatives increased beyond A and not-A, we can say that knowledge both is and is not (in the requisite senses) tacit, so that the *theorizing* of tacit knowledge does not emerge as inconsistent with the tenets of tacit knowledge.

A consistent pragmatism—or generalized agnosticism—that recoils before linkage with any particular version of reality also enables us to resolve the second dimension of the problem of reflexivity in relation to the theory of tacit knowledge. Such pragmatism can accommodate a theory of tacit knowledge that is parasitic upon the persistence of theories of explicit knowledge, because a pragmatic construal of tacit knowledge betrays no commitment concerning what the structure of the world is like. The world's actual structure might be appropriately mapped by multivalued logics that accommodate the suspension of the law of excluded middle so that knowledge both is and is not in the appropriate senses tacit.

A multivalued logic also helps us to resolve the third dimension of the problem. A consistently pragmatic construal of the *distinction* between tacit and explicit knowledge enables us to circumvent the issue of reflexivity, because knowledge of the world might be both tacit and not tacit, explicit and not explicit at the same time, so that the distinction between "tacit" and "explicit" that has validity in our notational universe might have no counterpart in the "real" universe. Another factor contributing to resolving the third dimension of the problem of reflexivity in relation to tacit knowledge is that the world itself might facilitate the construction of analytical grids that would enable us to trace possibilities intermediate between "explicit" and "tacit" knowledge that our current conceptual schemata are incapable of elucidating. This, in turn, might reflexively support the drawing of the tacit-knowledge/explicit-knowledge distinction itself.

Versions of all three dimensions of the problem of reflexivity are present in relation to the other four approaches mentioned earlier for achieving a consistent formulation of extreme skepticism. In addition, versions of the strategies for overcoming these three dimensions of the problem of reflexivity are also available for the remaining four approaches.

1a. With regard to the first approach—extreme skepticism cannot be stated; it can only be enacted through massive participation—a version of the first dimension of the problem of reflexivity is present because "enactment" cannot take place outside a linguistically ordaining interpretive context that establishes the link with participation. Therefore, the relationship between enactment and participation that this approach underscores is being begged rather than proved. "Enactment" cannot be the only appropriate translation of skepticism without transcending its character as mere enactment.

1b. The translation of skepticism as enactment through participation is parasitic upon an understanding of skepticism as not requiring a participatory translation in order for the first delineation of skepticism to have explanatory force. Otherwise, it constitutes a mere tautology.

1c. The *distinction* between the conceptualization of skepticism as crucially predicated upon enactment through participation and as not so predicated is not derivable from the content of either the participatory or the nonparticipatory half of the distinction. How can the distinction itself be reflexively justified?

A consistently pragmatic, or generalized-agnostic, construal of the first thesis—the only way to formulate skepticism is through enactment by collective participation in decision making—would emphasize that this statement harbors no commitments as to the nature of the world. The world might be such that experiences can only be linguistically mediated. This would give rise to the first dimension of the problem of reflexivity in relation to my first thesis concerning skepticism. Then again, the world might be such that experiences and their import can be perceived and grasped nonmediationally, and it is only our various cultural traditions that generate the illusions of the linguistically mediated nature of experience. Since a consistently pragmatic construal of the first thesis requires one to be unremittingly agnostic concerning the nature of the world, the first inconsistency attendant to my first thesis concerning skepticism falls by the wayside.

The second dimension of the problem of reflexivity with regard to my first thesis can also be resolved by acknowledging that the world might be most accurately mapped by a multivalued logic that accommodates the suspension of the law of excluded middle. The appropriate translation of skepticism could thus both be and not be enactment through collective participation.

The third dimension of the problem of reflexivity in relation to my first thesis can be resolved by recognizing that the *distinction* between skepticism as crucially predicated upon enactment through collective participation and as not so predicated has validity in our notational universe but might have no counterpart in the "real" universe. In addition, the world itself might facilitate the construction of analytical grids that would enable us to trace possibilities intermediate between the two extremes of "enactment" and "nonenactment" that our current conceptual schemata are incapable of elucidating. This might, in turn, reflexively support the drawing of the distinction.

I now proceed more schematically with my remaining three theses concerning how extreme skepticism might be philosophically accommodated:

3a. To theorize dialectical historicism is already to be behaving inconsistently with its tenets. If the break between current and future hegemonically mutually reinforcing paradigms of thought and action is as total as dialectical historicism predicates, then how would we have access to the intellectual tools to plot and theorize the nature of this break? To theorize cultural development as a movement of artifacts in a process of mutual self-consumption has to allow, inconsistently, for the persistence of one artifact that remains unconsumed—namely, the cultural artifact of self-reflection that enables the otherwise global cultural movement toward self-consumption to get recorded.

3b. "Dialectical historicism" is contingent upon a "nondialectical historicism" in order not to constitute a tautology and to wield explanatory force.

3c. The *distinction* between dialectical historicism and nondialectical historicism is not derivable from the content of either the dialectically or the nondialectically historicist half of the distinction.

4a. The tenets of intuitionism cannot be theorized without violating those same tenets. When one regresses the tenets of intuitionism into a background theoretical framework in order to gauge their sense and reference more reliably, it emerges that intuitionism is formulated as an alternative to realism. This means that intuitionism's suspension of the law of excluded middle is not something that can itself be suspended. A doctrine of reverse causation constitutes a local resolution to this problem because, if we can conceptualize the arrow of time moving from future to past (from effect to cause), then we can circumvent the movement of regression that discloses the inconsistency between intuitionism applied to other theoretical statements and intuitionism applied in relation to its own tenets.

4b. With regard to the concept of reverse causation, a version of my second dimension of the problem of reflexivity remains. The explanatory force of reverse causation is parasitic upon the continued existence of "regular causation"—moving from cause to effect. Otherwise, "reverse causation" emerges as a tautology. How, then, can "reverse causation" work to resolve the first dimension of the problem of reflexivity manifest in the formulation of the tenets of an intuitionistic logic when "reverse causation" itself is reflexively unsustainable?

4c. The *distinction* between intuitionism and realism is not derivable from the content of either the intuitionistic or the realistic half of the distinction.

5a. The theorist of Lyotardian or other related versions of postmodernism is already behaving in ways inconsistent with its tenets by metatheoretically demarcating the ways in which postmodernism differs from modernism. Such a theorist presents us with a justificatory metanarrative regarding the cogency and legitimacy of dispensing with justificatory metanarratives.

5b. In order for postmodernism to be an adequate metaphilosophical theory, it must presuppose the existence of modernism. Otherwise, postmodernism emerges as a tautology possessing zero explanatory power.

5c. The *distinction* between modernism and postmodernism is not derivable from the content of either the modernist or the postmodernist half of the distinction.

Regarding (3a) above, a consistently pragmatic, or generalized-agnostic, construal of the third thesis would preclude any linkage between one's statements and the world, so that a multivalued logic might provide the most accurate mapping of what the world is truly like. In that case, one could say that the movement of historical change both was and was not, in the appropriate senses, dialectically historical. The same strategy would apply with regard to (4a). A local response to this conundrum (as we have seen) is reverse causation. A more global response would be to say that the structure of the world might be such that the law of excluded middle fails to hold, so that the tenets of intuitionism can be construed both intuitionistically (in relation to all other statements) and nonintuitionistically (in relation to themselves). This means that the "rejection" of the law of excluded middle itself remains a qualified rejection—continually suspended between the two possibilities of affirmation and rejection of this rejection. This, in turn, suggests that my argument self-referentially encompasses itself—since its presupposing of the law of excluded middle in the course of rejecting it can be subsumed under an intuitionistic construal of the tenets of an intuitionistic logic. Concerning (5a), the tenets of postmodernism can be construed so that postmodernism both is and is not, in the requisite senses, affirmed.

Regarding (3b), (4b), and (5b), all can be resolved from the perspective of a multivalued logic, which a consistent pragmatism (or generalized agnosticism) affords, so that dialectical historicism, reverse causation, and Lyotardian postmodernism can conceptually recede to make room for their theoretical opposite numbers.

The issues in (3c), (4c), and (5c) become intelligible if one reflects that, in each case, the distinctions between dialectical historicism and nondialectical historicism, intuitionism and realism, and modernism and postmodernism have validity in our notational universe but might have no counterpart in the "real" universe. In addition, a consistent pragmatism underscores for us the possibility that the world itself might facilitate the construction of analytical grids that would enable us to trace possibilities lying between the extremes of dialectical and nondialectical historicism, intuitionism and realism, and modernism and postmodernism that our current intellectual schemata are incapable of elucidating, which in turn might reflexively support the drawing of the respective distinctions.

My five strategies for philosophically accommodating extreme skepticism have contradictory implications concerning the nominalism-realism dispute. A tacit-knowledge approach, by calling attention to certain permanently unrationalizable elements in discourse, might be appropriately linked with realism, in contrast to nominalism, in philosophy. Dialectical historicism, intuitionism, and postmodernism, on the other hand, clearly point in the direction of antirealism— of nominalism. In the light of our previous discussion, we can discern the three dimensions of the problem of reflexivity haunting the nominalism-realism debate.

First, one might argue that nominalism cannot be theorized without violating its own tenets. If only discrete particulars exist, then ascending to a theoretical level to be able to designate and justify those particulars, in contrast to universal essences or general terms, is already to be exceeding the warrant of nominalism. The demarcated, conceptualized, named particular is not in experience, but constructed out of our experience. In this sense, to be a nominalist is already to be committed to more than nominalism.

Second, in order for nominalism to have explanatory force as a philosophical theory, it is parasitic upon the continued granting of philosophical space to realism. It is the effect yielded by contrast with its opposite number that confers upon nominalism (or realism) whatever explanatory power each concept might possess. Reflexively considered, therefore, the theorist of nominalism is committed to the continued "existence" of realism in order for his elucidation of nominalistic theory to work—and not to constitute a tautology.

Finally, does not the *distinction* between nominalism and realism exceed the content of both halves introduced by the distinction? How can *it* be reflexively justified?

All three dimensions of the problem of reflexivity in relation to the nominalism-realism distinction can again, I think, be most satisfactorily resolved from the perspective of a consistent pragmatism, or a generalized agnosticism, that entails no commitments concerning the structure of the world. The world itself, therefore, might be most accurately mapped by a multivalued logic that accommodates the suspension of the law of excluded middle. If nominalism can both be affirmed and not affirmed, then the overlapping with realism that the first dimension of the problem of reflexivity calls attention to can be rendered intelligible. By the same token, the theoretically simultaneous existence of nominalism and realism—a further specification of the sense in which nominalism both is and is not affirmed—can begin to make sense.

With regard to the third dimension of the problem of reflexivity: When the dichotomy between nominalism and realism is translated into the notational terms of a multivalued logic, each side of the dichotomy recoils upon itself and each possibility can both be and not be at the same time. This signifies that the distinction between nominalism and realism that has validity in our notational universe might have no counterpart in the "real" universe. Another factor contributing to resolving the third dimension of the problem of reflexivity in relation to the issue of nominalism versus realism is that the world itself might facilitate the construction of analytical grids that would enable us to trace possibilities intermediate between nominalism and realism that our current conceptual schemata are incapable of elucidating, which in turn might reflexively support the drawing of the nominalism-realism distinction.

The upshot of my argument, therefore, is that all five theses accommodating extreme skepticism, in their nominalist and realist varieties, can be reflexively sustained in the senses that I have summarized.

By thus invoking extreme skepticism—and showing how a consistent construal of it eventuates in a generalized agnosticism, which leaves the world intact—we are able to have the world on the basis of the most reduced premise possible. The pursuit of a generalized agnosticism is thus defensible on grounds of parsimony. Is "parsimony" itself susceptible of a rational defense? I think the most that can be said at this juncture is embodied in Machiavelli's notion of *necessità*. The word "necessity" harbors both the descriptive connotation of choices being foreclosed and the normative connotation of the very restriction of choice being converted into a virtue, into a strategy of decision making, by opting for the most minimal approach.

A strategic philosophical advantage of my two-tier approach toward skepticism (I introduce what amounts to a generalized agnosticism at the second level of argument) over Nagel's one-tier approach (he introduces a generalized agnosticism at the first level of argument)[12] is that it enables me to make the point that skepticism is only sustainable as a generalized agnosticism. The only way that I can do this is by pursuing the circuitous route that I follow with my five theses, which try to keep skepticism afloat. Then I try to show that the theses themselves work only if they are agnostically interpreted. To follow Nagel's more direct route and introduce a generalized agnosticism at the outset of argument appears like a mere substitution— stipulatively substituting a generalized agnosticism for skepticism— rather than a demonstration that the latter is only expressible through (as) the former.[13]

I thus adopt a theoretical and logical strategy for dealing with issues of self-referentialism, in contrast to what we might call a pragmatic approach. Such an approach would emphasize that the skeptic's claim that there is no knowledge involves him, not in a logical, but in a pragmatic contradiction. Asserting the claim undercuts what is claimed, and the claim undercuts its assertion. One might argue that the virtue of treating the skeptic's claim as a pragmatic rather than a logical contradiction is that it "leaves the world as it is," whereas relating to the skeptic's claim as a logical contradiction necessitates the search for a higher level of generality in argument that incorporates within itself both contradictory halves of the skeptic's argument that my generalized agnosticism is designed to meet. I adopt a generalized agnosticism in order to accommodate the skeptic's "I know" and "I do not know"—both *A* and not-*A*. I therefore advocate substituting an intuitionistic logic (one version of a multivalued logic) for Aristotle's law of excluded middle—either *A* or not-*A*. As we have seen, in order for an intuitionistic logic to perform its strategic role in this argument, its tenets have to be interpreted intuitionistically—rather than as involving a categorical rejection of realism. However, at this point one might argue that I leave all truth and even probability hanging in air and introduce an unbridgeable gap between thinking and reality.

There are two defenses of my approach. First, the point of my going the logical route rather than the pragmatic one in grappling with paradoxes of self-referentialism is to be able to provide a full-scale philosophical vindication of a pragmatist reading of those paradoxes: that on philosophical grounds we need to recoil from more traditional modes of philosophizing and embrace pragmatism. My commitment to philosophical theory in dealing with paradoxes of self-referentialism is thus less substantive than heuristic.

Second, with regard to a pragmatic construal of the self-referentialist paradoxes surrounding skepticism (in the sense attributed to my would-be opponent), one can pose the question How can pragmatism itself be supported? There is an inescapable move from "pragmatism" to "theory" and "logic," if only for purposes of exposing their limitations and underscoring the virtues of pragmatism. It is a question simply of what we want to leave hanging—whether pragmatism without foundations or theorizing that opens a gap between thinking and reality. It is not a question of whether or not to leave something hanging, but of *what* is to be left hanging. Stated more pointedly, a pragmatism without foundations also harbors the prospect of opening a gap between thinking and reality, since the status of the pragmatic construals and formulations themselves remains unresolved. I try to grapple with this question and am left with a form of philosophical theorizing that does not make an unreserved connection with reality. But stopping earlier in one's philosophical inquiry does not mean that one is not left with something hanging. It means only that one is left hanging with it earlier.

The appropriate analytical-philosophical translation of postmodernism might therefore be that it is a thesis concerned with philosophy's relationship to the world and of the implications of that relationship for the traditional questions and categories of philosophy. Postmodernism in my second sense of a consistent pragmatism, or a generalized agnosticism, may be distinguished from postmodernism in my first (Lyotardian) sense of "suspicion of metanarrativity" as follows. In contrast to Lyotard's usage, which registers a rejection and thus gives rise to all those unresolvable issues of reflexivity that Habermas raises against postmodernism, my conceptualization of postmodernism as a generalized agnosticism affirms everything it denies and denies everything it affirms ("not knowing" means assigning equal weight both to something being the case and to its not being the case). It thus puts qualms about reflexivity effectively to rest.

One might sharpen the case for postmodernism by saying that consistency, at least with regard to skepticism, is most satisfactorily achieved with the renunciation of the global and local metanarrative force of skepticism and relativism and their conversion into merely immanentist narratives. Postmodernism in the sense of a generalized agnosticism enables us to withdraw instantaneously from our skeptical and relativist affirmations—without having to ponder or elucidate interconnections of any sort—and thus to be consistently skeptical and relativist. One can be consistent in philosophy only if one concertedly and effectively drops the requirement of consistency in a worldly, factual, realistic sense.

This defense of postmodernism requires us to distinguish between two construals of it, a modernist (Lyotardian) one and a postmodernist (generalized-agnostic) one. As I have indicated, postmodernism in Lyotard's sense strives to surmount the problem of reflexivity by scrapping altogether the requirement for justification. But if postmodernism is just another theory for mapping the intellectual terrain of modernity, then it, too, confronts a problem of reflexivity. If postmodernism is construed postmodernistically, then its remapping of the intellectual landscape in a consistent manner so that the requirement of justification can be dispensed with would have to be applied against postmodernism itself. Its particular negative redrawing would have to be seen as one possible redrawing among multiple others, enjoying no intrinsically compelling force over its competitors. A postmodernist reading of postmodernism would yield a classificatory scheme willing postmodernistically to withdraw in the face of other available and potential intellectual ordering schemes. In other words, a consistent postmodernism yields a generalized agnosticism.

In making the case for postmodernism in the latter sense, it might be possible to revise the notion of "regression" to render it harmonious with postmodernist tenets. Instead of tying the meaning and reference of the terms of an object theory to their intertranslatability with the terms of a background theory, one could say that the grounds for making a statement collapse into the uses to which a statement can be put. This formulation could be regarded as an alternative to Willard Van Orman Quine's notion of regression,[14] and by its orientation toward the future it could be easily fitted into the postmodernist position. Or else one could say that that formulation is merely a paraphrase of the Quinian notion—because the use to which a statement is put is merely an invocation of one of the preexisting theoretical frameworks that can be shown to be intertranslatable with the current statement. The virtue of my paraphrase of Quine's notion of regression might then be that it highlights the postmodernist uses to which that notion can be put. This would be especially true if the preexisting theoretical frameworks compatible with a current statement were not taken to be strictly fixed in number, but were, rather, a function of the new interpretive possibilities residing in the background theories disclosed by the current statement itself. The new statement would thus be taken as carving out, as it were, its own set of relevant antecedents, as well as its own set of relevant implications, with the distinction between antecedent and implication being strictly pragmatic (irredeemably arbitrary) in character.

Given a generalized-agnostic position in philosophy, there can be no escape from circularity. Given an "incompletely objective knowledge of the world," our conclusions have no alternative but to replicate our premises.

The legitimizing of circularity that I am advocating is evocative of Donald Davidson's famous move in his essay "On the Very Idea of a Conceptual Scheme." [15] Just as Davidson proposes that giving up the dualism between conceptual scheme and reality and referring only to language is philosophically more parsimonious while renouncing nothing of the richness and complexity of our sense of reality, so too giving up the conceptual distinction between *explanandum* (the term being explained) and *explanans* (the sentence doing the explaining) and openly acknowledging and embracing the circularity of all of our explanations is also philosophically more parsimonious while sacrificing nothing of our sense of reality. What justifies Davidson's reduced ontology (language *instead* of the conceptual scheme–reality distinction) and mine (acknowledged circularity *instead* of the *explanandum-explanans* distinction) might be an identical factor: a generalized-agnostic construal of objective reality that assigns philosophic centrality to what we have a large role in creating (language; circular defenses and explanations of our position) rather than to what we ordinarily regard as given (reality in the large sense; causal factors in the world that are held responsible for particular situational outcomes).

3 • Liberalism versus Communitarianism: Epistemological and Sociological Perspectives

Liberalism and communitarianism remain two salient types of political theory of the 1990s. In the first part of this chapter, I focus on their common logical-structural features and zero in on epistemological vulnerabilities shared by the two types of theory. In the second section of the chapter, I indicate how these vulnerabilities might be accommodated by the philosophical strategy developed by Thomas Nagel in *The View from Nowhere*[1] and by the philosophical approach pursued in my first two chapters; I also point to the common ground between my approach and Nagel's. In the third section of the chapter, I question whether certain features of the American and worldwide postindustrial socioeconomic context introduce a certain element of artificiality into the whole question of liberalism versus communitarianism, since a communitarian restructuring of liberalism (a further democratization of it) might constitute the most promising strategy for preserving liberalism in troubled economic times.

The convergence of the epistemological limitations of liberalism and communitarianism leads to primacy being assigned to participatory democracy as overcoming these limitations. A striking parallelism thus emerges between the epistemological and sociological arguments of the chapter. Just as, in the first case, skepticism is most compellingly salvageable as participatory democracy, so too, in the second case, in a postindustrial setting, liberalism is most effectively sustainable as participatory democracy.

• *Problems of Circularity and Reflexivity*

In an influential article in *Philosophy and Public Affairs*, Thomas Nagel raises a question—describes an intellectual project—that goes to the heart of the philosophical coherence of liberalism. "Part of the problem," he says,

> is that liberals ask of everyone a certain restraint in calling for the use of state power to further specific, controversial moral or religious conceptions—but the results of that restraint appear with suspicious frequency to favor precisely the controversial moral conceptions that liberals usually hold. For example, those who argue against the restriction of pornography or homosexuality or contraception on the ground that the state should not attempt to enforce contested personal standards of morality often don't think there is anything wrong with pornography, homosexuality, or contraception. They would be against such restrictions even if they believed it *was* the state's business to enforce personal morality, or if they believed that the state could legitimately be asked to prohibit anything simply on the ground that it was wrong.[2]

What Nagel appears to be focusing on is the problem of whether a genuine neutrality is possible. Does not the erection of neutrality itself into a supreme political value in the manner that liberalism delineates founder on self-contradiction? If one is to be consistently neutral, one has to be neutral about one's own neutrality as well—so that one becomes logically disbarred from formulating the position concerning neutrality that one was originally driven to formulate. The issue of self-referentialism in relation to the principle of neutrality is analogous to the role of "self-referentialism" in defeating philosophical formulations of extreme skepticism and extreme relativism generally. In order for such formulations to be self-referentially sound, they have to integrate skepticism of their own skepticism and relativism about their own relativism into their very formulations of skeptical and relativist principles. This suggests that self-referential considerations undermine formulations of extreme skepticism and extreme relativism at the very outset.

John Rawls's reformulations of liberalism in *A Theory of Justice*[3] and in later writings[4] confront analogous issues of self-referentialism at three points, at least.

1. The radical egalitarianism that serves as the starting point—the initiating phase—of Rawls's argument[5] and that recourse to contractarian imagery (original position; veil of ignorance) and styles of argument partially obscures, is a political expression of extreme skepticism. How can extreme skepticism be reflexively sustained without also engulfing itself?

2. Both the substantive ethical and political theory (the priority of the right over the good) and the metaethical theory (wide reflective equilibrium) of *A Theory of Justice* are grounded in relativism and skepticism.[6] Do not the extreme forms of skepticism and relativism needed to support Rawls's theories self-referentially collapse?

3. The movement of thought from *A Theory of Justice* to the "Dewey Lectures"[7] to the more recent essays[8] constitutes an attempt to substitute the internal-external distinction for (and have it do the job previously performed by) the certainty-skepticism distinction. Instead of placing strategic philosophical emphasis on how political certainty can be generated out of ethical and epistemological skepticism through the invocation of contractarian modes of argument, Rawls, in his later writings, stresses how his first principles (and the arguments he mobilizes in their behalf) really represent an "internalist" reading out of the implicit principles and priorities animating liberal-democratic society. The displacement of the justificatory apparatus of Rawls's argument from the skepticism-certainty distinction onto the internal-external distinction, however, does not yield the strategic utilities that he would like. The internal-external distinction confronts analogous problems of self-referentialism to the skepticism-certainty distinction. The internal-external *distinction* transcends the content of what it introduces under both its "internal" and "external" halves. How can *it* therefore be self-referentially justified?

I will elaborate on each of these points in turn.

1. "In order to find an Archimedean point," Rawls says, "it is not necessary to appeal to a priori or perfectionist principles. By assuming certain general desires, such as the desire for primary social goods, and by taking as a basis the agreements that would be made in a suitably defined situation, we can achieve the requisite independence from existing circumstances."[9]

Partially because of the difficulties encountered in formulating a skeptical position in philosophy that does not become self-refuting, Rawls (following Kant) wants to arrive at a "transcendental deduction" of his theory of justice as fairness by projecting an original position and invoking a veil of ignorance and assessing what the most rational decision-making procedure would be in such a hypothetical situation. However, the central device of his argument, the original position, facilitates a too-quick renunciation of the premise of radical equality that Rawls acknowledges on one level of argument. In his view, this social-contractarian context would yield allegiance to his two principles of justice—that of equal liberty for all and that of competition for resources and offices being open to all (with only those sorts of inequalities being acceptable that would benefit the least-well-off members of society). The justificatory procedure assumes the priority of the right over the good—the inviolability of the principle of separateness of persons over any individual's conception of what the good life requires. Both Robert Nozick[10] and Rawls accept the Kantian reformulation of skepticism in the ethical sphere—that each person is to be regarded as an end rather than as a means, that the plurality of persons inhabiting a particular political unit, with their conflicting views of the good life, constitutes the rock-bottom layer of justification in ethical argument—and differ largely over the issue of how far a denatured conception of the right might go and still be rendered philosophically plausible.[11] Rawls argues that "the two principles are equivalent . . . to an undertaking to regard the distribution of natural abilities as a collective asset so that the more fortunate are to benefit only in ways that help those who have lost out."[12] In contrast, Nozick argues that this sort of construal of natural abilities constitutes an illegitimate extension of the Kantian notion of the priority of the right over the good.

People will differ in how they view regarding natural talents as a common asset. Some will complain, echoing Rawls against utilitarianism, that this does not take seriously the distinction between persons; and they will wonder whether any reconstruction of Kant that treats people's abilities and talents as resources for others can be adequate. "The two principles of justice . . . rule out even the tendency to regard men as means to one another's welfare." Only if one presses *very* hard on the distinction between men and their talents, assets, abilities and special traits.[13]

The dispute between Rawls and Nozick concerning the moral defensibility and desirability of society engaging in redistributive schemes thus hinges upon their respective interpretations of the Kantian transcendental approach. Kant posits the inviolability of persons and asks us to consider how persons affirming their separateness and bereft of any particular conceptions of the good might justify a scheme of reciprocal rights and obligations. The theoretical disagreements between Rawls and Nozick depend upon the limits to state action that such parties to the original contract might impose. However, their Kantianism introduces a significant distortion into the argument. The skepticism concerning political knowledge that leads Rawls and Nozick to opt for varieties of Kantian transcendentalism is misleading. The Kantian skepticism (the justifying of political judgments by reference to what distinct individuals proclaiming the gospel of their separateness would sanction) has been made to look like a form of assurance—that a secure source can after all be fashioned for anchoring political judgments. In order for the full political implications of skepticism to become evident—that we are all, as it were, epistemological equals, and that industrial and governmental power cannot be invoked legitimately in furtherance of any particular individual's conception of the good unless that conception has managed to attract what we might call a participatory consensus—skepticism needs to be stated in and for itself in a raw, unblinkered idiom. The paradox underlying modern political thought, particularly the history of liberalism, is that from its inception skepticism could be suggested but never formulated as an independent philosophical thesis. In Kant's political thought, as its strategies of argumentation are refracted in the writings of Rawls and Nozick, the intractability of the problem of certainty is deflected onto a particular mode of justification: At least the separate individuals composing the political unit constitute, as bearers of the right of their separateness and ultimately as bearers of a plurality of rights stemming from this more basic right, a set of incarnated limits to what the state might legitimately do. The unstatability of extreme skepticism, having forced liberal political theorists into adopting a vocabulary of rights (which generates a sense of spurious certainty), has led them to jettison the original, albeit implicit, link between skepticism, equality, and participation.

2. In his trenchant review of *A Theory of Justice* in *Philosophical Review*,[14] Thomas Nagel argues that the philosophical devices of an

original position and a veil of ignorance employed by Rawls to justify the priority of the right over the good do not work. "Any hypothetical choice situation which requires agreement among the parties," Nagel writes, "will have to impose strong restrictions on the grounds of choice, *and these restrictions can be justified only in terms of a conception of the good.* It is one of those cases in which there is no neutrality to be had, because neutrality needs as much justification as any other position."[15] According to Nagel, there is no noncircular way to defend the choice of constraints operative within the hypothetical construct of the original position. Opting for neutrality among diverse visions of the good—assigning priority to the right over the good—can only be achieved at the cost of an antecedent commitment to a suppressed theory of the good that identifies the good with neutrality.

In pressing the argument concerning circularity, Nagel hits home on the individualist bias of Rawls's original position. "But given that many conceptions of the good do not fit into the individualistic pattern, how can this be described as a fair choice situation for principles of justice? Why should parties in the original position be prepared to commit themselves to principles that may frustrate or contravene their deepest convictions, just because they are deprived of knowledge of their convictions?"[16] Rawls thus precisely builds into his premises the individualism that is supposed to be an outcome of his argument.

The way Rawls distinguishes between utilitarianism and social-contract theory and the arguments he adduces in favor of the superiority of the latter are again circular. In the original position, the computation of probabilities proportional to the number of persons in each social position is ruled out. The only way that this assumption can be justified is "because it is not thought acceptable to sum advantages and disadvantages over persons, so that a loss for some is compensated by a gain for others."[17] Rawls distinguishes between utilitarianism and social-contract theory precisely on the grounds that the former is willing to extend to a whole society the principle of rational choice of one man. The distinction and the moral superiority of social-contract theory over utilitarianism are thus built into Rawls's depiction of the choice situation in the original position.[18]

In addition, the circularity of Rawls's stance is highlighted by the arguments he advances in rejection of the principle of utility and in favor of the difference principle. The principle of utility is cast aside because of the sacrifices it requires from those at the bottom of the social ladder.[19] At the same time, the difference principle is embraced despite the sacrifices it imposes on the well-to-do for the sake of those who are less well-off. The difference between the two arguments has to do with the class positions of those of whom sacrifices are demanded—the lower classes in the case of the principle of utility, the upper classes in the case of the difference principle. The drawing of the lines in this way, in turn, is only justifiable in the light of an antecedently accepted moral principle—"that sacrifices which lessen social inequality are acceptable while sacrifices which increase inequality are not."[20]

According to Nagel's deep reading of Rawls, then, what gets developed in *A Theory of Justice* is a rhetorical, as opposed to a more thoroughly philosophical, defense of liberal democracy. In Nagel's terminology: "The egalitarian liberalism which he [Rawls] develops and the conception of the good on which it depends are extremely persuasive, *but the original position serves to model rather than to justify them.*"[21] But to call *A Theory of Justice* a piece of political rhetoric does not diminish, but only helps to underscore, the problematic nature of its epistemological claims. For the concept of rhetoric presupposes that truth is relativized, and relativism is a reflexively unsustainable philosophical thesis.

Ronald Dworkin calls attention to what one might describe as the "structural circularity" of Rawls's argument by pointing to the vacuousness of the whole concept of hypothetical agreement. "But if I had not in fact agreed, the fact that I would have in itself means nothing."[22] The gap between hypothetical and actual consent cannot be adequately bridged conceptually unless one supplies the circular premise that one has in fact agreed to what the argument was designed to evoke acquiescence for.

Adina Schwartz maintains that in his notion of the desirability of "primary goods"—"liberty and opportunity, income and wealth and, above all, self-respect"[23]—which is supposed to be the only kind of substantive knowledge the contracting parties have access to under the veil of ignorance defining the original position, "Rawls inserts moral ideals and hypotheses about psychology and society which are as controversial as those of the utilitarian or perfectionist."[24] She argues that a preference for primary goods is not something endemic to all rational individuals but constitutes a circular reading back into the premises of Rawls's argument of the desiderata of liberal rationality. Socialist followers of the early Karl Marx, for example, would give their allegiance to a network of ideas including self-realization through labor and the determination of the political structure by the economic structure, which suggests that a person is morally harmed by possessing more than a minimal amount of wealth.[25] Rawls's response to Schwartz's criticism[26] successfully addresses the wealth component but not the radical-individualist aspect of Schwartz's argument.

Rawls's discussion of the choice of toleration and equal liberty of conscience under a veil of ignorance in the original position is called into question by Gerald Dworkin.[27] Nonneutral principles that allow for leeway of interpretation to determine which features of a situation come under the particular terms enshrined in the principles are rejected in favor of neutral principles that can be applied more directly and inflexibly to the situation at hand. Given the variety of moral, epistemological, and political views clamoring for assent, parties in the original position would favor the institutionalization of a neutral principle that guaranteed toleration of freedom of conscience rather than the establishment of nonneutral principles that immediately favored particular doctrines or groups. Dworking argues that an epistemological assumption motivates the circumstances of choice in the original position. The suppressed assumption of Rawls's argument is, in effect, the truth of skepticism. "Suppose the parties to the agreement know (or believe) the following: With respect to some areas of life (morals, science, aesthetics), there are people who are better placed than others to know the truth. Further, there are signs by which we may know them (they have red hair or they have an IQ of 200 or . . .). Would it not then be rational to choose these people as authorities with the right to suppress false views?"[28] The blocking out of such possibilities from the original position suggests an illicit smuggling into its conceptualization of a premise affirming the truth of skepticism. The problem for Rawls at this point becomes twofold. First, skepticism cannot be reflexively sustained as a philosophical thesis without also undermining itself; second, Rawls's argument in favor of toleration and equal liberty of conscience becomes circular. He has surreptitiously "read" back into the premises what is only supposed to emerge in the conclusion. As we have seen, the critical force of this second point fuses with the first. If Rawls is only "modeling" liberal arguments for us—giving us the most powerful rhetorical defenses in their behalf available—then that, too, presupposes the truth of skepticism, and extreme skepticism, taken by itself, is an incoherent philosophical thesis.

The specific metaethical position advanced in *A Theory of Jus-*

tice, wide reflective equilibrium, points Rawls in the internalist direction he has pursued in writings subsequent to his masterwork. The metaethical view of *A Theory of Justice* is marked by tension. On the one hand, Rawls elaborates a doctrine of wide reflective equilibrium as the justificatory schema undergirding his specific moral and political arguments.[29] On the other hand, Rawls argues that his theory was constructed sub specie aeternitatis, looking at the human situation "not only from all social but also from all temporal points of view."[30] The method of wide reflective equilibrium consists in a kind of local application of a coherence theory of truth, whereby maximization of coherence is attempted in relation to a triple set of beliefs held by a particular person: a set of considered moral judgments; a set of moral principles; and a set of relevant background theories. In wide reflective equilibrium, conflicting philosophical arguments are advanced to clarify the relative strengths and weaknesses of alternative philosophical theories that are compatible with the judgments. The "fit" between principles and judgments is determined to some extent in the light of one's construal of relevant background theories (usually of a scientific or commonsense sort) that impinge upon one's moral deliberation and theorizing. The theory of "wide reflective equilibrium" projects the agent as shifting back and forth between his judgments, principles, and theories—making mutual adjustments between them—so as to maximize the fit and coherence of the whole.[31]

A problem with wide reflective equilibrium, as Adina Schwartz has remarked, is that it can be used to justify atrocities: "Would not the judgments in reflective equilibrium of competent moral judges of Nazi society have accorded with Nazi principles of justice?"[32] Partially to avoid such a conclusion, Rawls in *A Theory of Justice* wants to say that there is somehow an ideal position in reflective equilibrium—one that duly integrates the constraints of the veil of ignorance and the original position—that is able to abstract from the particularistic and tainted value schemes of individual societies and approximate to the principles of justice that would be compelling in all times and places (which turn out, of course, to be the principles that animate the left of liberal-democratic society). It is ironic that Rawls, who has been such a forceful critic of utilitarianism, which often employs in relation to a whole society the principle of rational choice for one man (and which therefore often makes use of an ideal observer or spectator in arriving at its specific moral judgments and recommendations), should formulate his own contractarian alternative to utilitarianism from the position of a suitably purged and neutralized observer who is thus able to guarantee the requisite temporal and historical aloofness of the workings-out of the process of wide reflective equilibrium.

3: In the essays that have appeared since *A Theory of Justice*, Rawls pursues an opposite justificatory approach from that developed in the book. In his address of 1974, "The Independence of Moral Theory," Rawls says: "Although in order to get started various judgments are viewed as firm enough to be taken provisionally as fixed points, there are no judgments on any level of generality that are in principle immune to revision. Even the totality of particular judgments are not assigned a decisive role; thus these judgments do not have the status sometimes attributed to judgments of perception in theories of knowledge."[33] This passage represents a transposition to the fields of moral and political philosophy of Quine's theorizing of the field of knowledge in "Two Dogmas of Empiricism":

> The totality of our so-called knowledge or beliefs, from the most casual matters of geography and history to the profoundest laws of atomic physics or even of pure mathematics and logic, is a man-made fabric which impinges on experience only along the edges. . . . But the total field is so underdetermined by its boundary conditions, experience, that there is much latitude of choice as to what statements to reevaluate in the light of any single contrary experience. No particular experiences are linked with any particular statements in the interior of the field, except indirectly through considerations of equilibrium affecting the field as a whole. . . . Even a statement very close to the periphery can be held true in the face of recalcitrant experience by pleading hallucination or by amending certain statements of the kind called logical laws. Conversely, by the same token, no statement is immune to revision. Revision even of the logical law of the excluded middle has been proposed as a means of simplifying quantum mechanics; and what difference is there in principle between such a shift and the shift whereby Kepler superseded Ptolemy, or Einstein Newton, or Darwin Aristotle.[34]

According to Rawls's revised, more consistently Quinian-inspired reformulation of his argument in "The Independence of Moral Theory," the whole field of statements that the political theorist deals with consists of human inventions. From the most discrete and particular moral and political judgments to the most elaborate and abstract formulations of principle—as well as the fabric of external reality to which these judgments and principles relate in multiple ways—all consist of human verbal artifacts. The world of moral and political experience is a doubly created realm: The linguistic categories used to describe events and transactions—and also those through which they are evaluated—are fashioned by man and are shaped by historical and cultural factors. In contrast to the search for approximations to Archimedean points and universal perspectives that marks the argument of *A Theory of Justice*, in "The Independence of Moral Theory" Rawls frankly acknowledges that the universal element in moral and political theory is the factor of human making that establishes common ground between moral agents and political actors, on the one hand, and moral and political philosophers, on the other. It is the provisional nature of the constructs employed by both agents and philosophers that normalizes the vocation of theorizing by assimilating it to the vocations of choosing, acting, and responding to circumstances in the world that typify the moral agent and political actor.

Just as Quine's radical skepticism and relativism lead to a leveling of science and philosophy of science—neither the scientist nor the philosopher of science has a privileged access to reality; both are involved in the work of mutually adjusting human constructs so as to maximize coherence—so, too, according to Rawls, moral agents and political actors, on the one hand, and moral and political philosophers, on the other, are each trying to achieve wide reflective equilibrium among the judgments, principles, and perceptions that they take to be true, without harboring any antecedent commitments as to what the physical world and the moral universe are like, and indeed whether they exist in any stable, secure sense at all. Rawls's neo-Quinian rearticulation of the foundations of his enterprise, however, evokes the issue of reflexivity. How can skepticism and relativism be maintained without also undermining themselves—so that Rawls's argument remains suspended between a universalism it cannot support and a skepticism that self-destructs even before it can get formulated?

In the "Dewey Lectures," [35] Rawls resolves the immanentist-transcendental hedgings of his metaethical doctrine in *A Theory of Justice* in favor of a purely internalist reading of his two principles of justice: "We are not trying to find a conception of justice suitable for all societies regardless of their particular social or historical circumstances. *We want to settle a fundamental disagreement over the just form of basic institutions within a democratic society under modern conditions. . . . How far the conclusions we reach are of interest in a wider context is a separate question."* [36] In three subsequent papers, Rawls presents metaphoric redescriptions of his internalism, which are encapsulated in their titles: "Justice as Fairness: Political, not Metaphysical"; "The Idea of an Overlapping Consensus"; and "On the Idea of Free Public Reason." In the first essay, Rawls argues that "philosophy as the search for truth about an independent metaphysical and moral order cannot, I believe, provide a workable and shared basis for a political conception of justice in a democratic society," and that "the basic ideas of justice as fairness are regarded as implicit or latent in the public culture of a democratic society." [37] In "Overlapping Consensus," Rawls suggests that "this political conception needs to be such that there is some hope of its gaining the support of an overlapping consensus, that is, a consensus in which it is affirmed by the opposing religious, philosophical and moral doctrines likely to thrive over generations in a more or less just constitutional democracy, where the criterion of justice is that political conception itself." [38] In the last essay, Rawls links his political conception of justice as fairness with the idea of free public reason: "In a democratic regime, it [political power] is also the power of the public: that is, of free and equal citizens as a corporate body. Therefore, political power must be exercised in ways that all citizens can publicly endorse before one another in the light of their own reason. Only in this way can the political conception of justice provide a public basis of justification." [39]

From which metaphysical/political perspective is Rawls formulating his rejection of a metaphysical reading (and affirming a political construal) of the principles of justice as fairness? Rawls's argument appears to be inconsistent, because he is looking for a philosophical vantage point beyond philosophy from which to rebuff the claims of philosophy and advance the priority of politics. In addition, the *distinction* between politics and metaphysics appears to transcend the content of both categories, and thus cannot be reflexively sustained.

There are three more lines of criticism that appear compelling at this point. The first is, as I have been arguing throughout this chapter, that the skepticism and relativism that Rawls has openly embraced since the "Dewey Lectures" renders him vulnerable to the charge that skepticism and relativism are self-refuting philosophical doctrines—

that they are not reflexively sustainable. Second, in relation to the unambiguously Quinian approach that Rawls has adopted in "The Independence of Moral Theory," one can put the question to both Quine and Rawls: How do you preserve the autonomous identity of "philosophizing of science" and "moral and political philosophizing" so that the collapse of the former into science and the latter into moral and political deliberation and decision making ("metaphysics" into "politics" in Rawls's idiom) do not yield mere tautologies but constitute genuine explanations? How is the independence of the *explanandum* from the *explanans* in each case to be maintained?

A third difficulty with Rawlsian skepticism and relativism is that to talk about them is already conceptually to be exceeding them. Someone who truly lacks a basis for judgment is not able to codify the insufficiency of a basis for judgment into a bona fide epistemological doctrine on its own that highlights the unbridgeable gap(s) between data and judgment. If you do not have a basis for judgment, how do you *know* that you do not have a basis for judgment? Analogously, someone whose knowledge was truly relativized to historical and cultural context would not be able to codify the relativization of knowledge to context into a theory about the limits of knowledge. If your knowledge is thoroughly relativized as to context, how do you *know* as an intellectual datum about yourself that your knowledge is so relativized? In each case, the formulation of the tenets of skepticism and relativism exceeds the epistemological warrant of the premises of the positions.

Rawls's internalism is vulnerable to the same criticism that Joshua Cohen has leveled against Michael Walzer's internalism as formulated in *Spheres of Justice*[40] and that can be extended to Walzer's more recent *Interpretation and Social Criticism.*[41] Walzer tells us in the earlier work that justice consists in following our shared values, that a "given society is just if its substantial life is lived in a certain way— that is, in a way faithful to the shared understandings of the members."[42] Cohen argues that Walzer's internalism is either vacuous or conservative. "When social practices support a particular, coherent value interpretation—that is, when we have determinate values—it [Walzer's internalist approach] is conservative. When our practices do not support such an interpretation, it gives conflicting advice and, as a result, no advice at all."[43] Similarly, with regard to Rawls's two principles of justice, as he has reinterpreted their epistemological status in his later writings, one might say that they either represent a consensual reading of the values and allegiances animating liberal-democratic society (in which case they are conservative), or else, out of the fragmented, multilayered consciousness of democratic citizens, Rawls has arbitrarily crystallized his two principles—in which case the principles tell us a good deal about Rawls but illuminate far less than he can acknowledge about the nature of liberal-democratic society.

The groundwork for the communitarian critique of liberalism that gained prominence in the 1980s in the works of Alasdair MacIntyre and Michael Sandel[44] was laid in a critique of Rawls's Kantianism written by Bernard Williams in the mid-1970s.[45] Williams argues that if Rawls is correct that utilitarianism fails to take seriously the separateness of persons, Kantianism is equally vulnerable because it does not assign sufficient weight to their distinctiveness. According to Kant "our obligations are independent of our identity or character."[46] According to Williams, however, abstraction from character is a fundamental mistake. A person's character—his goals and values—are conditions for his taking any interest in the world at all and make sense of the obligations he voluntarily assumes and of their binding character. From Williams's critique of Rawls's Kantianism it is but a short step to the full-blown communitarian critique of the 1980s. Williams wants us to consider flesh-and-blood individuals with the richness of their characters intact as the subjects of obligation. Communitarians want us to expand our canvasses of inquiry and justification to make room for the roles of community and tradition in transmitting and inculcating identity and values and thereby shaping character.

The problem of reflexivity facing communitarian critiques of liberalism is analogous to the problem of reflexivity confronting Rawlsian liberalism itself. The primacy of internalism—and the rejection of abstract right—that communitarianism advocates cannot be established on internalist grounds. "Community" and "tradition" cannot be justified in the name of "community" and "tradition" without becoming circular concepts. There are thus analogous justificatory gaps affecting both Rawlsian liberal and communitarian political theories. Just as we have seen Rawls building into his conceptualization of the original position most of what he requires for his full-blown contractarian theory, so that his position emerges as implicitly circular, communitarianism explicitly affirms circularity in the primacy that it assigns to tradition and community. The later Rawls, as we have seen, is increasingly inclined to an internalist reading of his two principles of justice, which means that in many respects he is recommending his liberal theory to us on communitarian grounds. It is supposed to resonate with the shared understandings that animate participants in our political tradition considered as a whole.[47]

The additional dimensions of the issue of reflexivity that destablize liberalism also bedevil communitarianism. Like the later Rawlsian version of liberalism, it presupposes the validity (and the explanatory efficacy) of an internal-external distinction. This *distinction*, however, moves beyond the content of its "internal" and "external" halves and therefore cannot be reflexively justified. In addition, for Rawls, as we have seen, the collapse of the activities of moral and political theorizing into the activities of moral and political deliberation and decision making raises the methodological specter of tautology—that the *explanandum* merges so totally with the *explanans* that the *explanandum* loses its autonomous identity and the explanation consequently is reduced to a tautology. Analogously, for communitarians the wholesale redescription of outside forces impinging upon individual and social development in terms of the traditional and communitarian apparatuses through which they are mediated to individuals and to the community is suggestive of such a total overtaking of the category of the external by the category of the internal that the specter of tautology looms, calling the explanatory force of communitarian social and political theory into question.

Just as Rawlsian liberalism is predicated upon skepticism and relativism in the multiple and continuing ways analyzed above, so, too, is communitarianism founded upon skepticism and relativism. Cultural value is a community product and inheritance. Normatively and descriptively, there is nothing to appeal to beyond the mechanisms of community and tradition in affirming or accounting for a particular society's scheme of values. Skepticism and relativism, however, in addition to giving rise to issues of reflexivity, are incoherent in the sense that their premises exceed their own epistemological warrant. "Skepticism" codifies the truth of skepticism, which the skeptic is disbarred from knowing, and "relativism" enshrines the truth of relativism, which the relativist is denied access to.

The concepts of "tradition" and "community" are incoherent for analogous reasons. If all of one's learning and values, the whole process of self-formation, is mediated through the mechanisms of "tradition" and "community," then one remains oblivious of the structured, well-defined character of that which is molding one into the person he or she is becoming. The concepts of "tradition" and "community"—just like the notions of "skepticism" and "relativism"—also exceed their epistemological warrant by presupposing in their very formulation precisely what their overt content denies.

The notions of "tradition" and "community" deployed by MacIntyre and Sandel as central vantage points from which to depreciate the metaphysically individualist claims of liberalism are also simultaneously sociologically and epistemologically vulnerable. When examined with appropriate historical scrutiny, the monoliths of "tradition" and "community" usually stand exposed as a tissue of "traditionalisms"—multiple, self-conscious acts of affirmation by individuals. "Tradition" and "community" are often terms applied ex post facto to what were at the time of their actual occurrence manifold self-conscious interventions by individuals goaded by the tensions introduced between the values and loyalties they were brought up with and cherish and alternative ways of ordering the world with which they came in contact during their young adulthood and maturity. Sometimes people are motivated to affirm their older values and loyalties in the face of later challenges, and a "summing" of these self-conscious affirmations gets denominated by such collectivist, irrationalist terms as "tradition" and "community." But such terms often belie a Kantian abstraction from the immediate circumstances of the self in order to facilitate a traditionalistic, self-conscious affirmation of the past.

The enveloping character of "tradition" and "community" that communitarian critics of liberal individualism rightly proclaim does not just stop where communitarians say it stops. It goes on to encompass—and to influence and shape in rebellion (even in rebellion that has the face of affirmation) the multifarious validations of tradition by traditionalists that take place in response to subversive alternatives. MacIntyre and Sandel arrest "circularity" prematurely. They are not sufficiently aware of the complexity of the dialectic of affirmation and rebellion—not only (as they perceive) rebellion using the conceptual tools of tradition, of affirmation, but the very conceptual tools of tradition itself as the reification and residue of multiple individual acts of rebellion (of transcending the givenness of one's situation) conceived and realized *as* affirmation—in creating the fabrics of tradition and community.

In responding to communitarian or protocommunitarian critiques of liberalism, John Rawls, Charles Larmore, and Richard Rorty pursue a common strategy that is vulnerable at precisely the same point. In the "Dewey Lectures," Rawls acknowledges that in "personal affairs," in the private realm, the communitarian critique of liberalism is appropriate. Private selves are nurtured and formed, and carry on their deliberations, in traditional and communitarian settings. In the public realm, however, we must abstract from the communal accretions to some primal layer of being and individuality in order to make our moral and political deliberations conform to our most exalted conceptions of value. Rawls extols the virtues of this radical individualist-communitarian synthesis: "Within different contexts we can assume diverse points of view toward our person without contradiction so long as these points of view cohere together when circumstances require." [48]

Charles Larmore, in *Patterns of Moral Complexity*,[49] adopts an analogous strategy for accommodating the communitarian critique: "What is of paramount importance in the political realm need not have the same weight outside that realm. Neutrality can be our highest political value, without being the value we must strive to make supreme in other parts of our lives, without being, as I shall use this term, our highest 'personal ideal.' " [50] According to Larmore, the unsatisfactory legacy of Kantianism can be adequately overcome by applying the communitarian critique to the formation of the private moral self while preserving the Kantian priority of the right over the good for a delimitation of the public moral self and the protocols of self-restraint appropriate there.

Richard Rorty also endorses the later Rawlsian synthesis: "The compromise advocated in this book amounts to saying: *Privatize* the Nietzschean-Sartrean-Foucauldian attempt at authenticity and purity, in order to prevent yourself from slipping into a political attitude which will lead you to think that there is some social goal more important than avoiding cruelty." [51] Liberal public neutrality for Rorty paradoxically becomes the only basis for solidarity available to Nietzschean, endlessly plastic private men and women.[52]

The bifurcation of Kantian moral philosophizing supported in different ways by Rawls, Larmore, and Rorty is predicated upon the viability of a contextual ethics—one that accommodates the invocation of different moral standards for the disparate spheres where moral decision making takes place. Contextualism, in turn, is an exemplification of relativism—and relativism falls prey to all of those dimensions of the problem of reflexivity discussed in this chapter.

• *"Rezoning" and a Generalized Agnosticism*

The general approach pursued by Thomas Nagel[53] in reconciling conflicts between subjectivity and objectivity in various regions of philosophizing is extremely congenial for resolving the dilemmas concerning skepticism and relativism affecting both liberalism and communitarianism. I will describe in broad outline his approach in the case of one region of ethical theory (the role of reason in ethics), indicate where I think a dominant model for his overall philosophical strategy comes from, and suggest how it might be possible to extrapolate from his approach to the issues of skepticism and relativism.

According to Nagel, linguistic formulations of an agent expressive of his subjective value allegiances and preferences have to be regarded as part of an enlarged concept of objectivity: Our everyday descriptions of our experiences, of what we think we are doing, are as much a part of what is in the world as a physicist's or neurophysiologist's account of our actions. Nagel calls this approach a version of realism: "Physicalism," he says, "is based ultimately on a form of idealism: an idealism of restricted objectivity. Objectivity of whatever kind is not the test of reality. It is just one way of understanding reality."[54]

Ludwig Wittgenstein provides an important model for Nagel's conduct of philosophical activity as rezoning—assigning to a new rubric what was previously included under a different, conflicting category (in Nagel's case, detaching the reports of the agent involved in moral deliberation from the category of "subjectivity" and assigning them to that of "objectivity"). The movement of thought from the early to the later Wittgenstein can most illuminatingly be understood from this perspective. In the *Tractatus Logico-Philosophicus* (Wittgenstein's early work), he confronts the problem of rendering his skepticism consistent, which he partially resolves by an act of rezoning—separating unacceptable discourse (according to his criteria of meaning) into the two regions of a "higher" and a "lower nonsense." Since the philosophical statements that compose the metaphysics of logical atomism and articulate the picture theory of the proposition (which are expressive of Wittgenstein's skepticism in the *Tractatus*) cannot themselves be validated in accordance with that metaphysics and that theory, he attempts to slough them off after his philosophical theory has been fully laid out by relegating these statements to a realm of what might be called the "higher nonsense." The "lower nonsense" consists of those statements rendered invalid by logical atomism and the picture theory that are truly to be discarded. The "higher nonsense" consists of what Wittgenstein in the *Tractatus* calls *das Mystiche* (6.522)—the statements that emerge as problematic because of his philosophical theory but that he remains committed to, or ones that are otherwise indispensable (as the philosophical statements are) on other grounds.

The transition from the *Tractatus* to Wittgenstein's later philosophy can be seen as expressive of his emerging realization that the issue of consistency in relation to his skepticism could be most elegantly resolved by rezoning on the acceptable-discourse side of the divide that separates acceptable discourse from nonsense, rather than within the region of nonsense statements themselves. With the work commencing in the 1930s and culminating in the *Philosophical Investigations*, Wittgenstein deploys the resources of rezoning on the side of intelligible discourse—so that the category of the higher nonsense disappears, absorbed into the notion of disparate and incommensurable language-games. In the new terrain mapped by the *Investigations*, everything can be said as long as the different rules governing different language regions are observed. There are no sanctions higher than, and no court of appeal beyond, the disparate sets of rules governing different language-games.

Nagel's rezoning of subjectivity so that it becomes as constitutive of reality as more officially objective indications of reality helps resolve the dilemmas concerning skepticism and relativism discussed above. His pursuit of rezoning is suggestive of a philosophical position that we might term "generalized agnosticism in relation to the world," or "generalized agnosticism" for short. Nagel appears to be telling us that as long as human experience (including scientific experience) of the world continues, no definitive, exhaustive account of objective reality exists. All kinds of subjective ramifications of our experience belong as data in the objective account. From this perspective, liberalism and communitarianism are ultimately salvageable as historical emergences that have managed to carve out theoretical and social space for themselves. Justification in both cases is *a posteriori* and *ex post facto*—with commitment endlessly deferred as to what the nature of the world is like.

A generalized agnosticism enables us to accommodate the various manifestations of circularity in Rawls's argument—as well as in "internalist" political thought more generally—discussed previously because it suggests that so-called reality is never sufficiently defined or known to serve as an ultimate constraint upon theorizing. Therefore, theorizing itself (for example, Rawls's own theorizing) has to be construed as just another event in the world that later theorizing, *a posteriori*, can attempt to theorize and devise logical protocols for. From the perspective of a generalized agnosticism, the charge of circularity loses its sting. "Circularity" can be viewed as proceeding on the premises of the incompleteness and, therefore, also the at least partially unknown character, of objective reality. Since reality is incomplete and hence also partially unknown, "circularity"—building the salient point(s) of one's conclusion into one's premise(s)—constitutes an artful philosophical strategy for producing a symmetrically designed piece of argument that will provisionally fill in our objective-knowledge gap. If there is no firm external check against a premise or an argument as a whole (as there is not, according to a generalized-agnostic account), then "circularity" becomes a fact of (logical) life.[55] In Lyotard's words, "Supporting an argument means looking for a 'paradox' and legitimating it with new rules in the games of reasoning."[56] In a generalized-agnostic universe, circular argument yields a thought construct that serves as a surrogate for a reality that is not otherwise conceptually containable or referrable. The circular argument confers durability and weight upon its components when reality provides none.

A strategic metaphysical and psychological advantage of participatory democracy over other forms of communitarianism—and over liberalism—is that there is a much more straightforward fit between skepticism and participatory democracy than is true of the relationship between skepticism and other forms of communitarianism and skepticism and liberalism. As we have seen throughout our discussion, theoretical delineations of communitarianism and liberalism are not able to shed successfully a profound theoretical link with skepticism. In the case of liberalism and communitarianism, this link gets (inadvertently) camouflaged through invocation of the rhetoric of "rights" in liberalism and invocation of the rhetorics of "community" and "tradition" in communitarianism. Liberalism and communitarianism, though grounded in skepticism, take a rhetorical detour through metaphysical and political categories suggestive of certainty: "rights," and "tradition" and "community," respectively. Participatory democracy, by contrast, does not generate illusions of certainty. The connection between individual citizen involvement and decisional outcome is preserved throughout the whole circuit of political theorizing and institutional translation.

A generalized agnosticism—which seems to be the only consistent version of skepticism available to us—links up with the world through political participation. This medium enables us to fashion modes of living in the world that are congruent with our uncertainties, because they are dependent upon mutual agreement rather than being in harmony with something transcendent. Also, political participation—especially when understood in Peter Bachrach's sense of a striving toward equality in the sharing of power—constitutes an "enactment" of skepticism in a straightforward institutional sense: the continuing reestablishment of democratic consensus on a multitude of issues through the active intervention of democratic citizens.

A consistently skeptical (generalized-agnostic) approach to political participation calls attention to the incompleteness of thought in order to be able to make sense of and justify what we do. "The incompleteness of objective reality" invites human beings to perpetually do—to perpetually intervene in their natural and social orders— for the sake of engendering a more secure sense of who they are, what they want, and what they are capable of achieving. A generalized agnosticism envisages thought (the conceptualization of what is involved in thinking) as needing to be supplemented by action (a recognition of the centrality of an action-context) in order to emerge more coherently as thought. More specifically, we might say that participation in diverse forms of collective doing and decision making needs to be invoked in order to make sense of the process of thinking itself. A consistently skeptical (generalized-agnostic) approach to political participation seeks to provide an epistemological backdrop in which the naturalness and inevitableness of participation—the proliferation of forums for collective doing—seem especially persuasive and compelling.

As we have seen, the political implications of skepticism cannot be tightly, logically drawn, since the connection between skepticism and participation is largely rhetorical. Under whatever theoretical auspices the validity of skepticism is achieved, the stage is merely set for drawing informal connections between skepticism and political participation. The most significant of these connections is that if secure knowledge about life's most fundamental questions cannot be attained, then the most justifiable course is to follow the evolution of a collective rationality through the active participation of democratic citizens in networks of decision making affecting as many areas of their lives as possible. Natural-rights claims that have historically been advanced in liberal-democratic society, though they project an aura of certainty, can most fruitfully be seen as an outgrowth of skepticism. In the absence of secure knowledge about the central questions of life, we convert respect for persons in all of its manifold dimensions into a central organizing principle of democratic political life. In the absence of substantive certainty, skepticism yields the procedural norm of participation.

Since the transition between skepticism and widespread political participation can only be informally, rhetorically negotiated, there is also room within a political ontology assigning highest priority to participation for accommodating the countervailing political principles of majority rule, representation, protection of minority rights, and leadership. The impulse governing this accommodation should always be toward maximum possible integration of participation in the delineation and justification of these alternative concepts. For example, it is possible to sketch a theory of democratic leadership suffused with a recognition of the imperatives of equality. Leadership needs to emerge from within a participatory political setting so that the identities of leaders and led remain fluid and porous. This relationship can be theorized on analogy with Gramsci's construal of the relationship between teacher and pupil, which "is active and reciprocal so that every teacher is always a pupil and every pupil is a teacher." In order for a political movement to achieve greater equalization in the distribution of power, the way the movement itself is structured must already reflect the preeminence assigned to the value of equality. Therefore, leadership has to be delineated and actualized as temporarily crystallizing moments in the extension of democratic equality as shocks of recognition are registered between those less in the know and those more in the know concerning configurations of power. Moreover, such moments should set the stage for later exchanges of roles between the two groups, enabling the formerly less knowledgeable to exercise leadership roles of their own in relation to marginalized or excluded groups within society.

• *A Postmodernist Liberal Communitarianism*

A more consistently and coherently postmodernist revision of the tenets of liberal-democratic theory than is currently available in the Rawlsian or the communitarian literature would include the following four points.

Theory of truth and its relationship to politics. A generalized agnosticism is suggestive of a continaully emerging truth. The only truth that politics institutionalizes (and it institutionalizes it only because it *may* be true—it does not refuse to countenance the possibility that it might not be true) is the "truth" of openness. Openness has "lexical priority" over any particular political program that is submitted under an agenda favoring openness because of the continuing relevance of the agnostic question that perhaps this (formulated in relation to any specific policy proposal) is not so.

Justice. Justice is what one is trying to do now, the kind of program or vision one is trying to enact at the present moment. It is not just, as the later Rawls, Walzer, and the communitarians would have it, the reading out of the intimations of your own tradition, but would also consist in attempts to reconstitute that tradition in the light of particular visions concerning how it might be improved or transformed. Justice, however, is not constituted by the shadow structures of blueprints of change or canons of judgment through which current arrangements are condemned or criticized but by the efforts at change themselves. It is the doing that bespeaks the impulse to achieve justice. The rationalizations and reifications all have to be construed in the light of the agnostic imperative that questions both their accuracy as abridgements of concrete political experience and their comprehensiveness and accuracy as codifications of the ideal. Justice is engagement in a certain activity—a form of doing—and theorizing inevitably distorts and artificially delimits the nature of that doing.

Rights. Current limits on state action are as permanent and enduring as our willingness to mobilize such action in their defense. What we cannot do boils down to what we are unwilling to do at any given moment in historical time. At the base of a constitutional regime lies the tautologous, circular argument—we cannot do it because we cannot do it. We need to emphasize the agnostic seedbed of rights. It is not that we know certain things to be the case but rather that we are searching on a rhetorical plane for the appropriate institutional translation of openness. The vocabulary of rights that requires negative, adversarial opinion to be heard signifies continual openness to all possibilities—including our questioning of the validity of openness itself.

There is, however, only a rhetorical affinity between a generalized agnosticism and a political system that emphasizes the centrality of rights. The "grundnorm" of a liberal political system is a metaphysically arbitrary attempt to structure political institutions in the light of the theoretical image of a generalized agnosticism (which does not itself decree that only a liberal ordering of institutions is just).

Political obligation. According to the postmodernist approach I have developed in this and the previous chapters, political obligation becomes a function of one's obligating oneself in a series of successive presents. The circular statement—one is obligated to obey because one is obligating oneself to obey—becomes the only relevant comment to make with regard to the question of political obligation. This circumvents Ronald Dworkin's objection against contractarian, hypothetical obligation cited earlier. "Political obligation," like "justice," becomes a concept that is open to the future. It is a notion formulated in the present summarizing the content of future actions.

There is a real-world analogue to the phenomenon of convergence between liberalism and communitarianism—and a supersession of the whole debate, once deep continuities between the two antagonistic sets of theories are unearthed—that has been brought to the foreground by our epistemological investigations. Our postindustrial civilization is providing a new impetus for a coalescence (or merging) between liberalism and at least some forms of communitarianism. As our society scales down and restructures to adjust to the exigencies of an era of industrial decline and diminished economic growth, the likeliest outcomes appear to be greater class and economic polarization, leading to widespread cynicism and demoralization concerning democracy. This, in turn, could set the stage for the emergence of collectivism under the aegis of either a rightist or leftist ideology— or perhaps of pendular movements in first one direction and then the other.

There has been a tacit premise of abundance underlying the establishment and subsequent history of American constitutionalism. Such doctrines as separation of powers and checks and balances, which officially aim at inhibiting the fund of governmental power, could seem plausible in governing a republic as vast and heterogeneous as the United States only because the abundance of resources available for cultivation meant that governmental authority did not have to be immediately invoked to mitigate conflict and regulate distribution, since deprived parties could strive to rectify the balance on their own by seeking out new opportunities. Also, the abundance of resources in America has historically meant that where government has had to step in to regulate and distribute it has been able to preserve a façade of neutrality and powerlessness, because the economy was rich enough to sustain the entrenched positions of the already powerful *and* the basic demands of the powerless clamoring for an institutional stake in the game. In a context of diminished economic growth, the basic ground rules of American politics are becoming jeopardized. The façade of governmental neutrality and powerlessness—epitomized by the whole concept of American constitutionalism—that has been preserved with varying cracks throughout American history might have to be dropped in favor of more direct, continuous, and self-conscious intervention in structuring American economy and society in response to the pressures of diminished growth.

From a sheerly theoretical, comparative-historical perspective, the possibilities that become most alluring are either greater collectivization in the direction of socialism (with government controlling more and more phases of the acquisitive and distributive processes) or greater collectivization in a fascist direction (with radical national unity purchased at the cost of racial, religious, or class scapegoats). The preservation of liberal democracy is the option that seems least plausible in the context of reduced economic opportunity. It is at this juncture that a participatory reorientation of American society might offer the most promising strategy for maintaining some key values of liberal democracy in a drastically transformed economic setting.

During the period that the doctrines that we have come to denominate as liberalism were fashioned and institutionalized, they had limited opportunity to become actualized in a pristine form because of the historical convergence of liberalism with capitalism. The radical individualism that lies at the core of liberalism quickly assumed a spurious "ideological" reality behind which the insatiable dynamic of capitalism could work itself out. Efforts to disengage the valuational kernel of liberalism from a fully elaborated capitalistic network of practices and institutions have generally failed, as an advancing capitalism devised new strategies to co-opt protest movements and have them contribute new personnel, ideas, and energy to its own expansive dynamic. It might very well be that liberal individualism will have a chance to come into its own and influence events as an unalloyed historical entity only when its link with capitalism will have been severed by circumstances in an age of diminished economic growth. A participatory restructuring of American society—encompassing all levels of human organization from educational and social networks to the workplace and government—furnishes a most promising strategy for ensuring the survival of liberal-individualist values in a social and economic setting that on the surface appears grossly inhospitable to them. If the values of the cultivation of individuality, diversity, and freedom of expression can no longer be supported even in a partial and distorted way by a shrinking resource base of society, they can perhaps be nurtured by a participatory praxis that teaches human beings the value of these notions through doing—by actualizing them in a participatory framework and thereby developing allegiance toward them. The result would be in some sense the emergence of a true liberalism after the historical era of liberalism was over.

4 • *Rousseau and the Discovery of Reflexivity*

What are the internal roots in Rousseau's thought for the tremendous stress on political participation one finds expressed there? It seems to me that there is an instructive contrast here with Hobbes concerning the background argumentation that sets the stage for the theorizing of the proper political order. Since Rousseau formulates his political theory at several crucial junctures in conscious opposition to Hobbes, what I am about to summarize might not only be heuristically useful but might actually tell us something concerning Rousseau's inner struggles to formulate an independent position in relation to views adopted by a major predecessor.

Hobbes, as we shall see, derives his representative scheme of government—his conception of sovereign political authority and its rootedness in consent—directly from his nominalism. Rousseau rejects Hobbes's nominalism, and the doctrine of representation and the concept of law to which it leads. Rousseau attaches permanent metaphysical significance to a particular phase in human development, so that man's essence—who he is, what his authentic potential is—remains fixed with regard to all subsequent periods of human development. After this phase, which is elevated out of historical time and given enduring significance, whatever else occurs in human history has to be measured against its facilitating the realization of or thwarting the potential of what was disclosed in that privileged phase. The generative insight of Rousseau's political theory, what might be regarded as the counterpart of Hobbes's nominalism, is the paradigmatic role and essentialist value to be attached to the earliest phases of the state of nature. Here is the familiar description from the *Second Discourse:*

> From the little care taken by nature to bring men together through mutual needs and to facilitate their use of speech, one at least sees how little it prepared their sociability, and how little it con- tributed to everything men have done to establish social bonds. In fact, it is impossible to imagine why, in that primitive state, a man would sooner have need of another man than a monkey or a wolf of its fellow creature; nor, supposing this need, what motive could induce the other to provide for it, nor even, in this last case, how they could agree between them on the conditions. I know we are repeatedly told that nothing would have been so miserable as man in that state; and if it is true, as I believe I have proved, that only after many centuries could men have had the desire and opportunity to leave that state, it would be a fault to find with nature and not with him who would have been so constituted by nature. But if I understand properly this term miserable, it is a word that has no meaning or only signifies a painful privation and the suffering of the body or soul. Now I would really like some- one to explain to me what type of misery there can be for a free being whose heart is at peace and whose body is healthy? I ask which, civil or natural life, is most likely to become unbearable to those who enjoy it? We see around us practically no people who do not complain of their existence, even many who deprive them- selves of it insofar as they have the capacity; and the combination of divine and human laws hardly suffices to stop this disorder. I ask if anyone has ever heard it said that a savage in freedom ever dreamed of complaining about life and killing himself. Let it then be judged with less pride on which side true misery lies.[1]

Rousseau lacks a theory of knowledge in Hobbes's sense. He does not systematically explore the question of how we can validate our knowledge claims. What substitutes for an epistemology in Rous- seau is a metaphysics that runs counter to the central impulse of Hobbes's theorizing. Instead of regarding the sources of knowledge and of truth as being the functions of a naming process that is ame- nable to human control (as residing within us), Rousseau regards the source of truth about man and the fundamental datum of political knowledge as being the results of a developmental process over which humans exercise no veto and no control (as residing outside us). The early phases of life in the state of nature—characterized by dependence on things, rather than by dependence on people[2]—represent that maximal ordering of human energies that enable human beings to reach the highest degree of happiness of which they are capable.

From a negative, critical perspective, one might say that Rousseau's theorizing serves as a precursor text for postmodernism. His collapsing of the certitude of Hobbes's point of origin, the assigning of names and the drawing out and interweaving of their implications, onto a more "secure" starting point, the realist (historically evolutionary) phase of the state of nature, is suggestive of the illusoriness and permeability of both nominalism and realism as background metaphysical postulates in political theory. Given our incomplete knowledge of objective reality, the distinction between nominalism and realism is blurred. The brute "thereness" of phenomena that the realist depends on to validate his philosophical statements might be eclipsed and transformed in the course of time, disclosing just further manifestations of human making. Correspondingly, the nominalist's overt and self-conscious making might constitute such a persuasive delineation of reality that it defines reality for us for long stretches of historical time. "Nominalism" and "realism" therefore might most appropriately be construed as pragmatically inspired and ordained metaphilosophical categories—that are known by their fruits and not by the intrinsic compellingness of their philosophical structures. Rousseau is among the first in a long line of rebels to chafe against the excesses of Hobbesian individualism—and therefore substitutes an alternative set of metaphysical assumptions to yield a more acceptable set of political consequences.

The history of the individual, for Rousseau, recapitulates the history of the human race. Here too there is an "essentialist moment" of dependence on things rather than on people that, if properly harnessed, leads to an optimal human existence. There is a necessary developmental phase in childhood (one independent of human intervention or control) that if properly translated and integrated into the remainder of one's life spells happiness. *Emile*, it might be said, is devoted to the theme of how to achieve a proper translation and integration of this phase of childhood. All forms of human unhappiness, according to Rousseau, result from a failure to capture and capitalize upon the implications and potential of that period of childhood in which dependence on things rather than people is still felt:

> I have already said that your child ought to get a thing not because he asks for it but because he needs it, and do a thing not

out of obedience but out of necessity. Thus the words obey and command will be proscribed from his lexicon, and even more so duty and obligation. But strength, necessity, impotence, and constraint should play a great role in it. Before the age of reason one cannot have any idea of moral beings or of social relations. Hence so far as possible words which express them must be avoided, for fear that the child in the beginning attach to these words false ideas which you will not know about or will no longer be able to destroy. The first false idea which enters his head is the germ in him of error and vice. It is to this first step above all that attention must be paid. Arrange it so that as long as he is struck only by objects of sense, all his ideas stop at sensations; arrange it so that on all sides he perceives around him only the physical world. Without that, you may be sure that he will not listen to you at all, or that he will get fantastic notions of the moral world of which you speak to him, notions that you will never in your life be able to blot out.[3]

The principle of dependence on things rather than on people is also reflected in the Profession of Faith of the Savoyard Vicar.[4] If one has been brought up in accordance with Rousseauean principles, one can dispense with the personal faith of biblical monotheistic religion (which is a kind of magnification of the principle of dependence on man), and rest content with the natural religion described by the Savoyard Vicar (which is a kind of glorification of the principle of dependence on things), accepting the irreducibleness and beneficence of natural phenomena.

The role of the legislator in Rousseau's thought can be seen in a new light from the perspective that I am advancing. The legislator is an important personage in Niccolò Machiavelli's political thought as a founder and renewer of states. However, in the context of Rousseau's political thought, the role of the legislator assumes an added dimension of significance. This is the way Rousseau defines the role of the legislator in the life of states:

The legislator is an extraordinary man in the State in all respects. If he should be so by his genius, he is no less so by his function. It is not magistracy, it is not sovereignty. This function, which constitutes the republic, does not enter into its constitution. It is a particular and superior activity that has nothing in common with human dominion. For if one who has authority over men should not have authority over laws, one who has authority over laws

> should also not have authority over men. Otherwise his laws,
> ministers of his passions, would often only perpetuate his injus-
> tices, and he could never avoid having private views alter the
> sanctity of his work.[5]

Given Rousseau's essentialism, his search for external sources of certainty, with this concept of the legislator he is seeking a temporal, methodically certified surrogate for the early phases of the state of nature. In order to be sure that a particular set of social arrangements suits a particular people, with their unique mores and historically conditioned patterns of living, in such a way as to maximize that image of balanced happiness suggested by the early phases of the state of nature, Rousseau defines the politically ambivalent role of the legislator. The method followed in delineating and circumscribing his role— that he establish a constitution that a whole society must live by, but then have no voice in the implementation of the blueprint he lays down—ensures that the legislator will be guided by the most altruistic motives possible. The pattern of the external guarantee of certainty begun by the privileged status accorded to the early phases of the state of nature is continued by Rousseau in the actual life of states by the investiture of a privileged status in a legislator whose role is methodically guaranteed to issue forth in the most disinterested and benevolent judgments concerning the welfare of the community.

The original dependence on things that prevailed in the early phases of the state of nature slowly gets transformed into an emerging recognition of the value of a division of labor in the performance of daily human tasks. This in turn leads to intramural comparisons between human beings, and finally to the devising of strategies (such as staking out a piece of land as one's own) to justify a higher comparative rating for one's efforts in relation to those of one's fellows. For the original equilibrium between need and desire that prevailed in the early phases of the state of nature (where human beings were still dependent on things rather than on other people), a proliferation of desires that bear no immediate, palpable relation to basic human needs is substituted that feeds upon and augments *amour-propre*. The career of artificial *amour-propre*, in contrast to natural *amour de soi*, is thereby launched, and with it all the attendant vexatious competitiveness of civil society.

The stress on political participation in Rousseau is motivated at least to some extent by a desire to reappropriate the essentialist phase of the state of nature. Citizens participating in the assembly (guided in their deliberations by the desire to articulate and follow the general will) are, by their very action, artifically attempting to re-create the environment of the early phases of the state of nature, where there was no dependence on people but only on things. In trying to act in conformity with the general will, the citizens of Rousseau's ideal community are endeavoring to establish contact with a structure of necessity that moves beyond the whims, desires, and valuations of other people to what a most earnest reading of the collective good of the community would dictate. Rousseau's society of the social contract tries to rehabilitate the rhythms of necessity and independence—a genuine rather than a spurious necessity because it is built upon a lack of dependence of one human being upon the next—that typified the early phases of the state of nature.

Rousseau's essentialism leads to a denial of the proudest claim of modern political theory (from the time of Hobbes) to have discovered, through the application of right method, those principles of statecraft that would allow the state to endure forever. With Rousseau's political thought we experience a return to the cyclical rhythms of the life of the state that were an obsession and a torment of ancient and medieval political writers. With his rejection of nominalism Rousseau renounces the one strategy that enabled the moderns to proclaim their superiority over the ancients: Truth is a matter of pragmatic consensus, and since the tools of social and cultural creation are all man-made we can control the results to the extent of assuring the stability and longevity of our creations.

Rousseau retells the myth of the social contract to make a point different from that of Hobbes. The purpose of establishing the society of the social contact for Rousseau is not to get the passions to replicate themselves in the form of instrumental reason, thereby resolving the dilemmas introduced by the paramountcy of the passions within the structure of human personality. Fashioning such a society is intended to provide institutional extensions and embodiments through such agencies as the legislator and the articulation of the general will of the essentialist phase of the state of nature. In establishing the society of the social contract, members of a community do not shift their gaze from the inner self to an outward sphere of action; they facilitate the nurturing of the inner person by the same essentialist guidelines that prevailed in the early phases of the state of nature.

According to Rousseau the root problem of politics is that of consciousness—the emergence of self-consciousness gives rise to the whole official sphere of politics. *Amour-propre,* an outgrowth of human self-consciousness, generates the officially political realm concerned to adjudicate between competing claims of private interest. At the same time, the centrality of *amour-propre* as the motive force behind political life renders most political arrangements ultimately unsatisfactory.

As we have seen, Rousseau sketches an internal movement in man from complete unself-consciousness (an animal-like existence, in a nonpejorative sense) to a state of self-consciousness. In a fully self-conscious state, a man's instinct for natural pity becomes subordinated to the directive force of a cunning, artificial intelligence, bent on improving his own position with respect to his fellows. Through the workings of the general will—with each member of society subordinating himself to the general will, rather than to the will of any particular member of society—Rousseau's theory of justice attempts to reconstitute artificially the freedom, in the sense of lack of dependence, that prevailed in the early phases of the state of nature, and to ameliorate the rampant promotion of self-interest that typifies the self in its postlapsarian phase.

Rousseau's essentialist participationism issues forth in a different theory of law from Hobbes's nominalist representationalism. Hobbes advances a positivist conception of law as the command of the sovereign. As long as law emanates from the appropriately designated sovereign representative, it must be obeyed.[6] Rousseau, by contrast, affirms a natural-law conception of law. He refuses to acknowledge any separation between law and justice by identifying law with the expression of an infallible general will.

> But when the entire people enacts something concerning the entire people, it considers only itself, and if a relationship is formed then, it is between the whole object viewed in one way and the whole object viewed in another, without any division of the whole. Then the subject matter of the enactment is general like the will that enacts. It is this act that I call a law.
>
> Given this idea, one sees immediately that it is no longer necessary to ask who should make laws, since they are acts of the general will; nor whether the prince is above the laws, since he is a member of the state; nor whether the law can be unjust, since no one is unjust toward himself; nor how one is free yet subject to the laws, since they merely record our will.[7]

5 • Habermas and Reflexivity: The Modernist versus Postmodernist Debate in Metatheoretical Perspective

Jürgen Habermas wants to establish a cognitivist moral philosophy partially on the basis of Peter Strawson's argument in his essay "Freedom and Resentment."[1] Strawson "develops a linguistic phenomenology of ethical consciousness whose purpose is maieutically to open the eyes of the empiricist in his role as moral skeptic to his own everyday moral intuitions."[2] The legitimation of a moral phenomenology sets the stage for Habermas's inferring from ordinary linguistic usage the principles of a minimal rationality. How logically defensible is the notion of a moral phenomenology?[3]

• Issues of Reflexivity in Habermas's Moral Phenomenology

There are two arguments that seem to me central in defeating the attempt of Strawson and Habermas to sever the skeptical and relativist roots of moral phenomenology. The first has to do with some version of an incompleteness argument surrounding the tenets of moral phenomenology. This position is not able to account for its genesis and elaboration in its own terms—by invoking the categories of human agency—but only by historicizing and relativizing, and thereby limiting the scope of, its competitors for the role of adequate moral philosophy. This makes moral phenomenology vulnerable to those issues of self-referentialism that I shall discuss shortly.

A second argument indicating that questions of skepticism and self-referentialism remain appropriate in fixing the import of moral phenomenology has to do with a central ambiguity surrounding the concept of interpretation. Derrida, in his essay "Structure, Sign, and Play in the Discourse of the Human Sciences," distinguishes between two interpretations of "interpretation": "The one," he says,

> seeks to decipher, dreams of deciphering, a truth or an origin which is free from freeplay and from the order of the sign, and lives like an exile the necessity of interpretation. The other, which is no longer turned toward the origin, affirms freeplay and tries to pass beyond man and humanism, the name man being the name of that being who, throughout the history of metaphysics or of ontotheology—in other words, through the history of all of his history—has dreamed of full presence, the reassuring foundation, the origin and the end of the game.[4]

The first sense of interpretation presupposes the continued existence of something stable to be interpreted. The second sense of interpretation views it in an entirely pragmatic way. There is never any component of any text (very broadly conceived) that remains immune to further interpretation. It is just that for the sake of carrying on the activity of interpretation altogether we must proceed in a serial manner by cordoning off certain sectors for the application of our interpretive techniques—while leaving the rest suspended in an unavoidable but temporary state of givenness. It seems to me that the proponent of moral phenomenology adheres to this more global interpretation of interpretation in his practice as a moral phenomenologist, while tacitly—one might almost say surreptitiously—giving allegiance to the more restricted understanding of the activity of interpretation when it comes to metatheoretically defining and delimiting his own vocation as a moral phenomenologist. This is what enables him to believe that he can effectively skirt issues of skepticism and self-referentialism in delineating the sphere of moral phenomenology. If there is a substratum of givenness in what the moral phenomenologist interprets, this would seem sufficient to deflect issues of skepticism and self-referentialism. But if the moral phenomenologist also acknowledges (as, for example, Charles Taylor does) that "what a given human life is an interpretation of cannot exist uninterpreted,"[5] then issues of skepticism and self-referentialism inexorably arise.

The more global concept of interpretation that Derrida openly affirms and that moral phenomenologists implicitly embrace would appear to give rise to an insurmountable self-referentialist dilemma.

What is the status of this global interpretation of interpretation? If it reflexively engulfs itself—if the global interpretation of interpretation is just one more interpretation—then the point of the distinction between the omnipresence and the limited character of interpretation has been effaced. On the other hand, if this global theory of interpretation offers us a privileged insight into the scope of interpretation and is not ontologically interchangeable with the objects of its own theorizing, then a strategy must be found to accommodate the inconsistency.

It seems to me that the most persuasive move to make at this point is to invoke a generalized agnosticism. If we have only "incomplete knowledge of objective reality," so that all possibilities remain open, then perhaps a multivalued logic (such as intuitionism) that maps the suspension of the law of excluded middle encodes reality more faithfully than the classic Aristotelian law does. In this case, our alternatives would be increased beyond *A* and not-*A*. We could affirm the pervasive character of interpretation in all cases except the theory affirming that pervasiveness itself, which privileges a particular construal (or range of construals) of itself.

The moral phenomenologist takes a philosophical detour through the person as molded by particular philosophical and metaphilosophical paradigms as the rock-bottom layer of philosophical justification. This is what enables him to achieve his celebrated triumph of ontology over epistemology.[6] He argues that "it belongs to human agency to exist in a space of questions about strongly valued goods prior to all choice or adventitious cultural change"[7] and forges ahead with a quasi-objectivist account of moral personality and moral reasoning because of the perceived ontological limitations of modern (seventeenth-century) epistemology. A modern epistemological account of moral personality and moral reasoning begins with sense impressions; it thus continually seeks to validate the full-blown categories of the agent in terms of a "primary matter" that is qualitatively discontinuous with such impressions. The asymmetry between the categories of moral judgment and the antecedent layers of sense impressions from which the categories are derived generates irresolvable problems of skepticism and relativism. "Moral agency" from an epistemological perspective gets superseded by external, objectivist, scientistic, behavioral, and neurophysiological accounts of moral deliberation and action. The moral phenomenologist counterposes to the epistemological account of morality the argument (which is evocative of historicism) that epistemological reasoning exists in an ontological space of its own—

designed to meet certain purposes, concerned with certain historically defined ends—that is separate and independent from the ontological space typically regarded as definitive of (and by) the moral agent. The agent's range of concerns and categories, which are more explicit and holistic than the concepts employed by the epistemologist, nudge to one side the ontologically differentially accented vocabulary(ies) of the epistemologist. On ontological grounds, ontology has priority over epistemology, since the explanatory relationship between the two is asymmetrical. Epistemological terms can be appropriately explained from an ontological perspective, whereas ontological categories cannot be correspondingly illuminated by epistemological factors. (The greater, or more general in scope, enjoys explanatory priority over the lesser, or more restricted, in scope.)

The model for the moral phenomenologist's argument for overcoming epistemology is the Martin Heidegger of *Being and Time,* who appealed (in Fred Dallmayr's paraphrase of Habermas's paraphrase of his argument) to "the domain of 'ontological pre-understanding' as the matrix underlying different cognitive and practical pursuits. This pre-understanding surfaces . . . when we probe *behind* the categorial structure of things supplied by a (scientifically informed) transcendental philosophy. The analysis of pre-understanding yields those structures of the life-world or 'being-in-the-world' Heidegger calls 'existentials.' " [8]

This argument is vulnerable to the charge that Heidegger and the moral phenomenologists he has inspired need to use the old epistemological vocabulary, with its central categories of skepticism and relativism, in order to transcend them. Once they are invoked, they cannot be bracketed off without further ado—purged of their original sets of connotations and of the problems that they engender—without the argument becoming viciously circular, presupposing the very point(s) it is trying to prove. "Skepticism" and "relativism," with their attendant degenerative dynamics of self-referentialism, are already inserted in the Heideggerian and moral-phenomenological arguments at the moment when transposition to an ontological mode of argument is supposed to displace them. For this very reason (they are already violating protocols concerning self-referentialism at the very moment of saying that they need not be adhered to), the displacement cannot be negotiated in their terms without their arguments becoming viciously circular.

The moral phenomenologist relativizes epistemology to its historical context and moral deliberation and judgment to their recurring historical contexts. But relativism is a self-refuting philosophical thesis. To be a consistent relativist, one would have to be relativistic about one's own relativism—which means that the position disintegrates even before it can get adequately formulated.

The moral phenomenologist's refusal of temporally transcendent factors (what we might call simply rational factors) in adjudicating between the competing claims of the moral epistemologist and himself suggests both extreme skepticism and extreme relativism. According to the moral phenomenologist, historical settings and contexts by themselves, outside a process of interposition of so-called neutral protocols of rational argument, determine their own logics. The historical context of epistemology—both in its formulation as grand theory by René Descartes and by John Locke in the seventeenth century and in its multiple applications by individual reasoners straight down to the twentieth century—is one of reduction and instrumentalization. The epistemologist is concerned above all to limit and unify the number of principles required for an explanation and to gear those principles to the manipulation and control of practice. The determinative context for the moral phenomenologist—both the philosopher setting forth the position and individuals applying it in a multitude of daily contexts in their moral deliberations—is one that takes the richness of moral categories at their face value and marks the ways they are typically woven into patterns of argument. Assigning primacy to the defining characteristics that separate the contexts of moral epistemology from the contexts of moral phenomenology—and rejecting the possibility of overriding canons of reasoning resolving tensions and conflicts between them—makes the moral phenomenologist vulnerable to the scathing attack that Friedrich Nietzsche levels against historicism: "The past always speaks as an oracle: only as master builders of the future who know the present will you understand it." [9] The implicit epistemological critique of this passage can be filled in from various directions: In our present as historical investigators we confront tokens only from the past (from divergent historical contexts), so that their status as artifacts stemming from the past (or as defining different contexts) can be called into question by the radical skeptic; the meaning of these tokens is subject to varying interpretations by new generations of interpreters, so that what the tokens signify can never be established with certainty; and so on. Historical knowledge statements that claim to disclose the past—to reveal context—can therefore more correctly be viewed as disguised action statements that enable their adherents to do certain things in the present. Historical statements that officially describe what occurred in the past—that give shape to context—are to be assessed by their capacity to release energies that will transform the present.

But if historicism devolves into future or action-oriented interpretations of the past, of historical context—if it metamorphoses into skepticism—then it gives rise to a problem of consistency. To be consistently skeptical concerning historical and contextual knowledge, does one not have to be skeptical of one's own skepticism, which would disbar one from redefining the import of historical knowledge statements that I summarized in the previous paragraph?

The priority of ontology over epistemology translates for the moral phenomenologist into primacy being assigned to the individual person situated in particular contexts of moral reflection, deliberation, and decision making as he begins to take stock of what it means to be placed in such a situation grappling with these particular sets of constraints and requirements. There is no level of argument and justification to pierce through beyond this level of moral reflection and deliberation. The person placed in a particular recurring set of interrelated situations in human life has priority over philosophical arguments concerning the limits of argument put forward, for example, by the epistemologist. The moral phenomenologist thus purchases autonomy and objectivity for moral judgment and deliberation by radically subjectivizing them so that they enjoy the character of ultimacy in hierarchies of explanation.[10]

The moral phenomenologist's taking a detour through the person in his moral philosophy—his circumscribing argument to a specification of context—is expressive of extreme skepticism and extreme relativism, with their attendant problematics concerning issues of self-referentalism. We can make this point another way by saying that the moral phenomenologist's substitution of an ontological dimension, an ontological perspective, for epistemological ones is already suggestive of the workings of skepticism. The very move that the moral phenomenologist makes to defeat the skepticism that he associates with the rise of modern epistemology already bears strong traces of skepticism. If one can deliberate about which perspective to apply—if it is not something directly constrained by features of the situation itself, but there is argumentative slack concerning which perspective to apply—then one is implicitly moving within the ambit of skepticism.

The moral phenomenologist is not able to accommodate reflexively his own activity as a moral theorist. The content of his theorizing is in tension with the activity of such theorizing. The content of the theorizing addresses itself to finding a vocabulary for "agency," to elaborate upon what it means for us to be embedded in multiple, often overlapping, and sometimes conflicting cultural, communal, and familial contexts, with their ranges of moral categories and problem-setting and problem-defining terminologies more or less in place when we confront a moral dilemma, engage in moral deliberation, or need to reach a decision affecting some aspect of our (moral) lives. The moral phenomenologist wants to explicate the "thereness" of our moral experience and to evoke the richness of received vocabularies in the conduct of the moral life.

A central tension in the moral phenomenologist's approach is that his writing in this vein presupposes the very absence of that which his writing on an official level assumes to be present. If the orientating categories of moral deliberation and action were operative, the moral phenomenologist would not have to work so hard to spell out their content. The moral phenomenologist is providing us with a self-conscious articulation of what, according to his explicit analysis, is supposed to be irresistibly there. He is offering us a vocabulary, not for the inexpressible, but for the already defined and expressed. He is making an argument as to why no argument is needed—and this constitutes the form of his argument.

The moral phenomenologist's activity as a moral theorist (in contrast to the content of his theory) presupposes that the very nature of the moral life is jeopardized—that its boundaries and content are overwhelmed by contemporary technological-instrumental culture, and that therefore what appears as an exercise in retrieval might more plausibly be redescribed as a stipulative recasting of the central elements of moral experience. A "moral phenomenology" that places major emphasis on interpretation has to itself be seen as a colossal act of interpretation that through its very formulation evinces the hollowness of the idea of the givenness of moral experience.

Taking these self-referential concerns seriously leads to a refocusing of moral inquiry upon all the conditions, cultural and theoretical, that define its impossibility. If scruples surrounding self-referentialism disbar us from theorizing moral experience, then perhaps what we need to do is to engage in more attentive stocktaking of the implications of our argumentative condition. "Self-referentialism" emerges as an issue only if the law of excluded middle is presumed to hold. Under the constraints of this law, our alternatives are restricted to *A* and not-*A*: either the knowability or the unknowability of our "moral data." However, if we adhere to a generalized agnosticism, claiming that we have only "incomplete knowledge of objective reality" so that all possibilities remain open, then perhaps a multivalued logic (such as intuitionism) that maps the suspension of the law of excluded middle encodes reality more faithfully than the classic Aristotelian law. In this case, our alternatives are increased beyond *A* and not-*A*—and we can predicate the knowability of moral data in all cases except the theory predicating their knowability itself.

One might argue that in a crucially revealing sense from the moral phenomenologist's perspective, the self, too, is a theory. It is a gigantic, evolving, and resilient intellectual construct intended to make sense of our multifarious encounters with experience and the myriad insights and obstacles that these engender and occasion. But if the self is a species of theory, and under a generalized-agnostic dispensation theory enjoys no privileged (or even certifiable) contact with the world, then the concatenation of interrelated categories that we call a "self" has to already be at one unverifiable remove from experience in order to constitute a self. To attempt to bridge the gap here by positing further selves—more abstractly and interiorly situated, as it were, than the original self, and therefore capable of grappling with its dilemmas—only reintroduces the problem at a further level of removal from the one upon which it was originally noticed. The idea of a self, of an agent, thus becomes a hastily improvised notion to forestall awareness of an infinite regress that impugns the very possibility of a self.

The moral phenomenologist rests his case upon borrowed claims. Methodologically, the claims are living off the classic epistemological thesis that the moral phenomenologist avers his historicism has superseded and discredited. Historicism—the moral phenomenologist's assigning of primacy to ontology over epistemology—"works" because classic epistemology "works." One sets the stage, furnishes the background assumptions, for the other. ("Skepticism" makes "relativism" possible.) The moral phenomenologist cannot simply proceed as if they were antithetical to one another. The validating source for the historicist divestiture of the epistemological tradition is the epistemological tradition. The contextualization of historical data in historicism is the counterpart to the primacy assigned to impressions and sense data in classical empiricism. In both cases, we have a search for building blocks that are then assembled into broader syntheses. It is therefore extremely ironic that the moral phenomenologist attempts to impugn the project of classical epistemology by a historicization of it that consists in an application of its very principles in another domain.

The idea of a moral phenomenology in Habermas serves to carve out argumentative space for a rationalist reconstruction of ethics. A good deal of Habermas's recent theoretical work is devoted toward arguing for the presence of a beachhead of rationality within human communicative interaction. He seeks to generalize from this to the desiderata of an ideal speech situation and also to use it as a basis from which to attack postmodernism, which denigrates the Enlightenment project of cultivating a critical rationality.[11] Habermas associates the beachhead of rationality with the range of linguistic phenomena identified by speech-act theory, as developed primarily by J. L. Austin and John R. Searle.[12] According to this theory, one needs to distinguish between the propositional content of an utterance and its illocutionary force.[13] The "propositional content" refers to the cognitive message being transmitted between speaker and listener; the "illocutionary force" signifies the set of instructions or cues embedded or encoded in an utterance concerning how the statement is to be taken—the set of responses that are expected from the listener, or what the statement itself portends on the part of the speaker. Examples of the former are obedience and compliance where the illocutionary force of the statement suggests that it should be construed as a command or a request. Examples of the latter are what Austin calls performative utterances, such as promising, where formulating certain words signifies the enactment of a particular deed (in this case, the commitment to do something in the future). The presence of implicit validity claims in many of the utterances that we make that can be either confirmed or resisted is suggestive of the presence and efficacy of rationality. The role of illocutionary force and performatives in utterance provides Habermas with a limited case study of the functioning of rationality in everyday oral discourse with which to counter the postmodernist rejection of reason. It thus yields a positive set of considerations to augment his largely negative arguments against postmodernist philosophy to the effect that rejecting the claims of reason is reflexively unsustainable since it is also generally done on the basis of rational arguments, so that one cannot advocate postmodernism without simultaneously affirming the truth of modernism.

The implications that Habermas wishes to draw from speech-act theory can only be as solid as the inspiring model from which he draws them. If that model is inherently flawed, then the implications that Habermas wants to tease out of it cannot even be drawn. I wish to argue on the basis of a dialectically interrelated series of criticisms and objections that the model is deficient from a number of different directions and therefore that the case that Habermas wants to make for a limited beachhead of rationality cannot be established.

In the third section of the chapter I present a sketch for a reconstruction of Habermas's argument from speech-act theory along my revised postmodernist lines and point to convergences between his philosophizing and generalized agnosticism.

• *Habermas and Speech-Act Theory*

Habermas's position appears to be conceptually equivalent to a view that conflates the emission of sounds with the articulation of speech. If there were any rational apparatus inherent in the emission of sounds, then Habermas might be entitled to make his case for a minimal verbal infrastructure of rationality to refute the postmodernists. But the very term "pragmatic" in the title of Habermas's essay "What Is Universal Pragmatics?" (where his analysis of the rational content of speech acts takes place) is suggestive of his realization that communicative action, the whole speech-act vocabulary, is just that: a vocabulary, a set of terms invented to facilitate certain moves in response to certain blockages in the real world. An appropriate analogy to consider in this context is Wittgenstein's mobilization of the concept of "language as use" as a way of discrediting traditional metaphysics and neutralizing its most persistently vexing puzzles.[14] If the speech-act vocabulary is pragmatically motivated, it cannot offer us a thoroughly reliable clue as to what the world is like. At most, one is warranted in interpreting this vocabulary agnostically in relation to its subject matter, so that the world itself—in this case the sector of it denominated as "interpersonal communication"—might both be (for heuristic purposes as codified in speech-act theory) and not be (in terms of what interpersonal communication is like in and for itself) defined by the rudimentary rationality described by Habermas's theory of communicative action.

This line of attack assumes the validity of the cryptopositivist premise of Habermas's philosophy-of-language theorizing—that the object of theorizing and the activity of theorizing are logically independent of one another—and turns this positivist split into an argument against him. My next point calls this very split into question—and uses *that* as a basis for criticizing Habermas's argument.

It might be said that he is illegitimately smuggling in a positivist premise in order for his argument concerning universal pragmatics to work. Habermas is somehow assuming that people's talk is one thing and theorizing that how their talk is efficacious, how the utterance of words manages to get communicated, is something else. But if discourse were just seen as what it is conceptualized to be, then a nonrational or an antirational conceptualization of discourse would simply reshape what we take discourse to be, would redefine our canons of "rationality," without in any way calling into question on a metatheoretical level our ability to communicate. Interpersonal communication might only exist in relation to an interpretive framework, so that "nonrational" construals of utterance and communication might just end up reshaping what we consider utterance and communication to be.

Austin's distinction between the "propositional content" of an utterance and its "illocutionary force" appears to be naïve and positivistic. It assumes that "propositional content" can be open textured and ambiguous and that "illocutionary force" as a set of stage directions concerning how to take the utterance (how to respond to it) is uniformly straightforward and unequivocal. The theory of tacit knowledge as developed by Michael Polanyi (with philosophical antecedents stretching back to Plato) alerts us, however, to the possibility that on a theoretical level the problem of making sense of "illocutionary force" is as intractable as that of making sense of "propositional content"—and for analogous reasons. What proves so vexatious in accounting for how "propositional content" manages to get communicated has to do to an important extent with the theoretical prospect of an infinite regress of interpretation opening up before us, preventing "meaning" from ever getting pinned down. The ambiguity and multivalence of language evoke the specter of the inability of even an infinite series of interpretive texts to confer stability of meaning upon any primary text. Analogously, in the case of "illocutionary force" responding to and applying a text or utterance in the appropriate ways raises the specter of an unbridgeable gap between theory and practice—since even the most detailed and elaborate of theoretical texts cannot substitute for the context of decision making and application that confront an agent at the moment of practice, the moment of actual doing or responding. The infinite regress in interpretation that confronts interpreters of "propositional content," and the infinite regress affecting *theoretical* attempts to close the gap between theory and practice that surrounds the notion of "illocutionary force," point to the primacy of the dynamics and dialectics of tacit knowledge over Austin's bifurcation of utterance into "propositional content" and "illocutionary force."

"Tacit knowledge" underscores how most of our statements and utterances in the world betray characteristics of being partially tacit, contextual, and submerged. From the perspective of tacit knowledge, even the "propositional content" of an utterance has to be viewed as, at least to some extent, a "performative." Since no statement can say everything that it is officially geared toward saying, our statements— even their most obdurately cognitive components—have to be viewed as species of doing, posting markers against the opacity of language of what we are striving to express and articulate. "Tacit knowledge" suggests the need for deconstructing even our most labyrinthine theoretical utterances as deeds. Correspondingly, since the "illocutionary force" of an utterance has to be interpreted and applied before an appropriate response can be forthcoming, there are vast regions of tacit lore that have to be invoked before one can make sense of how "illocutionary force" can get integrated into the appropriate individual behavior patterns. From the perspective of "tacit knowledge," therefore, both "propositional content" and "illocutionary force" are symptomatic of the limitations and opacity of *language*, of its insurmountable inadequacies as a vehicle of communication. "Tacit knowledge" points to the necessary theoretical subversion of reason before one can begin to make sense of the role of reason and the mechanics of communication in human life.

If the illocutionary force of an utterance is part of the universal pragmatics of discourse, then its rational content is reduced to zero. The use of the term "pragmatics" suggests an unbreachable antiessentialism. We really do not know what is going on when successful communication takes place, but the term "illocutionary force" and its split from "propositional content" gives us as good a handle as any in gaining conceptual mastery of the situation. If "illocutionary force" is construed pragmatically, then no implications whatsoever follow concerning the nature and scope of human rationality.

Even if, *per impossible*, some rational content were yielded through an examination of the role of "illocutionary force" in utterance, the inclusion of the concept as part of a "universal pragmatics" suggests that it is fashioned after the fact of successful communication having taken place as an explanation of how consummated discourse (discourse that has been properly "received" by a listener) works. This means that the notions of "illocutionary force" and "performatives" are hypothetical. One can then mobilize against Habermas an argument made familiar by Ronald Dworkin—that the rational constraints that are binding hypothetically in no way carry over to actual human discourse and communication. What Dworkin says in rejecting contractarian arguments for political obligation[15]—that hypothetical arguments demonstrating consent harbor no implications for citizens' behavior in existing societies—can be transposed to Habermas's universally pragmatic argument in defense of a minimal infrastructure of rationality. What can be shown to obtain hypothetically does not illuminate existing human personality structure, mental functioning, or patterns of interaction.

It is ironic that in order to counter postmodernism and to show that rationality has a foothold in human discourse Habermas uses speech-act theory, which is itself based upon a radically skeptical metaphysics. Speech-act theory does not so much resolve Habermas's problem of being able to attest to the presence of rationality in human life as present him with a paradigm case of it: Only on the basis of what appears to be extreme skepticism can one begin to make sense of human communicative competence and efficacy.

In order to become aware of the skeptical metaphysics that underlies Austin's theorizing of speech acts and performatives one needs to consider how Austin would seek to refute a "bizarre skeptic" who, in all cases of speech acts and performatives (commanding, requesting, promising, etc.), would deny the existence of the illocutionary force of utterances and would say that the way to make sense of the fact that commands were obeyed, requests complied with, promises kept, and so forth had to do with sheer coincidence or with a set of factors that were in no way captured by the vocabulary of speech-act theory and performatives. The rule-bound character of the workings of "illocutionary force" and of performatives would in no way deter the skeptic, because he would question the very concept of what it means to follow a rule. At that juncture, Austin presumably would have had recourse to Wittgenstein's argument in the *Philosophical Investigations*.[16] As Saul Kripke has shown in his book on Wittgenstein,[17] a characteristic and influential argument in the *Investigations*—that against the notion of a private language—constitutes a skeptical response to the challenge articulated in section 201 of the book: "This was our paradox: no course of action could be determined by a rule, because every course of action can be made out to accord with the rule." Kripke illustrates this paradox by a mathematical example. He refers to the word 'plus' and the symbol '+' to denote the ordinary mathematical function of addition. Kripke, explicating Wittgenstein, says that "one point is crucial to my 'grasp' of this rule. Although I myself have computed only finitely many sums in the past, the rule determines my answer for infinitely many new sums that I have never previously considered. This is the whole point of the notion that in learning to add I grasp a rule; my past intentions regarding addition determine a unique answer for indefinitely many new cases in the future."[18]

Suppose now that the wielder of this simple arithmetical rule concerning the plus sign is confronted by a "bizarre" skeptic. All of us in our previous instances of learning and applying the rule have dealt only with finite examples. Surely, for each of us there exist problems in addition both of whose arguments exceed numbers we have previously worked with. For the sake of argument, Kripke assumes that $68 + 57$ constitutes a problem in addition that a particular person has not worked with in the past and that these numbers represent magnitudes greater than the person has dealt with before. It is now open to the skeptic to argue against the person performing the addition problem that the sum of $68 + 57$ is not 125 but 5. The counterargument would go as follows: Since all the numbers the person doing the addition had previously been involved with were all less than 57, perhaps when the person was saying "plus" what he meant was "quus." The latter could be defined as requiring that when dealing with integers that were less than 57, addition should be performed in the normal way; with integers greater than 57, the "quus" sign always yielded a result of 5.

How could such a skeptic who questioned whether any course of action could be determined by a rule be refuted? According to Kripke, the private-language argument found in the *Investigations* constitutes Wittgenstein's answer to the imaginary skeptic. "The impossibility of private language," according to Kripke, "emerges as a corollary of his skeptical solution to his own paradox, as does the impossibility of 'private causation' in Hume. It turns out the skeptical solution does not allow us to speak of a single individual, considered by himself, and in isolation, as ever meaning anything."[19] Wittgenstein accepts the skeptic's challenge concerning the possibility of communicating in accordance with a rule to the extent of acknowledging that meaning is never individual in character. In the course of jettisoning the concept of individual meaning, Wittgenstein is also deflating our traditional conception of truth. Normally, we take the utterance of truth to be the result of a particular action conforming to the intention(s), principles, judgments, and the like present to the mind of the individual actor as she or he goes about performing a particular action. But if meaning is not appropriated or validated individualistically, neither can truth be what is at stake in the discourse individuals employ to communicate and describe their intentions and achievements. Assertability and utility must take the place of truth. "Wittgenstein replaces the question, 'What must be the case for this sentence to be true?' by two others: first, 'Under what conditions may this form of words be appropriately asserted (or denied)?'; second, given an answer to the first question, 'What is the role, and the utility, in our lives of our practice of asserting (or denying) the form of words under these conditions?' "[20]

For Kripke, the movement from Wittgenstein's *Tractatus* to the *Philosophical Investigations* can be most reliably characterized as a movement from a limited to a more extreme skepticism—from a philosophy that left a safe preserve of statements that were securely anchored in reality to a philosophy that eroded even that preserve. Given that the modifications in Wittgenstein's philosophy all take place within the purview of skepticism, a compelling question to raise is how does he deal with the self-refuting nature of extreme skepticism. Even the *Tractatus*, which does allow for a privileged class of statements—the elementary propositions—evokes the question of how one can sustain in the metalanguage of philosophy the destructive arguments that invalidate all save elementary propositions and truth functions of them without having that destructive force turn inward and undermine the philosophical language itself for failure to consist of elementary propositions or truth functions of them. Grappling with the problem of being able both to adhere to skepticism and to state it coherently forms one of the major motive forces of Wittgenstein's philosophy from beginning to end.

The *Philosophical Investigations* exemplifies an implicit form of radical skepticism. Its skepticism is implicit in the sense that a deceptive tolerance pervades the surface of Wittgenstein's argument, which leads one to think that epistemologically "anything goes." But epistemologically "anything goes" only because metaphysically—ontologically—nothing matters. Whether the topic is the laws of logic or the foundations of mathematics, religion or aesthetics, the moves that we make in these disparate regions of discourse are ultimately grounded in "the linguistic practices which embody them"[21]—and nothing else.

Wittgenstein can finally establish a charmed circle of secure knowledge invulnerable to logical attack—the original project of empiricism inaugurated in England by Hobbes and elaborated in a more sophisticated fashion by David Hume—simply because for him this charmed circle is coextensive with the realm of ordinary language itself. The "outside" has been turned "inside." (There is no longer any "outside.") There is no level of certainty beyond what is secured by linguistic convention within particular regions of discourse. Wittgenstein emasculates all special philosophical concepts and makes all forms of activity—all forms of life, including the philosophical— metaphysically equal, uniformly leveled by the irremediable opacity of language.

Wittgenstein needs to invoke a doctrine of showing versus saying in the *Investigations* in order to render his philosophical case more coherent. He argues that the notion of language-game yields the appropriate sanction for correct linguistic usage in each sphere of discourse: "Our mistake is to look for an explanation where we look at what happens as a 'proto-phenomenon.' That is, where we ought to have said: This language-game is played. The question is not one of explaining a language-game by means of our experiences, but of noting a language-game."[22]

Wittgenstein also says that "we may not advance any kind of theory. . . . We must do away with all explanation, and description alone must take its place. . . ."[23] And further: "Philosophy may in no way interfere with the actual use of language; it can in the end only describe it. For it cannot give any foundation either. It leaves everything as it is."[24]

Given the pivotal role assigned to the concept of a language-game in guiding the philosopher in performing his therapeutic task, a crucial question becomes what status to assign to those statements I have just marshaled out of Wittgenstein (and others like them I could have cited) that stake out the central philosophical role assigned to "language-games." If these statements are merely illustrative ("descriptive," in Wittgenstein's word) of how the philosophical language-game is played, then why should they be normative—why should they provide the controlling model—for analyzing and restoring coherence to nonphilosophical regions of discourse? In what sense can Wittgenstein's many statements in the *Investigations* about how philosophy should be practiced legitimately obtrude upon other regions of discourse and set them in order when incoherencies of various sorts threaten?

Wittgenstein's answer would appear to be that by analyzing how language-games work in particular cases he has *shown* rather than *stated* what has gone wrong to generate the traditional philosophical puzzles and the therapy that needs to be applied to restore language to a condition of health.

It appears, however, that Wittgenstein has succumbed to a myth of the given. Now all regions of discourse are officially declared to be within the semantic pale—no region is consigned at the outset to the realm of nonsense—and the depth grammar of troublesome words, phrases, and sentences is also a given that is disclosed by minute examination of the language-games in which these words, phrases, and sentences are typically employed. Because there is a double given here—the different regions that periodically give rise to perplexities and the depth grammar revealed by close scrutiny of the language-games deployed within particular language regions [25]— Wittgenstein believes that he has successfully evaded the necessity of stating and generalizing his skeptical principles. Through the proliferation of examples culled from diverse regions of discourse and disparate language-games, he has dramatized skepticism, as it were, without having to confront the necessity of stating it.

It is precisely here, however, that I believe Wittgenstein has committed a blunder. The double structure of the given that he discerns still does not license him to extrapolate from the practice of one language region (philosophy) to all other language-games.[26] The concepts of language region and language-game, after all, are originally at home in a philosophical setting. They were fashioned to help resolve some of the perplexity growing out of Wittgenstein's first formulation of his skepticism. Their extension to other spheres of discourse outside philosophy is not a function of natural necessity—it is a deliberate act. What is suggested by Wittgenstein's initial image of separate regions of discourse governed by their disparate language-games are self-contained, Foucauldian mini-epistemes. There is nothing inevitable about their all being orchestrated through the extension of the philosophical technique of unraveling the implicit rules of language-games to their separate domains. This imperialistic takeover did not have to happen. Its occurrence is neither vouchsafed nor legitimated by the double structure of necessity Wittgenstein points to in the linguistic landscape around him.

If, then, the notions of language region and language-game are extended from philosophy to other areas of discourse (so that they are remade in philosophy's image)—if this move is not self-evidently justifiable in terms of the double-barreled structure of necessity Wittgenstein discerns—then he cannot resort to the vocabulary of showing, in contrast to saying, to ward off the dilemmas associated with formulating a consistent version of skepticism. He must be able to justify in an explicit idiom why the vocabulary appropriate to philosophy is licensed to establish an imperium over other regions of language and thought. If Wittgenstein is cutting other language regions and language-games down to size through the application of his linguistic therapy—if this is skepticism in action—why are the philosophical language-games allowed to loom larger than the rest? Wittgenstein cannot say that philosophy is merely being deployed in action, that there is no doctrine that is being advanced here, because, as we have seen, the extension of the imperium of philosophy to encompass other areas of language and thought takes him beyond what is strictly validated by his double-barreled structure of necessity. The skepticism at this point is being directed toward all other language regions except philosophy.

Austin's "speech-acts" and "performatives" constitute particular language-games among the many that are played within language. But the concept of "language-game" itself is grounded in an extreme skepticism that denies reality to an external world in favor of language. Wittgenstein's strategy for effacing the skeptical roots of the vocabulary of language-games by claiming that he is merely showing and describing (certain features of language) rather than stating (certain philosophical theses) does not work. This critique transfers to Austin's usage of this vocabulary as well. The crucial question to address to Habermas at this point then becomes: Since speech-act theory already presupposes the same extreme skepticism that Habermas's invocation of it was intended to combat, how can speech-act theory help him establish his limited rationalist case against the postmodernists?

An additional internal strand of criticism to bring to bear upon Habermas's use of speech-act theory is that, given the nature of his critique of Hans-Georg Gadamer,[27] would it not be possible to say that the cognitive content as well as the illocutionary force of the utterances that are made within society—as well as the whole range of performatives that are uttered—are manifestations of a distorted communication? If the real interests of members of the middle and lower classes have been systematically beclouded through a range of hegemonic political and cultural apparatuses, would it not be reasonable to suppose that most members of society were speaking in a class-tainted way, and that the assumption of a common rationality that performatives betoken would represent a truncated and distorted rationality? What is the hedge in Austin's and Searle's philosophical discourses against such a possibility? Cannot the sort of argument that Habermas invokes against Gadamer's hermeneutics be mobilized equally tellingly against Habermas's theory of communicative action?

• *Habermas and the Now-Time*

Habermas's negative argument against postmodernism—that the very formulation of (rational) arguments against modernism attests to the endurance of issues of self-referentialism to haunt and undermine postmodernist critiques of modernism—can be met most effectively by the generalized-agnostic construal of postmodernism I am advocating in this book. Not only does a generalized agnosticism accommodate the inconsistently modernist elements in postmodernism[28] but it also legitimates recourse to circularity, which might be the most revealing way to construe speech-act theory. Given the difficulties involved in making sense of and justifying speech-act theory that we have been considering, perhaps the best way to proceed is to deliteralize speech-act theory and to formulate an openly circular argument, a tautology: Certain sentences (such as those relating to commanding and promising) work because they work. Perhaps this circular approach is the most charitable way to construe Austin and Searle—the philosophers of speech-act theory—themselves. Given a generalized-agnostic position in philosophy, there can be no escape from circularity. Given an incompletely objective knowledge of the world, no arguments can aspire to a higher status than circularity. If this is the way to construe Austin and Searle, then Habermas, who bases his argument for a beachhead of rationality within human communicative interaction upon them, emerges as a postmodernist in spite of himself.

This construal of Habermas as someone who at least implicitly endorses a generalized-agnostic position in philosophy receives support from his metaphilosophical paper "Philosophy as Stand-In and

Interpreter."[29] Habermas argues that "it makes sense to suggest that philosophy, instead of just dropping the usher role and being left with nothing, ought to exchange it for the part of stand-in [*Platzhalter*]. Whose seat would philosophy be keeping, what would it be standing in for? Empirical theories with strong universalistic claims."[30] Habermas then goes on to inventory those areas where philosophy can effectively perform this "Platzhalter" role:

> From the vantage point of my own research interests, I see such a cooperation taking shape between philosophy of science and history of science; between speech-act theory and empirical approaches to pragmatics of language; between a theory of informal argumentation and empirical approaches to natural argumentation; between cognitivist ethics and a psychology of moral development; between philosophical theories of action and the ontogenetic study of action competences.[31]

The conceptualization of philosophy as laying the groundwork for the cultivation of particular sciences (and in this sense having its basic insights merge into what later turn out to be ongoing, fruitful sciences) suggests that outside an ambit of continual human theoretical assertiveness the world always maintains an at least partially unknown character. Philosophy as a motive force in the generation of new sciences (Habermas mentions in this connection the work of Noam Chomsky and Jean Piaget) evokes an image of our incompletely objective knowledge of the world, which is continually supplemented and renewed by philosophic vision and inventiveness.

In his "Review of Gadamer's *Truth and Method*,"[32] Habermas, in sympathetically elucidating large segments of Gadamer's theorizing of hermeneutics, cites with approval the following passage in Arthur C. Danto:

> Any account of the past is essentially incomplete. It is essentially incomplete, that is, if its completion would require the fulfillment of a condition that simply cannot be fulfilled. And my thesis will be that a complete account of the past would presuppose a complete account of the future so that one could not achieve a complete historical account without also achieving a philosophy of history. So that if there cannot be a legitimate philosophy of history, there cannot be a legitimate and complete historical account. Paraphrasing a famous result in logic, we cannot, in brief,

consistently have a complete historical account. Our knowledge of the past, in other words, is limited by our knowledge (or ignorance) of the future. And this is the deeper connection between substantive philosophy of history and ordinary history.[33]

There thus appears to be convergence between Habermas's philosophy of science and his philosophy of history—both equally pointing in a generalized-agnostic direction.

Habermas's fascination with Walter Benjamin's conception of a "Jetztzeit" ("now-time"), as disclosed in *The Philosophical Discourse of Modernity*,[34] betrays strong affinities with my "generalized agnosticism" and Nagel's "incompleteness of objective reality." Benjamin's conception "is shot through with fragments of messianic or completed time."[35] The way that this is paradoxically accomplished is through use of an " 'imitation' motif":

> The French Revolution viewed itself as Rome reincarnate. It invoked ancient Rome the way fashion evokes costumes of the past. Fashion has a flair for the topical, no matter where it stirs in the thickets of long ago; it is a tiger's leap into the past. . . . The same leap in the open air of history is the dialectical one, which is how Marx understood the revolution.[36]

Every present state of human history is a microcosm of all future and past states of human history. One important sense in which this is so is captured by the generalized-agnostic position that I have been developing in this book. From a generalized-agnostic perspective, our future states of being are haunted by the prospect of being as insurmountably incomplete in terms of knowledge of ourselves and of the world as our present states are. In this sense, past, present, and future states subsist in a condition of a "now-time." Messianic redemption is paradoxically bound up with a locking into place of our limitations. The reconceptualization of our history as one long qualitatively homogeneous moment sets the stage for an efflorescence of human creativity that is adequate to the authentic powers and limitations of man.[37]

It is interesting to note the relationship between Benjamin's approach to history and Plato's original metatheoretical project of discerning and cultivating a mode of thinking—the pursuit of interconnections—that would enable us to achieve theoretical mastery over self and social environment. The stationary character of the world as evinced in Benjamin's metaphor of a "now-time" testifies in an ironic and inverse way to the enduring influence of the Platonic vision and project. Benjamin reinvents human history in the light of the Platonic image concerning the powers and capabilities of thought. If human beings cannot achieve the mastery glimpsed by Plato, they can at least cogently redesign their image of their habitation in the world as one protracted stationary moment.

Our discussion of a generalized agnosticism and its relevance for Habermas leads to a new perspective on the Gadamer-Habermas debate.[38] One can construe this debate as revolving around the issue of ultimacy in philosophical explanation. For Gadamer, the "transcendental conditions of history" are ultimate; for Habermas, "the universal history in which these conditions are constituted" is more ultimate still.[39] In their respective philosophies of explanation, both men appear to be inclined in a skeptical, reductionist direction while claiming to give due obeisance to those factors to which they do not assign ultimacy. Gadamer gives priority to the organizing categories of mind in shaping linguistic and all other cultural traditions and in making sense of the innovations that take place within those traditions and of the reciprocal interplay between innovation and tradition. Habermas, on the other hand, views "language, labor and domination" as equally primary, searches for the distorting effects of domination in all traditions (including the linguistic), and assigns as a central task of social criticism the uncovering of such systemic patterns of domination. The de facto reductionisms of Gadamer and Habermas are each founded upon the truth of skepticism: that a particular range of explanatory phenomena (mental in the case of Gadamer, material for Habermas) are more real than alternative or competing ranges of phenomena, so that the philosophical quest can be brought to a satisfactory arrest in relation to them.[40] Skepticism, however, as we have seen, is an unsustainable philosophical thesis, because to be skeptical in a self-referentially sound sense requires one to be skeptical of one's own skepticism.

The approach that I am taking suggests that Gadamer and Habermas are misguided for an analogous reason: They fail to appreciate how dilemmas of skepticism wreak a comparable effect on their officially opposed positions. The most persuasive move to make at this point—which, politically speaking, would be more acceptable to Habermas than to Gadamer—is to acknowledge a generalized agnosticism as most successfully redeeming the promise of modernism by enabling us to formulate a consistent version of skepticism. Only an ultimacy that refuses to take its own ultimacy for granted can be satisfactorily ultimate. Politically, this translates into assigning centrality to political participation as the most fitting institutional analogue to the resistance of ultimacy. Methodologically, it would require elaboration of a demillenialized Marxism that renounced the vision of deliverance into a historical after-time for the sake of the undimmingly hopeful and unremittingly ambiguous cultivation of our universal and unending "now-time."

6 •   *Strauss and Reflexivity*

I will try to conceptualize common elements among Leo Strauss's broad range of concerns—and a continuing strategy for grappling with theoretical problems emerging in these diverse areas—in relation to the formal, metatheoretical issue that I have been calling reflexivity. Throughout his extraordinarily productive career, Strauss adverted again and again to a recurring set of themes and topics (the nature of philosophy, the nature of revelation, the appropriate methodology for textual study, the nature of political philosophy, the most justifiable methods and norms for studying political life and for practicing it, the nature of Judaism and Jewish philosophy, and modernity and its relationship to ancient and medieval experience and thought) that did not on the surface always bear an immediately compelling relationship to one another. One way of appreciating the links between these topics that is grounded in Strauss's texts is to invoke the theme of reflexivity. At its simplest level, "reflexivity" signifies the requirement to be utterly consistent. Critical canons that are directed outward need to be shown as susceptible of accommodation by the formulation of the critical canons themselves. This sort of critical requirement can be invoked against any articulation of theory in the humanities and the social sciences. For example, one can question whether the formulation of the Marxist theory of historical materialism itself conforms with that theory, since it does not acknowledge that it is materially tainted. The problem of reflexivity is also manifest with regard to theoretical formulations of extreme skepticism and extreme relativism, as we have seen. To be consistently skeptical requires one to be skeptical of one's own skepticism—which means that a position of extreme skepticism is in a certain sense self-refuting. Analogously, to be consistently relativistic requires one to be relativistic concerning one's own relativism—which defeats formulations of extreme relativist positions. Strauss is often explicit about the implications of "reflexivity" construed as a general requirement of consistency in argument; he is frequently oblique and indirect when dealing with the larger implications of the requirement of reflexivity in relation to skeptical and relativist positions in philosophy and social theory. In the course of my argument I try to reconstruct Strauss's strategies for grappling with reflexivity in relation to skepticism and to relativism and to show that he is consistent in the philosophical consequences he draws from the theme of reflexivity.

I begin with an analysis of Strauss's demarcation of the disparate spheres of theology and philosophy and proceed to a discussion of his concepts of philosophy and revelation, using his "Lectures on Socrates" as a basis for the former and his Introduction to Moses Maimonides' *Guide of the Perplexed* as a textual underpinning for the latter. I then analyze the theme of reflexivity in Strauss's writings, incorporating into my discussion a new reading of the import of his distinction between exoteric and esoteric teaching. Then I consider the implications of the approaches adopted for Strauss's politics.

• *In Pursuit of the One*

In his essay "The Mutual Influence of Theology and Philosophy," Strauss observes: "Generally stated, I would say that all alleged refutations of revelation presuppose unbelief in revelation, and all alleged refutations of philosophy presuppose already faith in revelation. There seems to be no ground common to both, and therefore superior to both."[1] On an overt level, therefore, Strauss seems to be advocating that philosophers and theologians cultivate a mutual openness, with each group remaining receptive to the challenge posed by the other.

His statement of this position, however, confronts a dilemma of reflexivity, of self-referentialism. If Strauss's formulation of his premises—that different fields of discourse evolve in relation to a set of premises that they privilege, and that therefore the furthest reaches of argument within particular fields of discourse cannot impinge upon the validity of a field of discourse that has developed in relation to an alternative set of premises and that remains permanently incommensurable—is correct, then his conclusion does not follow. According to his own postulates, Strauss is either moving in the universe of theology or in the universe of philosophy. What enables him to transcend the particularity of his field of discourse to pronounce upon the mutual incommensurability of philosophy and theology?

Before indicating how I think Strauss might respond to this question, I would like to dwell further on the theoretical pedigrees of the two halves of the dichotomy, "philosophy" and "revelation." According to Strauss, Socrates is the inventor of the activity of philosophizing. "He is the first to grasp the significance of the *idea*, of the fact that the whole is characterized by articulation into classes or kinds, whose character can be understood only by thought, and not by sense perception."[2] Socrates helps to delineate a human mental activity (theorizing) that is characterized by abstraction from particulars and an attempt to locate those particulars within larger wholes that are not immediately given in experience. Thus, from its very inception the relationship between theory and reality emerges as problematic, setting the stage for skepticism as the most faithful substantive correlative to the philosophical impulse. The discursive doctrine that most accurately reflects the ascent from the discrete particulars of experience involved in philosophical activity is skepticism. Philosophical inquiry in an important sense is coterminous with skepticism.

This is borne out on a formal, stylistic level in the irredeemable ambiguity surrounding Strauss's account of Socrates. There is no real Socrates, so to speak—only the Socrates of Aristophanes, or Xenophon, or Plato. This mirrors (or parallels) an irremovable dimension of givenness or arbitrariness present in even our most ardently affirmed intellectual constructions. Intellectual positions come out the way they do because of our antecedent commitment to certain premises, lines of inquiry or argument, questions, symbols, metaphors, and so on. If these commitments change—if the configuration of our intellectual landscape gets modified—the relocation of urgency in our deliberations will issue forth in a completely reinflected set of compelling and unavoidable conclusions. The pursuit of truth therefore is inseparable from a search for premises whose centrality is so unassailable that it obviates altogether the need for reasoned argument in defense or support of those premises. To philosophize, to pursue the truth of things through reasoned argument, is to be situating oneself intellectually in such a way as to be forever displacing what one is in the process of doing. The issue—or theme—of reflexivity is thus also coextensive with the activity of philosophizing itself.

In Strauss's continually provisional image of Socrates, there is a dialectical countermove that limits and contains the implications of the above picture of Socrates as the theorist—the abstracter and generalizer—par excellence. Strauss says that

> Socrates is distinguished from all philosophers . . . by the fact that he sees the core of the whole, or of nature, in noetic heterogeneity. The heterogeneity is not sensible heterogeneity, like the heterogeneity of the four elements, for example, but noetic heterogeneity, essential heterogeneity. The discovery of noetic heterogeneity permits one to let things be what they are and takes away the compulsion to reduce essential differences to something common. The discovery of noetic heterogeneity means the vindication of what one could call common sense. Socrates called it a return from madness to sanity or sobriety, or, to use the Greek term, *sophrosynē*, which I would translate as moderation.[3]

The corrective to the philosophical impulse, according to Socrates, is to integrate into the activity of theory construction itself the insight concerning the irremediable arbitrariness of the theoretical constructs that we develop to enhance the intelligibility and coherence of individual items in our experience. This means that the activity of philosophizing is bound up with an inexorable movement of recoil, as the initial unitary and unifying impulse of philosophizing gets fragmented on unitary grounds into an awareness of the irreducible diversity of experience. Pluralism-heterogeneity-diversity becomes, in Socrates' hands, the most trustworthy deliverance of philosophical reason.

The pattern of Strauss's own philosophizing recapitulates the Socratic dialectic as I have just summarized it. Before developing this argument further, I will focus on the content of the other major concept in Strauss's mapping of intellectual experience—the idea of revelation. When scrutinized under the prism of Maimonides' account of monotheistic principles in *The Guide of the Perplexed*, the concept of revelation works to unhinge certainty even more than the idea of philosophy does. With regard to Maimonides' intention and achievement in the *Guide*, Strauss says two apparently contradictory things. On the one hand, he maintains that "the nonidentity of the teaching of the philosophers as a whole and the thirteen roots of the Law as a whole is the first word and the last word of Maimonides."[4] On the other hand, he asserts that what Maimonides means "by identifying the core of philosophy (natural science and divine science) with the highest secrets of the Law (the Account of the Beginning and the Account of the Chariot) and therewith by somehow identifying the subject matter of speculation and the subject matter of exegesis may be said to be the secret par excellence of the *Guide*."[5] Thus, according to Strauss, a radical discontinuity between philosophy and revelation that Maimonides affirms on an explicit level of argument is just as radically denied on an implicit or latent level. How does Strauss decipher the latent content concerning revelation of the *Guide?*

Strauss points to a major paradox in Maimonides' construal of the nature of God when he says that "God thus understood [in Maimonides' final portrait of him] is precisely God as presented in the doctrine of attributes."[6] I would like to paraphrase in my own terminology what the sources and ramifications of this paradox are and set forth its implications for the issues of skepticism and reflexivity.

In denying the possibility of extrapolation from our human vocabularies to descriptions of God, Maimonides says: "Now everything that can be ascribed to God, may he be exalted, differs in every respect from our attributes, so that no definition can comprehend the one thing and the other."[7] Yet, according to Maimonides, we can state definitely that these attributes do not apply to *him*. Here the problem of consistency emerges in all of its sharpness. If this statement is true (that God is denied all humanly characterizable attributes) then it is false (that we can know nothing about God). Maimonides' articulation of monotheism would appear to be a doctrine whose formulation implies its own falsity.

"Self-referentialism" emerges as an issue only if the law of excluded middle is presumed to hold. Under its constraints, our alternatives are restricted to *A* and not-*A*. We cannot reject attributes in relation to God and affirm them in some sense so that we have a valid subject, God, concerning whom the disavowal of attributes can take place. However, if we adhere to a generalized agnosticism—claiming that we have only "incomplete knowledge of objective reality," so that all possibilities remain open—then perhaps a multivalued logic such as intuitionism (itself intuitionistically interpreted) that maps the suspension of the law of excluded middle encodes reality more faithfully than the classic Aristotelian logic does. In this case, our alternatives are increased beyond *A* and not-*A*—not-attributes in the case of the predicates of negative theology and attributes in some sense, on some level, with regard to the subject of negative theology so that the parings down and shavings off have a subject to latch on to.[8]

Maimonides also attacks the imputation of "existence" to God: "Similarly, as I shall make clear, the term 'existence' can only be applied equivocally to his existence and to that of things other than him."[9] In order for God to exist, he (logically) must not exist. One of the conundrums to which attributing reality to his existence gives rise is his passing over "from potentiality to actuality," which suggests that there is something anterior to God that enabled him to pass over from potentiality to actuality. As soon as one begins to attribute reality to the notion of God as creator, one ends up with an infinite regress. The infinite regress is resolved by purging the concept of God of both secure meaning and reference. The notion of God, we might say, becomes a paradigm of the lack of conceptual self-sufficiency of all of our concepts, which can be seen as being merely rhetorically manipulable but drained of unequivocal meaning and certain reference. "God," as it were, becomes the norm of our ontologically unmoored-detached vocabularies.

Maimonides' project thus involves the leveling of philosophical and theological discourse to the same metaphysical plane—illustrating that "God" does not represent an intrusive, nonrationalizable presence that prevents assimilation of religious talk to philosophical talk and vice versa. His project of regarding Judaism and philosophy as forming a seamless web of inquiry also suggests that for Maimonides the criteria by which they can be fitted together will emerge in relation to a life devoted to their merging. A presupposition behind his intellectual project would seem to be a skeptical denial of the objective rightness of criteria of judgment, ethical or epistemological, that were not strictly immanentist or retrospective in character.

As we have seen, Maimonides' critique of the popular concept of God, which ascribes attributes to him, cannot be formulated consistently. He says that none of the traditional theological terms applies literally to God—God does not see, hear, or even exist in the way that traditional religious understanding projects—yet Maimonides wants all of his negative criticisms to apply to *God:* The subject of all of his negative, paring-down work is the traditional (mono)theistic God. In order for Maimonides' critical apparatus to have a viable target, he needs precisely to maintain in some form, to some extent, whatever it is that apparatus shoots down.

The problem of consistency would not arise in relation to a philosophical attack against unicorns (comparable to Maimonides' attack upon the popular conception of God), because Maimonides would concede that unicorns are stipulated by the literary imagination. The issue of consistency arises, however, with regard to monotheistic theology because Maimonides does not want to say that God is merely stipulated as a philosophical or literary fiction. God is more than a projection.

How does Maimonides analyze the emergence, and significance, of the monotheistic principle (God's absolute otherness)? He traces it to the patriarch Abraham, who is depicted in Maimonides' intellectual-biographical sketch of him in his "Laws Concerning Idolatry and the Ordinances of the Heathens" as a proto-Aristotelian philosophical inquirer in search of an indubitable first cause:

> But the Creator of the Universe was known to none, and recognised by none, save a few solitary individuals, such as Enosh, Methuselah, Noah, Shem and Eber. The world moved on in this fashion, till that Pillar of the World, the Patriarch Abraham, was born. After he was weaned, while still an infant, his mind began to reflect. By day and by night he was thinking and wondering: "How is it possible that this (celestial) sphere should continuously be guiding the world and have no one to guide it and cause it to turn round; for it cannot be that it turns round of itself." He had no teacher, no one to instruct him in aught. He was submerged, in Ur of the Chaldees, among silly idolaters. His father and mother and the entire population worshipped idols, and he worshipped with them. But his mind was busily working and reflecting till he had attained the way of truth, apprehended the correct line of thought and knew that there is One God, that He guides the celestial Sphere and created everything, and that among all that exist, there is no god beside Him. He realised that the whole world was in error, and that what had occasioned their error was that they worshipped the stars and the images, so that the truth perished from their minds. Abraham was forty years old when he recognised his Creator. Having attained this knowledge, he began to refute the inhabitants of Ur of the Chaldees, arguing with them and saying to them, "The course you are following is not the way of truth." He broke the images and commenced to instruct the

people that it was not right to serve any one but the God of the Universe, to Whom alone it was proper to bow down, offer up sacrifices and make libations, so that all human creatures might, in the future, know Him; and that it was proper to destroy and shatter all the images, so that the people might not err like these who thought that there was no god but these images. When he had prevailed over them with his arguments, the king (of the country) sought to slay him. He was miraculously saved, and emigrated to Haran. He then began to proclaim to the whole world with great power and to instruct the people that the entire Universe had but one Creator and that Him it was right to worship. He went from city to city and from kingdom to kingdom, calling and gathering together the inhabitants till he arrived in the land of Canaan. There too, he proclaimed his message, as it is said "And he called there on the name of the Lord, God of the Universe" (Gen. 21:33). When the people flocked to him and questioned him regarding his assertions, he would instruct each one according to his capacity till he had brought him to the way of truth, and thus thousands and tens of thousands joined him. These were the persons referred to in the phrase, "men in the house of Abraham. . . ."

The essential principle in the precepts concerning idolatry is that we are not to worship anything created—neither angel, sphere, star, none of the four elements, nor whatever has been formed from them.[10]

What motivates Maimonides' formulation of the monotheistic principle—God's absolute otherness—is a desire to bring the philosophical/scientific quest to a halt. As long as the stuff to which the *explanans* makes reference is in any way continuous with the material to which the *explanandum* refers, the search for reasons and for causes can proceed indefinitely without any letup in the search for a more primary explanation. The only way that the philosophical/scientific quest can be brought to a satisfactory arrest, and philosophical repose achieved, is by postulating (arriving at) an *explanans* that invokes an entity that is totally unassimilable to human conceptual schemata. For Maimonides, the origin of the monotheistic God who is depicted as being wholly other from humankind arises out of the need to achieve release from philosophical anxiety by postulating an entity as first cause that embodies absolute difference.[11]

One might say that the understanding that Abraham advances in opposition to the animistic outlook of the rest of the world is the centrality of dialectical tension itself for a proper construal of human beings' situation in the world. The rest of the world are monistic reductionists, inveterate naturalizers of the phenomena within and around them. They want all aspects of their existence to have a qualitative sameness. They want the created and the Creator to be composed of the same stuff, to be reducible to the same material. What Abraham's compatriots sought to do was to annul the metaphysical "distances" (in Nietzsche's sense) of human life. Abraham is an advocate of the reality, the permanence, the ineradicableness of those distances.

Since Maimonides acknowledges that the central themes of the *Guide* are an elucidation of *Maʿaseh Bereshith* (the Work of the Beginning) and *Maʿaseh Merkebah* (the Work of the Chariot),[12] which heretofore had constituted the staples of Jewish esotericism and mysticism, the recourse to writing of the *Guide* itself constitutes a momentous metaphysical act that can at least to some extent be interpreted in the light of our discussion concerning the significance of monotheism. As Jacques Derrida has emphasized, writing betokens a "metaphysics of absence," in contrast to speech, which presupposes a "metaphysics of presence."[13] A good deal of the content of the *Guide* relates to the nature of God. The choice of writing over speech figures the endless series of displacements that the Jewish monotheistic conception of God requires and facilitates. Monotheism points in the direction of a metaphysics of absence that assigns primacy to writing above speech.

As summarized so far, there appears to be a grave incoherence in Maimonides' systematization of monotheistic teaching, as alluded to in the quotation cited earlier from Strauss where he questions the motivations that lead Maimonides to reject divine attributes. Since the central point of Maimonides' argument is to emphasize God's otherness, his total difference from man, this is accomplished just as much by endowing him with humanly comprehensible attributes as by denying him those attributes. God, who is essentially totally other than man, endowed with (or manifesting) such traits as omnipotence, omniscience, and benevolence, is as fundamentally unfathomable by us as God deprived of these humanly compassable attributes. The incomprehensibility, the otherness, is preserved either way. Why the staunch stand against the attribution of qualities?

It thus appears that God is not truly wholly other in Maimonides' conception, because otherwise he could possess the panoply of the highest human attributes to their fullest extent and still be God. What nullifies this possibility for Maimonides is his steadfast adherence to God as first cause, necessarily existent, as a strategy for bringing the philosophical quest to a satisfactory halt.[14] It is this holding of God answerable to a human intellectual need that forecloses the acceptance of the wholly other, monotheistic God with a full range of the highest human attributes.

There appears to be a schizophrenic split in Maimonides' argument for deriving and conceptualizing God. With regard to the emotions, the affections, Maimonides formulates his famous denial of attributes. God's goodness, compassion, anger, power, and so forth are not to be construed literally, but are merely figures of speech conforming to ordinary human conceptions of divinity that in no way refer to or capture God's essence. Only a rigorous process of denial of the literal relevance of these attributes can help us to see God's nature clearly. With regard to the human intellect, however, Maimonides' theorizing points to the reverse conclusion. God is the necessarily existent (whose existence coincides with his essence) because otherwise there would be no satisfactory arrest in the search for reasons and causes. The philosophical/scientific quest, the continual search for the causes and reasons for phenomena, can only come to a satisfactory conclusion in the postulation of God as necessarily existent or as first cause. God's character as necessarily existent thus makes him answerable to the explorations and conundrums of the human intellect. While Maimonides vehemently denies any point of contact or resemblance between man's emotions and God's, there is an urgently compelling link between man's intellectual ruminations and God. If Maimonides were more thoroughly consistent and denied that intellectually there was any point of contact between our mental probings and God, then he could have rehabilitated the conventional understanding of God with all of its manifold attributes in their full pristine literalness. If God is not answerable to our intellectual canons and standards of judgment, if he is not conceptualized as the necessarily existent or first cause, then he does not have to be coherent in accordance with our versions of coherence. He can be compassionate and powerful in a sense fully comprehensible to us and still be God. By being consistent in his dissociation of God from human attributes—by severing him from our intellectual exertions and postures, as well as from our emotional qualities—Maimonides paradoxically would have been able to salvage the concept of God in its full human literalness. God would simply be a humanly unfathomable entity to whom the traditional array of theological attributes applied. The "sense" of such a formulation would be clear to us, even if the reference remained inscrutable. However, by denying only the affective attributes (and preserving common ground between our intellectual ruminations and God's existence), Maimonides removes from view the possibility of imputing the traditional attributes to God while remaining faithful to the conception of God's total otherness.

Given this inconsistency, a principle of charitableness in inter-pretation would counsel reading Maimonides in such a way that there is no overarching background narrative through which to place or to locate the argument of the *Guide*. There are only immanentist nar-ratives temporarily spun out to more effectively gauge the import of the specific arguments he is making. If severed and immanentist narratives are adequate and sufficient in an ontologically relativized universe, then Maimonides can coherently argue for a rigorous affir-mation of God's otherness as well as for the nonresemblance of any attributes imputed to him to anything displayed by human beings. Pursuing this approach to Maimonides' monotheism, one could say that the utter existential removal of the monotheistic God issues forth in a paradigm of construal of worldly phenomena that is defined by thoroughly rampant "ontological relativity." If God is wholly other, not only does the decision whether to impute human attributes to him become completely arbitrary but all other theological formulations concerning his relation to the human world become equally arbitrary. Thus, in his rejection of the Aristotelian position concerning the eter-nity of the world, Maimonides opts for a monotheistic alternative that in effect becomes the functional equivalent of the Aristotelian view-point. Maimonides says that the concept of time cannot be literally applied to God because otherwise an infinite regress would open up, since time is a function of motion and movement would have to be postulated of a force behind, above, or outside God that facilitated his existing in time. Therefore, according to Maimonides, we must say that the universe has an absolute beginning—that God created the world in time—but that the notion of time in relation to God is as devoid of meaning and reference as is the concept of God itself. Time in relation to God has to be construed "monotheistically," just as God himself has to be so construed. Maimonides then goes on to say that there is nothing theologically offensive about postulating that the world will exist forever. The conjunction of the "monotheistic" con-strual of God's creating the world in time with the literal construal of the world's subsisting forever yields the Aristotelian doctrine of the eternity of the universe, while registering a formal rejection of it.[15]

Maimonides' oblique, ambivalent affirmation of the eternity of the world contradicts his search for an acceptable first cause, which to a large extent motivates his monotheistic theorizing. One possible strategy for reconciling these conflicting strands of argument is to point to the role of "esoteric teaching" in the theoretical economy of the *Guide*.[16] Maimonides' indirect affirmation of the eternity of the world in partially "monotheistic" terms dislodges the quest for a first cause from the central position that it occupies in the formulation of monotheistic principles. We could say that this is one juncture in which an esoteric teaching is being intimated by the argument of the *Guide*. Problems and solutions, as Plato argues in the *Meno*, are correlative notions. If the prospect of a solution has been foreclosed, a problem remains unformulable. If in a "monotheistic" paraphrase Maimonides gives his allegiance to the doctrine of the eternity of the world, then the search for first causes has been rendered beside the point. On a submerged, implicit level, Maimonides appears to be undercutting the very problematic that seems to provide the motive force of the argument on an explicit level.

The significance of the modifier "esoteric" in the phrase "esoteric teaching" might be to call into question the possibility of fully elaborating a background justificatory narrative that will suitably undergird the statement at hand. It is in terms of what can be done with a hypothesis or problem that an approach is metatheoretically validated, not in relation to the strength or impeccability of its credentials or pedigree. Statements, theories, hypotheses, questions, and problems thus have content to the degree that they can be correlated with other statements, solutions, and so on. "Esoteric teaching" construes our knowledge statements as abridgements out of a stream of experience that remains unbounded in relation to both past and future. By delegitimating the search for justification and by lowering the stakes for coherence, such teaching allows each statement to be taken by itself without considering its implications for the larger web of theories and assertions.

Maimonides' indirect affirmation of the eternity of the universe also contradicts his rejection of an infinite regress of cause and effect.[17] The upshot of his argument concerning the issue of creation is to affirm the legitimacy of an infinite regress. Our agnosticism extends backward as well as forward. We are unable to trace in our deliberations either a necessary starting point or a necessary point of termination. A generalized agnosticism thus invalidates "infinite regress" as a basis for rejecting arguments in philosophy. We might say that "infinite regress" constitutes a species of circularity. If one is not able to locate a justificatory premise in the argumentative background to one's current statement, then the conclusion in effect is being tacitly smuggled into one's premise to enable the conclusion to follow. If circularity is permissible under the metatheoretical dispensation of a generalized agnosticism, so is infinite regress.

I have been arguing that God's otherness and denial of attributes are totally severable concepts and that Maimonides' conflation of the two requires us to articulate the coherence of the argument of the *Guide* along lines other than those officially advanced by Maimonides. Perhaps a more charitable way still of interpreting Maimonides would be to say that he uses the "denial of attributes" as an instrumentality for stating the thesis of God's otherness. Attributes are denied as a way of providing a humanly accessible conceptual handle on the idea of God's otherness. But Maimonides would acknowledge the conceptual dispensability of the "denial of attributes" construed on a fully literal level. The numerous passages where he vehemently assaults conventional understandings of God that attribute qualities to him on a literal level would then have to be reinterpreted as heuristic devices for providing a point of entry into the notion of God's otherness, but should not be taken literally on their own terms.

Can a case for an ontologically relativized reading of monotheistic teaching be made that is independent of Maimonides' supposed conflation between "God's otherness" and "denial of attributes"? Aside from the theoretical impact of his ambivalent affirmation of the principle of the eternity of the world discussed previously, one can say that Maimonides' articulation of the principle of God's otherness establishes a model of conceptual ontological unmooring that appears to inspire and encompass the articulation of whatever immanentist narratives we temporarily expand upon in advancing the sorts of arguments that we are concerned to make. All of these immanentist narratives (including skeptical and relativist ones) are relative to the points we wish to make; they have no validity or permanence beyond them. The premodernist Maimonidean monotheistic universe and a postmodernist ontologically relativist universe converge in their shaping of a world in which the ultimate props of argument are relocated from extrahuman theological and metaphysical levels to an unabashedly human realm where human exigencies and needs prevail.

Our analysis of the theoretical terrain of "revelation" discloses a more extreme skepticism than is true of "philosophy." We might say that the move from philosophy to revelation reflects a shift from a more confined to a more unrestricted skepticism. Philosophical activity, as we saw earlier, is predicated upon the relatively arbitrary relationship subsisting between words and things. There are many different— sometimes conflicting—strings of words that can theoretically circumscribe a particular region of fact or experience. That philosophizing serves as an occasion for ascent from the immediate stimuli of experience guarantees that the theoretical slack and variation governing the relationship between philosophical concepts and things will never be fully overcome. "Revelation" introduces a more extreme skepticism into theoretical speculation, because inquiring into its meaning and conceptual ramifications engenders despair concerning the status of words themselves. Probing the concept of God leads us to become aware of the stark disconnectedness of some of our most frequently invoked words. "Philosophy" at least holds out the prospect of working to maximize the fit between words and things. "Revelation" underscores the possibility that some of the words that are being deployed in the project of maximizing coherence are themselves so devoid of manageable sense and reference that they are inadequate for the more humble tasks of philosophy. Words can do the job that philosophy assigns to them if one postulates that because of their deliberately fashioned character ambiguity can be more firmly sealed off and precision achieved with greater efficacy than is true in the case of the raw stimuli themselves—the "things" of human existence. Maimonides' treatment of the concept of God, however, shows that arbitrariness is no refuge. Fashioning a concept is no guarantee that its sense will remain stable and coherent enough to enable the concept to "work" in the dialectical stratagems of philosophers. The activity of concept formation lurches toward a beyond, a realm of internally necessary concepts, whose most consummate expression is the idea of God, which destabilizes itself and ends up signifying nothing and referring to nothing. "Revelation" nudges to center stage of the theorist's attention how the words and concepts that are the tools of philosophers stand poised on the brink of imminent self-dissolution.

How the formation and refinement of concepts, which is integral to philosophical activity, leads to the postulation of the idea of a totally unique one—the Maimonidean-Straussian bridge between philosophy and revelation—is presaged in Plato's *Parmenides:*

> And if the one is absolutely without participation in time, it never had become, or was becoming, or was at any time, or is now become, or is becoming, or is, or will become, or will have become, or will be, hereafter.
>
> Most true.
>
> But are there any modes of partaking of being other than these?
>
> There are none.
>
> Then the one cannot possibly partake of being?
>
> That is the inference.
>
> Then the one is not at all.
>
> Clearly not.
>
> Then the one does not exist in such way as to be one; for if it were and partook of being, it would already be; but if the argument is to be trusted, the one neither is nor is one?
>
> True.
>
> But that which is not admits of no attribute or relation?
>
> Of course not.
>
> Then there is no name, nor expression, nor perception, nor opinion, nor knowledge of it?
>
> Clearly not.
>
> Then it is neither named, nor expressed, nor opined, nor known, nor does anything that is perceive it.
>
> So we must infer.
>
> But can all this be true about the one?
>
> I think not.[18]

The pursuit of interconnections that defines theoretical activity leads to the envisioning of a master concept that contains within itself *in potentio* all of the ramifications and extensions that come to define

not only the theoretical realm but also ultimately the domains of practice as well. The idea of the one—what eventually emerges as the
concept of God in the hands of the theologians—begins as a kind of
natural development out of the philosophical impulse that comes in
the course of time to theorize a unitary and singular entity that concentrates within itself the multiple interrelationships delineated by philosophical reason. The one (what eventually comes to be called God) is
conceptualized as the ultimate interconnection. However, at this stage
of theorizing—and this is the burden of the Platonic-Maimonidean
argument—the idea of the one, of the irreducibly singular and unique,
becomes incoherent. If the one is truly to qualify as one, it must be
bereft of all human attributes and even be deprived of existence. The
rigors of philosophical thought legislate the one into nonexistence.
The exercise of theological construction serves as a kind of reductio
ad absurdum of philosophical thought. Philosophy, which begins as
a search for a more secure foundation for knowledge than is available
in commonsense judgment, ends up in theological speculation confronting the limitlessness of its own uncertainty—with all the masks
torn away.

From this perspective, perhaps the most persuasive way to
read Maimonides is as someone intensely driven to believe (someone
utterly fascinated and preoccupied by the God-man relationship) who
must yet acknowledge that the content of belief is hair-raisingly interchangeable with the content of nonbelief. I think it makes the most
sense to see Maimonides (including Strauss's Maimonides) not as an
atheist or rejector of religion but as someone who desperately wants
to believe—or, in Strauss's idiom, wants to preserve the autonomy
and distinctness of revelation in contrast to philosophy—who in all
honesty needs to affirm that, conceptually considered, philosophy
achieves a nearly total overtaking of revelation. What confers upon
revelation its special character as a way of life and mode of being in
the world is almost entirely dependent on such extrarational factors
as the roles of tradition and community in shaping individual belief
systems rather than on some unique set of conceptual traits intrinsic
to revelation. The approach that I am outlining here would also help
explain why Maimonides' *Code*, which provides us with a systematic exposition of Jewish beliefs and practices, constitutes the ideal
companion volume to his *Guide*.

Both philosophy and theology can be understood as highlighting
continually expanding areas of human ignorance. Just as philosophy

expands the area that remains impervious to the achievement of theoretical certainty, emphasizing the persistently imperfect fit between words and things, so too does revelation in the Maimonidean sense signify the rational impenetrability of the primary ingredient in the activity of theorizing, the fashioning of names. The ultimate theoretical ascent—the fashioning or invocation of the idea of God—deconstructs itself (is not able to sustain the weight of its own contradictions) and derails beyond retrieval the whole point and purpose of theoretical activity. Whereas the sphere of philosophy, which is concerned with the relationship between words and things, issues forth in mitigated skepticism, revelation, which is preoccupied with the prior level of theorizing having to do with the validity of words (names) themselves, conjures up the specter of extreme skepticism. Strauss's preference for a life devoted to philosophy in contrast to one centering around the claims of revelation might be symptomatic of his desire to remain within the orbit of moderation rather than to enter into the region of the extremes. On religious grounds, therefore, Strauss might be said to renounce the claims of religion in favor of those of philosophy.

If skepticism is present from the start of Western philosophical speculation, then we can perhaps argue that what unites the West's different theoretical paradigms is more deep-seated and revealing than what divides them. What unites them are mechanisms of displacement: Something has to be not where one is in order for one to be where one is and to be able to do what one is about to do. In Plato, the Ideas are elsewhere—ostensibly reflective of cosmic ordering principles in order to enable theorizing as an ascending, synthesizing activity to take off. In monotheistic theology, God is elsewhere in order to enable the recognizable human scene to get formed and to become an appropriate setting for the efflorescence of human creativity. In Descartes and Locke, mind is elsewhere—the interior has been thoroughly exteriorized or externalized—in order to enable an analogously rampant theoretical activity to take place: the instrumentalization of the person and the consequent emergence of the "punctual self" of which Charles Taylor speaks in his recent book, *Sources of the Self*.[19] By "displacement" in these diverse contexts, I mean the interjection of an act of theorizing—the Ideas, God, the removal of mind from the concept of a person. We need to distinguish positive displacement from negative displacement and point to the theoretical coalescence of the two. The negative displacement of modernism is prefigured by the positive displacement of ancient philosophy and revelation. Upon close scrutiny, the positive categories that Greek and Jewish thought displace onto—the Ideas and God—turn out to be tissues of negative disownings. The highest theoretical notion—the concept of the one, which is a kind of discursive translation of the highest Ideas both epistemological and ethical (or the unity subsisting between them) in a technical Platonic sense—gets derailed out of the weight of its own incoherence and can only be negatively specified and delineated. The same, as we have seen, is true of the concept of God.

Alternatively, it might be possible to read Strauss in such a way that his thesis concerning the incommensurability of philosophy and revelation masks an antithetical esoteric teaching. Perhaps, at the highest levels of theorizing, Strauss wants us to see his dualism of philosophy and revelation collapse into a barely articulable unity. Perhaps, qualms about self-referentialism are finally put to rest by a negative theology that in its infinite openness—its infinite recognition of infinite distance between God and ourselves—facilitates the emergence of an equivalence between our ceaseless historicizing and relativizing and the presence of God, whose impact is felt in the relentless nullification and qualification of our thought. Instead of violating the protocols of self-referentialism in our historicism and relativism, we are in a negative, oblique way (the only way possible) affirming God. The ultimate perspective to bring to bear on things human is the continual receding of all perspectives. The ultimate human identity is the suspension and erosion of that identity in the acknowledgment of the possibility of God. In this sense, Strauss provides a Heideggerian "clearing" for God.

In pursuit of this more unified strategy of interpretation, we might also say that in monotheistic theology, history—humanly fashioned and humanly told—constitutes a kind of monotheistic residue that exudes an afterglow of sanctity and holiness. Because God's presence and purpose remain permanently removed from human grasp and comprehension, a premium is placed on endless doing in a succession of theoretically uncompleteable acts of retrieval. The lack of official and explicit confirmation of connection with the divine is built into the very tenets of monotheistic theology, so that secular history (an engagement in and recounting of human action without reference to divine intervention) is ontologically interchangeable with sacred history (a setting forth of divine imperatives and involvements with

human beings). Human life pulsates with a tension of not knowing whether tension is appropriate—a self-referential anxiety about
anxiety—that is a pervasive but negative trace of its being touched by
the sacred.

• Strauss's Mitigated Skepticism

I would now like to sort out in a neutral philosophical idiom Strauss's
strategies for dealing with skepticism and reflexivity and to underscore the political implications that he draws from them. Strauss
clearly rejects extreme skepticism. On what grounds does he do so?
To use shorthand terms that I have been employing throughout this
book: on grounds that it fails to meet the test of reflexivity, of self-
referentialism. The argument of the consistent skeptic founders on
the paradox that if skepticism is correct (that it is justifiable to doubt
everything) then skepticism too becomes a valid subject of doubt, so
that skepticism gets aborted even before it can be formulated. The
reduction to language of a consistently skeptical position seems to
self-destruct before the targets of skepticism can be negotiated.

I would like to present a sampling from Strauss's writings of
his grappling with skepticism and relativism, and of his rejection of
extreme skepticism and extreme relativism in favor of mitigated versions of both doctrines. With regard to social science, Strauss says
that it "is always a kind of self-knowledge. Social science, being the
pursuit of human knowledge of human things, includes as its foundation the human knowledge of what constitutes humanity, or rather,
of what makes man complete or whole, so that he is truly human." [20]
The continuity of the "stuff" linking the investigator to what he is
investigating inhibits the emergence of a completely neutral, objective social science. Several factors are at work here. One is that since
the subject matter of social science is human beings, human bias is
too pervasive and deep rooted to facilitate a completely neutral and
disinterested study of human and social phenomena. Another factor
minimizing the "objectivity" of social science is almost the antithesis
of the first. In social science we would not want a thoroughly unbiased
account of a particular issue, because the human and social entities
and interactions that social scientists study—and the personality of
the observer—are so completely suffused with overlays of human interpretive reconstructions that a totally neutral study would distort
and efface the very phenomena it sought to comprehend. The idea

of scientific neutrality seems to be hopelessly out of place within the sphere of social science. Third, the metaphysical continuity between the investigator and what is being investigated suggests the possibility that the identities of both might be transformed as a result of the investigation at hand, thus defeating the possibility of a neutral study. The upshot of all three factors is a skeptical attack on the idea of social science, but Strauss ends up roundly endorsing certain forms of social inquiry and investigation. He says that "to treat social science in a humanistic spirit means to return from the abstractions or constructs of scientistic social science to social reality, to look at social phenomena primarily in the perspective of the citizen and the statesman, and then in the perspective of the citizen of the world, in the twofold meaning of 'world': the whole human race and the all-embracing whole." [21] For the external perspective of the scientistically motivated observer, Strauss substitutes the internal perspective of the citizen or statesman who builds on the commonalities subsisting between himself and his subject matter to formulate an agenda of interesting questions and to come up with a series of answers that are deliberately qualified as to time, place, and historical location. What such a suitably redefined social inquirer comes up with will also be subject to doubt and reinterpretation, but nevertheless Strauss finds it immensely more acceptable than the global aspirations of the external observer. The knowledge base and claims of such an internally situated observer are mitigated, in contrast to the claims put forward by the scientistically motivated observer, so that the skeptical counterarguments that one can address to the internal observer are correspondingly deflated and reduced.

Strauss's critique of relativism can be succinctly stated: It fails to meet the test of reflexivity.

> I fear that the field within which relativists can practice sympathetic understanding is restricted to the community of relativists who understand each other with great sympathy because they are united by identically the same fundamental commitment, or rather by identically the same rational insight into the truth of relativism. What claims to be the final triumph over provincialism reveals itself as the most amazing manifestation of provincialism.[22]

Instead of relativism turning out to be a true universalism, Strauss unmasks it as one additional variety of provincialism. The relativist that Strauss criticizes is relativist about everything except the truth of relativism. To be consistently relativistic, however, requires one to be equally relativistic about the truth of relativism. Extreme relativism is in a certain way self-refuting—in the way that extreme skepticism is self-refuting. Only modified versions of both can withstand philosophical criticism—can meet the test of reflexivity.

In his critique of Isaiah Berlin's classic "Two Concepts of Liberty," the nub of the issue for Strauss is reflexivity. "Liberalism, as Berlin understands it, cannot live without an absolute basis and cannot live with an absolute basis."[23] According to Strauss, the paradox from which Berlin's presentation of liberalism cannot extricate itself is that liberalism must be committed to the truth of relativism at the same time that it is relativistic about truth. A less compressed formulation of this criticism is found in the recent writings of Thomas Nagel examined in Chapter 3.

With regard to Nietzsche, Strauss identifies a central issue of reflexivity:

> I have in mind his interpretation of human creativity as a special form of the universal will to power, and the question that this interpretation entails, namely, whether he did not thus again try to find a sufficient theoretical basis for a transhistorical teaching or message. I have in mind, in other words, his hesitation as to whether the doctrine of the will to power is his subjective project, to be superseded by other such projects in the future, or whether it is the final truth.[24]

Nietzsche's concept of the will to power confronts a daunting paradox of self-referentialism. If he intends that all human exertions—including intellectual exertions—be regarded as manifestations of a will to power, then what is to exempt Nietzsche's own formulation of the theory of the will to power from being subsumed under the category of "Expression of a Will to Power"? If, on the other hand, Nietzsche wants to privilege his theory of the will to power from falling under the rubric of "Will to Power," on what basis can he consistently do so? The paradox surrounding Nietzsche's work is directly evocative of the self-referential paradox concerning skepticism. If one is being consistently skeptical, is one not compelled to doubt the truth of skepticism as well?

In his diagnosis of existentialism, Strauss points to the vexing consequences of reflexivity. "Existentialism admits the truth of relativism, but it realizes that relativism, so far from being a solution or even a relief, is deadly. Existentialism is the reaction of serious men to their own relativism."[25] Since to be consistently relativistic requires one to be relativistic about one's own relativism, the relativist is not even able to deduce an ethic of simple toleration from his own moral principle. In a frenzied recognition that relativism cannot even sanction its own putative self-realization, the relativist invokes "commitment" as his touchstone for the organization of the moral life. But "commitment," from Strauss's perspective, becomes an involuted testament to the intractability of "reflexivity" as an issue bedeviling moral deliberation and action.

In the case of Heidegger, a variation of the paradox surrounding reflexivity emerges into full prominence:

> The analytics of *Existenz* had culminated in the assertion that the highest form of knowledge is finite knowledge of finiteness; yet how can finiteness be seen as finiteness if it is not seen in the light of infinity? Or in other words, it was said that we cannot know the whole; but does this not necessarily presuppose awareness of the whole?[26]

Heidegger's critique of our ability to know the whole—his pursuit of a theory of a "finite knowledge of finiteness"—both has to allude to knowledge of the whole in order to adduce a content for itself and has to concede intellectual space to what it rejects in order that the theory that it affirms might have explanatory power. If all that we ever have is "finite knowledge of finiteness," then this theory constitutes a gigantic tautology. In order for a "finite knowledge of finiteness" to retain its explanatory force and for invocations of this concept to constitute more than tautologies, the metaphysical approaches that a "finite knowledge of finiteness" rejects must somehow continue to exist even after Heidegger has affirmed that all we ever have access to is a "finite knowledge of finiteness." The explanatory force of a "finite knowledge of finiteness" is parasitic upon the continued existence of contrasting metaphysical understandings concerning the possibility of our achieving a knowledge of the whole. Issues of reflexivity thus come to undermine Heidegger's stress on a "finite knowledge of finiteness."

Strauss invokes the issue of reflexivity in his critique of historicism—in his discussion of its destructive impact upon natural right:

There cannot be natural right if human thought is not capable of acquiring genuine, universally valid, final knowledge within a limited sphere or genuine knowledge of specific subjects. Historicism cannot deny this possibility. For its own contention implies the admission of this possibility. By asserting that all human thought, or at least all relevant human thought, is historical, historicism admits that human thought is capable of acquiring a most important insight that is universally valid and that will in no way be affected by any future surprises. The historicist thesis is not an isolated assertion: it is inseparable from a view of the essential structure of human life. This view has the same trans-historical character or pretension as any natural right doctrine.[27]

Historicism inconsistently asserts that all the products of human culture have to be construed historically—except the historicist thesis itself, which provides us with a transhistorical key for understanding human culture.

What are some of the logically and metaphysically specific features of a mitigated skepticism that enable Strauss to surmount the difficulties he diagnoses in other philosophers' arguments? I will begin by trying to show how the version of mitigated skepticism that I am calling a generalized agnosticism enables Strauss to accommodate the difficulty introduced at the start of this chapter. The problem posed there was how Strauss could pronounce upon the mutual incommensurability of philosophy and revelation when, according to his implicit mapping of the theoretical terrain, these two approaches were mutually exhaustive. According to this implicit premise, Strauss would have to stand either in the domain of philosophy or in the domain of revelation. From what higher perspective, therefore, was he licensed to pronounce upon their mutual incommensurability?

The inconsistency that I have pointed to is only present in Strauss's argument if the law of excluded middle is presumed to hold. In that case our alternatives would be restricted to A and not-A (philosophy and revelation). But if the law of excluded middle is regarded as suspended, so that our alternatives are increased beyond A and not-A, then the inconsistency is resolved. Strauss could then legitimately affirm both that philosophy and revelation were the only alternatives available and also that they were not the only alternatives available. A generalized agnosticism would have to acknowledge that at any given moment we had only an incomplete knowledge of objective reality, which leaves the door open for all possibilities. In that case, a multi-valued logic like intuitionism that mapped the suspension of the law of excluded middle might appropriately capture what the world was like—and Strauss would legitimately be able to both affirm and not affirm his restriction of alternatives to philosophy and revelation.

Strauss almost openly embraces a generalized agnosticism in his essay "Relativism" when he asks: "Can there be eternal principles on the basis of empiricism, of the experience of men up to now? Does not the experience of the future have the same right to respect as the experiences of the past and the present?"[28] A consistent skepticism requires one to be open to the possibility that the future will totally not resemble the past. If we are properly skeptical of our skepticism, we have to entertain the possibility that what we have ruled out on the basis of our critical canons will actually happen. What we thought we knew, we might not have known. At the same time, what we consigned to the alien and the exotic and even the unintelligible might come to pass.

An agnostic is committed to the permanence of questions and to the transitoriness and insubstantiality of answers. Strauss's generalized agnosticism is thus reflected in *Natural Right and History*[29] when, in opposition to historicism, he speaks about certain enduring questions:

> Far from legitimizing the historicist inference, history seems rather to prove that all human thought, and certainly all philosophical thought, is concerned with the same fundamental themes or the same fundamental problems, and therefore that there exists an unchanging framework which persists in all changes of human knowledge of both facts and principles.[30]

Strauss's advocacy of a nonscientistic, internalistic, interpretive social science as discussed previously also encounters a problem concerning circularity that can be most satisfactorily accommodated by a generalized agnosticism. Strauss's internalism, his arguing that we "look at social phenomena primarily in the perspective of the citizen and the statesman,"[31] cannot be defended on internalist grounds. The communities and traditions of citizens and statesmen cannot be justified in the name of "community" and "tradition" without these terms becoming circular concepts. Strauss, however, implicitly affirms circularity in the primacy that he assigns to tradition and community in his internalist social science. Here again, as I argue in earlier chapters, a generalized agnosticism enables Strauss to legitimize a recourse to circularity.

Strauss's conceptualization of Socrates' innovation as consisting in "the discovery of noetic heterogeneity"[32] also gives rise to a problem of reflexivity. The issue of reflexivity that Strauss himself identifies in Heidegger—that Heidegger cannot theorize a "finite knowledge of finiteness" without simultaneously invoking an awareness of the whole (a position that he rejects)—can also be raised in relation to Strauss's presentation of Socrates' position. The "noetic heterogeneity" of Socrates has to concede intellectual space to what it rejects in order that the theory that it affirms might have explanatory force. If "noetic heterogeneity" is definitive of reality, then the theory constitutes a gigantic tautology. In order for "noetic heterogeneity" to retain its explanatory force and for invocations of it to constitute more than tautologies, the metaphysical approaches that this theory rejects must somehow continue to exist even after Socrates affirms (in Strauss's version) that the world is characterized by "noetic heterogeneity." The explanatory force of the theory is parasitic upon the continued existence of contrasting metaphysical understandings that articulate a more homogeneous and unified vision of reality.

Strauss's generalized agnosticism offers him an overall framework for accommodating this dimension of the issue of reflexivity. "Generalized agnosticism" suggests that at any moment we have only an incomplete knowledge of objective reality, and therefore that it is possible that a multivalued logic that maps the suspension of the law of excluded middle accurately captures the structure of reality. Our alternatives would then be increased beyond A and not-A. We could thus accommodate a theory of "noetic heterogeneity" that was parasitic upon the persistence of more homogeneous and unified metaphysical theories in order to retain its explanatory force. The Socratic underpinnings for Strauss's "qualified relativism"[33] will have been preserved.

In the light of our discussion so far, it will also be possible to provide a new gloss upon Strauss's doctrine of "esoteric teaching."[34] From the perspective that I have been advancing in this chapter, "esoteric teaching" is not only a politically and ethically motivated concept but is also responsive to important epistemological and metaphysical requirements. In the latter sense, it holds strong affinities with Michael Polanyi's notion of "tacit knowledge."[35]

Given the dilemmas concerning reflexivity that we have been considering throughout this chapter, a paradigm of knowledge that emphasizes how the full extent and import of one's teaching is not fully formulated seems especially attractive. "Tacit knowledge" and "esoteric teaching" help to dissolve reflexivity as a source of anxiety in philosophy because they place this problematic in a context where our models of knowledge are statements that are more "knowing" than anything they directly state or justify. The inability to unravel the presuppositions and implications of some of our statements to render them more fully coherent with the explicit statements themselves that the dilemmas concerning reflexivity call attention to have now, through the medium of "esoteric teaching," been accommodated to a model of discourse in which not everything is—or can be—stated. Instead of the dilemmas surrounding reflexivity constituting an aberration, they have now been reconceptualized as defining a significant norm of discourse.

• *Liberalism and the Limits of Reason*

Strauss's politics is forged in the image of the epistemological concerns that we have been considering throughout this chapter. The political implications of a generalized agnosticism are to try continually to dissociate the positive value commitments of liberalism from its negatively formulated, methodologically inspired, process-oriented precepts. Thus, Strauss aims for what he called a "rational liberalism,"[36] one that is completely institutionally self-aware of the limitations of reason. He is critical of the secularist value overlay of modern liberalism, which engenders a false sense of certainty that is inimical to its broader value commitment to openness. Strauss is critical of behavioral political science—as well as of modern liberalism generally—because they rest "on a dogmatic atheism which presents itself as merely methodological or hypothetical."[37] He says that "just as our opponents refuse respect to unreasoned belief, we on our part, with at least equal right must refuse respect to unreasoned unbelief."[38] He therefore advocates a liberalism that is open to the regenerative powers of religion.

Because of his epistemological commitments, Strauss is equally opposed to the rarefied technical vocabularies in which modern liberal politics is both conducted and criticized by governmental bureaucrats and social scientists, as well as by humanists. He would like to see the public life and discourse of liberal democracies characterized by the triumph of common sense over technical philosophy—the triumph of the generalized vocabularies of everyday life over the specialized vocabularies of philosophy and the natural and social sciences. He praises the classical political philosopher for not abandoning "his fundamental orientation, which is the orientation inherent in political life."[39] "Classical political philosophy," Strauss says, "was essentially 'practical.'" Its primary concern "was not the description, or understanding, of political life, but its right guidance."[40] A primary motivating factor in the mistrust of technical vocabularies and the affirmation of everyday, commonsense vocabularies is that the former claim to achieve (and betoken independently of their official pronouncements) premature closure, whereas commonsense vocabularies maintain a fluidity and an openness to experience that suggests that reality, or individual sectors of it, has not yet been fully grasped or defined. The mistrust of technical vocabularies and the promotion of commonsense talk also harbors a tremendous democratic potential in theoretically extending the promise of democratic life to encompass more and more strata of the population.

The pace of social change in a liberal democracy has to be modulated to accommodate to the ideal of democracy as "an aristocracy which has broadened into a universal aristocracy."[41] Elsewhere, Strauss says that "only choice, in contradistinction to mere desire, makes something a man's value."[42] In order to facilitate the emergence of a democratic mass capable of making wise and informed choices, and not merely being swayed by momentary impulses and desires, time and public nurturance are required. Public policy has to be assessed at least in part by its likelihood to evoke thoughtful responses from citizens and to enrich public discourse, not just by its promotion of some sort of felicific calculus.

Strauss's affirmation of liberal democracy is partially based upon his awareness that a life bounded by the category of tradition has become increasingly inaccessible in the modern age. "We have lost," he says, "all simply authoritative traditions in which we could trust, the *nomos* which gave us authoritative guidance, because our immediate teachers and teachers' teachers believed in the possibility of a simply rational society. Each of us here is compelled to find his bearings by his own powers, however defective they may be."[43] The acids of an extreme rationalism have corroded the viability of tradition so that it cannot be artificially rehabilitated in the modern world. The kind of politics that is compatible with our social and psychological condition, which disbars us from deliberately re-forming traditions, is the mutually restraining individualism of a liberal-democratic society. This, according to Strauss, becomes the only viable political surrogate for tradition—a primary negative effect of tradition is achieved, without its emotional aura or value overlay.

The case for democracy in Strauss rests upon the skeptical limitations of philosophical reason. The case for liberalism in Strauss rests upon the implications of reflexivity. Skepticism itself cannot be fully trusted. Liberal brakes on democratic rule are therefore required to ensure that not even a democratic reading of the common good is translated into public policy in its entirety. Ultimately for Strauss, politics—like knowledge and understanding—represents movement toward a continually receding shore.

There is an analogous interweaving of the multifarious strands of a generalized agnosticism that maximizes the coherence of Robert Dahl's *Democracy and Its Critics*.[44] Dahl does not need to rely on the ad hoc theoretical strategies he develops in that book to reconcile, on the one hand, the limitation of democracy by such institutional principles as representation and the protection of minority rights and, on the other hand, the expansion of democracy by extending it to the economic sphere or workplace.[45] Both the limits and the expansion can be rooted in one unitary epistemological model—that of a generalized agnosticism. "Reflexivity" (the logical brakes on skepticism) is suggestive of limitation of direct expression of majority will. "Incomplete knowledge of objective reality" supports continual expansion of forums of democratic decision making to enable new possibilities to become crystallized and to get acted upon.[46]

In the end, Strauss's "rational liberalism" becomes its own theodicy. "All evils," he says,

> are in a sense necessary if there is to be understanding. It enables us to accept all evils which befall us and which may well break our hearts in the spirit of good citizens of the city of God. By becoming aware of the dignity of the mind, we realize the true ground of the dignity of man and therewith the goodness of the world, whether we understand it as created or as uncreated, which is the home of man because it is the home of the human mind.[47]

Since we can never proceed beyond understanding toward a serene expectation of its realization or toward a secure practical translation of our insights—and since we are also bidden by Strauss not to become

bewitched by large-scale programs of social and economic meliora-
tion, which always embody an imperfect and imprecise reason—in
the end all we are left with are the consolations of the understanding.

The most enduring image that emerges from Strauss's writing is
that of all of Western intellectual experience forming a seamless web—
an eternal now, a series of completely reversible menus of speculation and action—where it is just as intelligible to move from religion
as a way of life to philosophy as a way of life as it is to move from
philosophy to religion. The project of modernity of fashioning out of
the resources of the self a set of guidelines for thought and action is
forever taking place—and is forever renewed.[48]

7 • Freud: A Postmodernist Reconciliation of Theory and Therapy

Daniel Yankelovich and William Barrett aptly describe a central tension of psychoanalytic theory in *Ego and Instinct:*

> The most abstract level of psychoanalytic theory, its metapsy-chology, represents in almost pure form the late nineteenth century version of scientific materialism (i.e., the human person is conceptualized in analogy with a material object as "psychic apparatus" powered by energies whose accumulation and discharge are as lawfully regulated as any machine). Psychoanalytic practice, on the other hand, is, in psychoanalyst Avery Weisman's apt phrase, "existential at its core" (i.e., it is dominated by the human encounter between two subjects and the transformations that take place in both of them). Thus, psychoanalysis has one foot firmly planted in scientific materialism and the other equally firmly in existentialism, which is at violent odds with the former and indeed was largely conceived in opposition to it. A rigorous adherence to both philosophies would tear psychoanalysis apart.[1]

Breaking down this large tension in Freudian thought pointed to by Yankelovich and Barrett into more manageable terms, we begin, against the backdrop of psychoanalysis's dual claim to be both theory and therapy, to raise some questions concerning the theory. After attempting a more coherent rearticulation of some of the central terms of the theory, we confront a more specific set of tensions growing out of the simultaneous theoretical as well as therapeutic claims of psychoanalysis.

What is the relationship between intellectual enlightenment and action in Freudian theory? Does psychoanalytic theory rest upon a naïve positivist metaphysics—so that if enough nudgings of psychic energy take place in the course of an analysis, previously repressed (or sublimated) energies can be brought to light and made to interact realistically and creatively with our own latent energies, as well as with those of other human beings? How can we use elements of Freudian theory to rehabilitate psychoanalysis along nonpositivist lines?

One promising avenue is the Freudian notion of the unconscious. This concept is extremely fertile. As Sigmund Freud writes in elucidating it: "There is no need to characterize what we call 'conscious': it is the same as the consciousness of philosophers and of everyday opinion. Everything else psychical is in our view 'the unconscious'. . . . This reminds us that consciousness is in general a highly fugitive state. What is conscious is conscious only for a moment."[2]

The almost inexhaustible richness of the Freudian unconscious invites a hermeneutic approach to it. It is as if we as individuals were provided with a built-in set of tools to reconstruct our lives constantly. The idea of the unconscious might be employed mechanically in the context of Freud's own system—with forbidden thoughts and desires being repressed into the unconscious and finding their release in the course of psychoanalysis. However, the notion of the unconscious suggests that traces of whatever has happened to us, whatever we have felt, remain stored within us. Through the medium of the Freudian unconscious we harbor within ourselves the emotional and imaginative wherewithal to complete and define our lives in different ways in response to the exigencies of the moment. The notion of the unconscious hermeneutically conceived suggests the idea of "power as rationality"—with our willful invocation of certain unconscious images or themes rendering our lives more intelligible and coherent in response to temporary crises of incoherence.

According to Freud, one of the most deeply repressed memories in the human unconscious is the killing of the primal father.[3] Freud personalizes this putative anthropological datum for the life history of every human being with his notion of an Oedipus complex. It appears that for him an almost metaphysical necessity attaches itself to the act of killing the father. Generalizing this aspect of Freudian theory, we might ask: Why does the existence of others—and specifically of progenitors and influencers—constitute a threat and embarrassment to us, inducing primordial anxiety?

Jean-Paul Sartre, in *Being and Nothingness*,[4] points to an existential longing for self-sufficiency—a craving for the fixity of thinghood. It is possible to reinterpret Freud's tripartite division of our psyches into id, ego, and superego to be in consonance with this insight. His typology of the psyche can be construed as referring to three internal voices rooted in three different time dimensions. The id is the voice of the past—of drives, needs, and desires emanating from our child- hood. The ego is the voice of the present. It engages in reality testing and tries to reconcile the unregenerate drive toward pleasure lodged in the id with the exigencies of the reality principle. The superego serves as an ally of the ego. It is the voice of the future—trying to get us to assess the implications of present action for longer range principles and values.

From a more structuralist perspective than Freud's, one might say that the basic source of tension and conflict in human life is the in- stitutionalization of distance evident in the functioning of our psychic economies. Freud's invocation of the Oedipus myth might be con- strued as a metaphoric way of describing what I am talking about. The child's desire to kill the father and sleep with the mother represents a quest for self-origination—to be the source of his own being—to overcome contingency and dependency, to annul distance. The Oedi- pus myth refers to an attempt to heal the rupture of consciousness through reintegration in a world entirely circumscribed by the self, where other people (save the desired and necessary partner from the opposite sex) have been eliminated.

Living in a world characterized by distance means that we are doomed to be creatures of metaphor—forced to connect and contrast, indeed, even to locate and identify—present moments of existence in relation to a before and an after. Freud's employment of radical images, myths, and metaphors to diagnose the human condition forces us to confront the ontologically necessary—and ontologically unen- durable—metaphoric nature of human existence. Man, for Freud, is indeed a "useless passion." He self-destructs as soon as he begins to think about himself with any degree of seriousness. Man, for Freud, is a creature in search of an underlying reality—whose reality is metaphor.

Another aspect of the problematics of Freudian interpretation has to do with the epistemological claims of psychoanalytic theory— where we confront versions of the problem of reflexivity. How can we evolve a set of diagnostic psychological categories that would be psychoanalytically untainted, categories that would not simply represent the unconscious aggressive drives of particular individuals as they sought to impose their will upon other individuals in the name of some spurious ideal of scientific objectivity? What would logically disallow an exercise of psychological reductionism being directed against Freudian theory itself—to the effect that if true, it must according to its own terms (emphasizing such key psychological factors as repression, sublimation, and aggression) be false, and therefore it is false—which would have the effect of relativizing psychoanalytic theory in the same way that psychoanalysis itself relativizes other historical absolutes? How can Freud salvage the exalted epistemological pretensions of his own theory while denying independent, objective validity to most other theories?

Freud's response to this dilemma of theorizing, of how to justify claims for his own theory that he denies to others, might be to say that it is precisely the unconscious nature of the drives originating in the id that allows us to convert these psychological categories into norms through which to criticize prevailing theories and practices of individual and social psychological organization. It is the fact that id-related concepts are prerational that confers upon them a special moral psychological status. Rational argumentation distorts and falsifies id-level categories of mental life. They are both below and beyond rational argumentation.

The problem with this approach, however, is that discourse about id categories is not the same thing as the id categories themselves. To conceptualize about what is present in mental life (even, and perhaps especially, with regard to the most basic substratum of one's depth psychology) is in an important sense already to be repressing and sublimating—that is, creating some distance with regard to the id level of consciousness and establishing the locus of one's personality elsewhere than in the id. If the id categories taken by themselves are logically exempt from rational criticism, one's talking and conceptualizing about them is not. From what perspective, then, can Freud legitimate his psychoanalytic critique of individuals and of society?

I have just criticized psychoanalytic theory as saying too much, and therefore as not being able to withstand the barrage of its own criticism. It is also possible to attack psychoanalysis from the opposite perspective—as saying less than it appears to say and therefore as not capable of effectively criticizing any established social position at all. The reason for this theoretical paralysis before the given can be traced, I think, to the instrumentalist character of the theorizing of mind. Given the Hobbesian antecedents of Freudian ideas, the structure and dynamics of the psyche is to a large extent conceptualized in instrumentalist terms—which renders psychoanalytic theory parasitic on reigning value systems and therefore incapable of formulating a critical judgment against them.[5] The ego (the main conscious psychic mechanism, according to Freud) mediates between the instinctual urges of the id, the demands of the superego, and the exigencies of a perpetually changing, largely indifferent reality. The ego posits no ends or values of its own and therefore seems to be at the mercy of these three subjectively grounded value systems: the instinctual drives lodged in the id; the societal and familial values channeled through the authority figures in one's immediate environment and later reified as the superego; and evolving social norms themselves as limits to aggressive behavior grasped by the ego. The highest personality type in psychoanalysis—the genital type, whose ego functioning is least impaired—is the person thoroughly in harmony with the prevailing norms of his society, and deprived by psychoanalysis of a critical basis by which to criticize those norms.

Perhaps the most promising route out of our difficulties is to raise another set of questions—not with regard to psychoanalysis as theory, but in relation to it as therapy—and to see where our exploration leads. Concerning the relationship between Freudian theory and psychoanalytic practice, one might ask: Are there exercises of power in Freudian theory that are neither repressive nor sublimative? Does Freud envisage less ambivalent, more authentically constructive uses of power beyond repression and sublimation? How are such uses manifested? Can they be reconciled with the more basic mechanistic theory concerning the structure and organization of the psyche—whose tone is captured by the terms "repression" and "sublimation," which suggest a pushing downward or a pushing upward of psychic energies? What sort of power is being manifested by the individual as the result of a successful therapy? What sort of power is being manifested by Freud himself qua psychoanalytic theorist? Where does Freud's own theorizing stand in relation to his psychoanalytic theory? Has he made sense out of his own activity as a psychoanalytic theorist?

A basic tension with Freudianism appears to be between its deterministic and indeterministic elements. On the one hand, we find Freud as theorist trying to capture psychological interactions within a determinist framework deriving ultimately from Hobbes, which places emphasis on such concepts as power and energy being pushed and pulled along rigidly prescribed channels in response to anticipated or experienced feelings of pleasure and pain. Counterposed to this image of Freud, we have him as therapist, who in relation to his patients (and in the relationship that he tries to induce them to cultivate in their intrapsychic lives) must transcend all determinist conceptual frameworks, including the specifically Freudian one.

Traditionally, the role of the transference has been stressed by Freud and his interpreters as crucial to the therapeutic process. He defines the phenomenon of the transference as follows:

> The most remarkable thing is this. The patient is not satisfied with regarding the analyst in the light of reality as a helper and adviser who, moreover, is remunerated for the trouble he takes and who would himself be content with some such role as that of a guide on a difficult mountain climb. On the contrary, the patient sees in him the return, the reincarnation, of some important figure out of childhood or past, and consequently transfers to him feelings and reactions which undoubtedly applied to this prototype. This fact of transference soon proves to be a factor of undreamt-of importance, on the one hand an instrument of irreplaceable value and on the other hand a source of serious dangers. This transference is ambivalent: it comprises positive (affectionate) as well as negative (hostile) attitudes towards the analyst, who as a rule is put in the place of one or other of the patient's parents, his father or mother.[6]

What emerges from Freud's discussion of the transference is highly puzzling and paradoxical. On the surface, the role of the transference appears to be tautologous. Whatever neurotic symptoms the patient has he acts out in relation to the analyst. The analysis simply provides him with a new forum to display and manifest those symptoms. Why should such a continued enactment of the symptoms itself constitute the cure?

It seems to me that the true dynamics of therapy are built into the interstices of Freud's descriptive analysis of the transference. The therapeutic moment would appear to consist fundamentally in new insight that restructures the whole field of action for the patient. What the patient learns in the course of an analysis, even if he is not able to fully articulate it, is how our actions—and the field of action generally—are theory dependent: The natures of our actions are dependent upon the antecedent intellectual categories we employ to demarcate our world and the significant elements within it. That our theories are underdetermined by experience indicates the strategic role assigned to will in the making and remaking of our selves. The manifestation of power for Freud is indeed the distinct form of human rationality. The neurotic would appear to be fixated on the determined character of his existence, and release from neurosis consists precisely in becoming aware of the undetermined character of existence. The neurotic is in search of a new starting point upon which to build his life. He has forgotten how to act—how to engage in what Hannah Arendt calls new beginnings.[7] The implicit metaphysics of psychoanalysis as therapy is that determinism itself is a man-made category—created to further human ends. As Hobbes says in *Leviathan*, determinism enables one to do certain things to nature, to maximize most effectively on certain observed correlations.[8] The concept of "correlation" itself provides one with a lever for maximization. There are also internal psychological benefits to be reaped from the category of causality because of the element of necessity that it introduces, which serves as a most potent goad to action.

With regard to the difficulties described earlier concerning the epistemological foundations of psychoanalysis, one might say from our current perspective that, as traditional theory, psychoanalysis is fundamentally incoherent—impaled on the dilemma of either saying too little or saying too much, but in either case not being able to validate its own epistemological claims. It is as therapy that psychoanalysis displays its greatest coherence. As therapy, the dilemma that I adduced earlier concerning the shaky epistemological basis of the theory—how it is bereft of a defensive strategy against turning its unmasking mechanism inward and thus undermining its own claims—disappears. The therapeutic moment for Freud seems akin to the theoretical moment as experienced and articulated by such epic theorists as Plato, Thomas Hobbes, G.W.F. Hegel, and Karl Marx,[9] where the very categories of thought and action dissolve into each other—where thought itself is perceived as the integrating and synthesizing moment of action. What is truly theoretical in Freud according to this perspective is the structuring and conduct of the therapeutic relationship, rather than psychoanalytic theory per se, which is in many ways mechanistic and derivative. Psychoanalysis, we might thus say,

126 • A GENERALIZED AGNOSTICISM

is "postmodernism" in advance of the historical advent of postmodernism. A generalized agnosticism that does not have to be theoretically accountable beyond the adumbration of individual statements leads to a displacement of theory onto therapy—with the theory embedded in the therapy—and individual therapeutic acts themselves, constituting the real theory of psychoanalysis.

8 • Wittgenstein's Postmodernist Theory of Action and Conceptualizations of the Relationship between Past and Present

- *Intellectual History, Postmodernism, and the Concept of Action*

In what is perhaps the most influential systematic restatement of a historicist position in the twentieth century—*The Idea of History* by R. G. Collingwood[1]—a withering tension emerges between the means and the end of historical understanding. The end can be described as the rooting of the subject of inquiry (whether a political event like a war or revolution, or a document in intellectual history) in its immediate historical context. The chief means toward this end, however, is the reenactment of the past in the historian's own mind, which suggests the superimposition of a present context over the past. The means (the reenactment process taking place in the historian's mind, which reflects her own needs, vision, and perception of the world) would appear to have a tendency to obliterate the end, so that what emerges partakes more of the nature of a fabrication than a re-creation.

How does one evolve a theory of historical interpretation that is able to face up squarely to the subjectivist implications inherent in the historicist analysis of the process of historical understanding that does not smother its insights in talk about "reenactment of past experience" and other vestiges of an exploded objectivist understanding of history? It seems to me that what is needed is a concept of human action generally that severs forever the privileged relationship of an agent to her or his own action and that regards all actions as essentially incomplete, susceptible to limitless interpretations by ever-more imaginative interpreters. In short, what is required to remedy the deficiencies of historicism is a postmodernist theory of action.

The outlines of such a philosophy of action are present, I think, in Wittgenstein's *Philosophical Investigations*. The central teachings of this work concern the ultimacy of language and of the disparate sets of rules governing its employment in different regions of discourse. Basing herself upon these views, Elizabeth Anscombe in a classic paper draws a distinction between brute facts and institutional facts.[2] "That a man has a bit of paper with green ink on it is a brute fact, that he has five dollars is an institutional fact."[3] Brute facts refer to a class of events or activities that exists as such, for example, eating. The marriage ceremony, money, promising, baseball and chess, on the other hand, as well as transactions pertaining to them, all involve reference to institutional facts, since the moves that one makes under the particular rubrics of marriage, money, and so on are constituted as such by the particular institutions creating and defining them in the first place. That my lifting an oblong wooden object and attempting to hit a thrown round one constitutes a "strike" becomes intelligible only within the larger institutional, man-made framework of the game of baseball and is totally devoid of sense outside it.

Expanding upon this distinction between brute fact and institutional fact, one might say that, strictly speaking, the only things that are past, that are irrevocably done, are brute facts. However, the set of institutional contexts under which particular sequences of brute facts might be subsumed is potentially infinite. The set of brute descriptions of a particular event is sufficiently indeterminate to square with an indefinite range of institutional characterizations of the same event. In an institutional sense, therefore, no action is ever complete, since the class of possible descriptions of what happened remains open. The possibilities for fashioning institutional contexts to frame a particular sequence of brute facts are coextensive with the resources of language itself, which provides us with the intellectual wherewithal to generate ever-new conceptual frameworks through which to organize our experience.

With a revised philosophy of action, we will be better able to appreciate the extent to which the test of truth to be applied to a work of history is not one of correspondence, as Collingwood and his disciples are frank to admit, but is thoroughly pragmatic in character. What level of coherence, of personal integration, has the historian been able to achieve with her image of the past? What has her image of the past done for the historian? Has it enabled her to achieve a more satisfactory relationship to the tensions and anomalies stemming from her own environment? The past—either as an unknown, menacing shadow cast by what went before or as a particular ordering of thought, imagination, and feeling contravening emotional imperatives in the present—needs to be confronted and assimilated so as to make a flourishing present possible. The historian in a sense serves as a public therapist unblocking our relationship to the past so as to create a clear path for successful action in the present. By rethinking the past in Collingwood's terms, we are enabled to repossess it—to make it continuous on some emotional level with our needs and projects in the present.

In interpreting texts in intellectual history, specifically, there is an inescapable paradox that confronts us which is resolved from the perspective that I am advancing here. A major component in the self-image of many of the creators of these texts is that they are grappling with (and perhaps even expressing) truth. By interpreting these texts historically, by rooting them as fully as possible in their own immediate context, one in a sense does justice to the external environment of creation at the cost of falsifying a crucial element in the internal environment—the author's sense of himself as transmuting finite, relativized materials into something that he recognizes as truth. A historical approach to texts in intellectual history captures the circumstances of creation while being untrue to the spirit of creation, which is defined in many instances by precisely its antihistorical drive. The paradox emerges that, on the deepest level, the process of retelling what others have said and thought requires one to divest oneself of historical methodology in order to achieve the end that historians have traditionally sought—namely, reproducing the thought world of those who created works coming down to us from the past.

By positing a wedge between brute fact and institutional fact, between utterance and interpretation, and abolishing an author's privileged relationship to the interpretive schema to be invoked to frame a particular utterance, we in effect recapture an essential element in the context of creation. It is precisely the fluidity of the intellectual context—the lack of fixed correlations between words and combinations of words and the ideas that they are intended to convey—that makes it possible for an author to manifest his creativity and to make his leap from an idiom of approximation to an idiom of truth. Working in the interface between words and their meanings (between utterance and interpretation) establishes common ground between writer and interpreter, enabling the latter to reenter in the fullest possible sense into the creative process of the former, and in that way to represent and complete—to represent *by* completing (for his generation and his time)—the creative efforts of an author. By reworking the same set of tensions (between word and meaning, utterance and interpretation) that an author had to traverse in order to produce the text, complete fidelity is preserved between the act of writing and the act of interpreting, by allowing the process of grappling with truth to remain central to both.

One might ask, concerning this approach: Does not psychoanalysis end up being the queen of the historical sciences? And does not, paradoxically, a work of history reveal more about the present (of its author) than it does about the past (that he is writing about)? In that case the history of historiography becomes the true work of history (if its aim is taken to be the record of past events), rather than a study of the original events or documents themselves. History could therefore only study its own subject matter (i.e., other works of history) and would be denied access to a philosophically neutral concept of "raw data" or "raw material."

But perhaps what I am saying is not paradox but platitude. The most we can approximate toward a neutral, objective description of the past is through a comparative study of what various authors writing at different times and from different points of view have had to say about it, rather than through a direct examination of source material emanating from the past itself.

Perhaps we might say in the light of the distinction between brute facts and institutional facts that this is what we are always doing. The typical documents stemming from the past, such as letters, legal and governmental papers, accounts of certain key events written by participants, and so on are not the brute facts of history but are already institutional historical facts. There is only a difference in degree (and not a difference in kind) between such material, typically employed by the historian and labeled by her "primary sources," and interpretive works on the events (or texts) she is interested in done by other historians. From a rigorous philosophical perspective, once the instant of action vanishes everyone is interpreting. The concept of action itself might be an ideal limit to an ongoing, uninterrupted process of interpretation. With the breakdown of an ironclad distinction between primary and secondary sources, we can more easily see that historical knowledge consists every step of the way in indirect, retrospective retrieval of events, rather than in an examination of hard tokens of events, granting participants a metaphysically superior relationship to events over later observers. From the perspective advanced here, everyone—including participants in historical events themselves (and authors of texts)—is simultaneously retrieving (through reporting and interpreting what is happening) and acting, and their relationship to events from a strict philosophical vantage point is not qualitatively superior to that of later historians.

The problematic of the interpretation of theoretical texts is analogous to the problematic of the interpretation of more standard forms of "primary evidence," such as letters, diaries, and other sorts of memorabilia. Every text is simultaneously a statement and an explication—with the development and more precise formulation of an idea in many ways constituting its true statement. From the moment one begins to write, to communicate any idea, one is already interpreting (i.e., expanding, refining, revising, detailing, condensing, extrapolating, connecting). Every text is an institutional elaboration of a point instant that merely constitutes the ideal limit, the vanishing point, of an omnipresent and unending process of interpretation. This constitutes the historical analogue to the endless deferral that postmodernism in other areas of thought both encodes and advances. The communication of ideas through the institutional medium of language suggests that every text, no matter how systematically argued, is a fragment—susceptible of further elaboration, refinement, and articulation by the author as he gains new insights into what he is saying or as he discovers new ways of deploying the resources of language to clarify his conception(s), or as other interpreters discover these ways and proceed with further elaborations of their own. There are only differences in degree (but not in kind) between an author's interpretation of his text and a later person's reading of it. Institutional elaboration through language is all—encompassing both later and earlier interpretations and leveling the privileged status of any one vantage point, of priorities claimed on the basis of temporal or spatial location.

In order to grasp the ramifications of the approach to the concept of action and to the past that I am advocating more fully, it is appropriate to delve more deeply into some key aspects of Wittgenstein's philosophy—a metaphysical seedbed for the perspectives that I am advancing.

• Meditations on Wittgenstein

One of the major problems of Wittgenstein interpretation is reconciling the philosophic teachings of the *Tractatus Logico-Philosophicus*[4] with those of the *Philosophical Investigations*.[5] The traditional view, which follows Wittgenstein's own analysis of his philosophical development, is to regard the later work as a recantation of the earlier one. This understanding has become so far entrenched that the words "early" and "later" have become staples of Wittgensteinian criticism. From the organizing perspective outlined previously, however, it is possible to perceive an underlying pattern of unity linking the *Tractatus* with the *Investigations*. The doctrine of logical atomism, which is integral to Wittgenstein's argument in the *Tractatus*, leads to the exclusion of certain regions of experience (the ethical, the aesthetic, the religious, and the philosophical) as falling outside the scope of rational resolution within language. These areas of experience have become completely "privatized," being confined to inner states of feeling and having no objective translation in the shared resources of language. One might say, in the light of my analysis of Wittgenstein's concept of action discussed previously, that the *Investigations* completes the project begun in the *Tractatus*. In the earlier book, a good deal of ordinary language can still be salvaged as a vehicle of knowledge and of truth; in the *Investigations*, ordinary discourse itself emerges as problematic. There are no external points of reference by which to verify even our typical, everyday assertions, so that with regard to the brute facts of any given situation the agent's institutional description enjoys no logical priority over that of any other observer. The "privatization" of our experience begun in the *Tractatus* is extended in the *Investigations* from the more specialized realms of aesthetics, religion, ethics, and philosophy to encompass our everyday transactions with the world, staked out and captured by ordinary language.

Viewed in this way, Wittgenstein's thought becomes symptomatic of one aspect of our modern predicament in politics—that our keenest pleasures and sorrows are regarded as so intensely personal that no ground for action and discussion with other people can be established on their basis. The progressive "privatization" of experience exemplified in Wittgenstein's thought points to the metaphysical and epistemological underpinnings of our world that inhibit the emergence of a viable concept of the public.

> 97. We are under the illusion that what is peculiar, profound, essential, in our investigation, resides in its trying to grasp the incomparable essence of language. That is, the order existing between the concepts of proposition, word, proof, truth, experience,

and so on. This order is a super-order between—so to speak—super-concepts. Whereas, of course, if the words "language," "experience," "world," have a use, it must be as humble a one as that of the words "table," "lamp," "door."

109. And we may not advance any kind of theory. There must not be anything hypothetical in our considerations. We must do away with all explanation, and description alone must take its place. And this description gets its light, that is to say its purpose, from the philosophical problems. These are, of course, not empirical problems; they are solved, rather, by looking into the workings of our language, and that in such a way as to make us recognize those workings: in despite of an urge to misunderstand them. The problems are solved, not by giving new information, but by arranging what we have always known. Philosophy is a battle against the bewitchment of our intelligence by means of language.

116. When philosophers use a word—"knowledge," "being," "object," "I," "proposition," "name,"—and try to grasp the essence of the thing, one must always ask oneself: is the word ever actually used in this way in the language-game which is its original home?—What we do is to bring words back from their metaphysical to their everyday use.

118. Where does our investigation get its importance from, since it seems only to destroy everything interesting, that is, all that is great and important? (As it were all the buildings, leaving behind only bits of stone and rubble.) What we are destroying is nothing but houses of cards and we are clearing up the grounds of language on which they stand.

119. The results of philosophy are the uncovering of one or another piece of plain nonsense and of bumps that the understanding has got by running its head up against the limits of language. These bumps make us see the value of the discovery.

121. One might think: if philosophy speaks of the use of the word "philosophy" there must be a second-order philosophy. But it is not so: it is, rather, like the case of orthography, which deals with the word "orthography" among others without then being second-order.

122. A main source of our failure to understand is that we do not command a clear view of the use of our words.—Our grammar is lacking in this sort of perspicuity. A perspicuous representation produces just that understanding which consists in "seeing connexions". Hence the importance of finding and inventing intermediate cases.

The concept of a perspicuous representation is of fundamental significance for us. It ear-marks the form of account we give, the way we look at things. (Is this a "Weltanschauung"?)

123. A philosophical problem has the form: "I don't know my way about."

124. Philosophy may in no way interfere with the actual use of language; it can in the end only describe it.

For it cannot give it any foundation either.

It leaves everything as it is.

It also leaves mathematics as it is, and no mathematical discovery can advance it. A "leading problem of mathematical logic" is for us a problem of mathematics like any other.

126. Philosophy simply puts everything before us, and neither explains nor deduces anything—Since everything lies open to view there is nothing to explain. For what is hidden, for example, is of no interest to us.

One might also give the name "philosophy" to what is possible before all new discoveries and inventions.

127. The work of the philosopher consists in assembling reminders for a particular purpose.

128. If one tried to advance theses in philosophy, it would never be possible to debate them, because everyone would agree to them.

129. The aspects of things that are most important for us are hidden because of their simplicity and familiarity. (One is unable to notice something—because it is always before one's eyes.) The real foundations of his enquiry do not strike a man at all. Unless that fact has at some time struck him.—And this means: we fail to be struck by what, once seen, is most striking and most powerful.

132. The confusions which occupy us arise when language is like an engine idling, not when it is doing work.

133. It is not our aim to refine or complete the system of rules for the use of our words in unheard-of ways.

For the clarity that we are aiming at is indeed complete clarity. But this simply means that the philosophical problems should completely disappear.

The real discovery is the one that makes me capable of stopping doing philosophy when I want to.—The one that gives philosophy peace, so that it is no longer tormented by questions which bring itself in question.—Instead, we now demonstrate a method, by examples; and the series of examples can be broken off.—Problems are solved (difficulties eliminated), not a single problem.

There is not a philosophical method, though there are indeed methods, like different therapies.[6]

The conquest of metaphysics cannot succeed when the elements of the inquiry that pose the problems of metaphysics in the first place—human beings, language, world—are allowed to retain their independent status. The problems of metaphysics must remain unresolvable as long as the terms generating them retain their individual identities. To fully dispel the problems of metaphysics (such as the nature of logical necessity, the problems of other minds, the existence and nature of an external world) is not just a matter of discerning new patterns of relationship between the key terms that give rise to the problems. One must destroy the very form of the questions. One must internalize, cannibalize, the highly distinct terms generating the questions, showing them to be reducible to a monistic entity— language—for the problems of metaphysics to be subdued properly. The solutions, to be persuasive (and effective), must totally displace the origin and plausibility of the problems. The *Investigations* successfully resolves a problem that was not successfully met in the *Tractatus*. The *Investigations* renders unintelligible (by breaking down the distinctiness of) the very terms of the problems of metaphysics. There is no longer human beings, language, world—but only language. What appears to be the most artificial of the three entities is the only one that can be philosophically vindicated. The other two entities succumb to what in the *Investigations* is an implicit form of radical skepticism.

What Wittgenstein does in an important sense is to "metaphysicalize" ordinary language—ordinary reality. By abolishing the distinction between philosophical concepts and language, on the one hand, and everyday concepts and language, on the other, he has not destroyed philosophy but only sown it into the center of everyday discourse. Ordinary discourse itself is now estranging, distancing, philosophical—since from Wittgenstein's perspective it is disbarred from pointing to anything beyond itself. What language ends up doing is to keep the individual perpetually at one remove from himself, rendering intrapersonal distance (our relationship to ourselves) logically insurmountable. Language is both the enemy and the permanent guarantor of our self-estrangement. It generates the illusion of mastery over self and environment only at the cost of warding off forever hopes of eventual mastery.

> 125. It is the business of philosophy, not to resolve a contradiction by means of a mathematical or logico-mathematical discovery, but to make it possible for us to get a clear view of the state of mathematics that troubles us: the state of affairs before the contradiction is resolved. (And this does not mean that one is sidestepping a difficulty.)
>
> The fundamental fact here is that we lay down rules, a technique, for a game, and that then when we follow the rules, things do not turn out as we had assumed. That we are therefore as it were entangled in our own rules.
>
> This entanglement in our rules is what we want to understand (i.e. get a clear view of).
>
> It throws light on our concept of meaning something. For in those cases things turn out otherwise than we had meant, foreseen. That is just what we say when, for example, a contradiction appears: "I didn't mean it like that."
>
> The civil status of a contradiction, or its status in civil life: there is the philosophical problem.[7]

What governs philosophical practice is the internal rule of preserving order (or, in philosophical language, restoring coherence), rather than the external constraint of squaring language and concepts with the world.

The point of Wittgenstein's political metaphor at this phase of his argument is to underscore the lack of an external point of reference in going about the tasks of resolving puzzlement and ironing out contradiction. Just as civil society by its very nature is coterminous with the task of imposing order—it is problematic whether we would call a contiguous group of human beings living together a civil society at all unless they possessed this ability—the therapeutic work of language that the philosopher engages upon is just one additional moment in the development of language without which language could not function. Avoiding breakdown is not a second-order task assigned to the state: It is the state at its most rudimentary level. Similarly, avoiding breakdown and contradiction does not require a second-order piece of machinery appended to language—using a special group of concepts and techniques. The periodic restoration of coherence—the unfreezing of puzzles and contradictions—is just what language is about at its most elementary level.[8]

One of the paradoxes about Wittgenstein is that he ends up explaining how we are blocked on a depth-psychological, existential level—and why the blocking is inevitable—rather than being the philosopher of release, of consummated linguistic therapy. Wittgenstein's underlying metaphysics is in tension with his philosophical practice. The therapeutic moment in the life of a language is inevitable, given the perennial human temptation to extend the meanings of words beyond their original, literally ordained boundaries. Yet the restorative, therapeutic work of the linguistic philosopher does not introduce repose once and for all. Part of the reason for this in Wittgenstein's conception is that there is no stable point of reference through which the therapeutic task can be carried out. Because the materials remain lowly, man-made, instrumentalist throughout (the contradictions and puzzles are generated within language, the philosophically therapeutic strategies are carried out through the use of language, and the resultant clarified piece of discourse, concept, or set of concepts are again a linguistic product), it is almost inevitable that contradictions and anomalies will crop up again and again indefinitely. There is no external source of support to secure the work of the linguistic philosopher. This is another ramification of the political analogy. Just as in human civil societies the problem of order is recurring—most equilibria achieved will have to be rearticulated as the constellation of forces within society changes—so too with language the problem of restoring clarity is recurring, with no solution having the prospect of creating indefinite stability. In Wittgenstein's picture of things, we are always at one remove from ourselves, using language to chase and clear up language in an endless series of necessary but futile gestures.

The political metaphor in this section of the *Investigations* also serves as an ironic and tragic commentary on Plato's statement in *The Republic* that perhaps the ideal commonwealth can only be established in the confines of one's own soul.[9] The Greek polis was founded after all because man was neither a beast nor a god, and participation in statecraft represented the highest vocation for a creature capable of the kind of creativity—and the depths of depravity—that man was. Wittgenstein's radical skepticism, his denial of ultimate reality to anything but a continually evolving language, renders grossly implausible the Greek faith in heroic political action and in political participation generally as the highest form of actualization of human potential. For Wittgenstein, what captures human beings' peculiar estate as intermediate between beast and god is not political participation but recognition of the centrality of language. The ultimacy of language for Wittgenstein suggests both the indispensability of language for structuring and conferring meaning on human life and the fruitlessness of the drive toward structure and meaning in human life altogether, given the reflexive nature of language and the lack of secure external referents through which to underwrite or reject particular linguistic formulations. The status of contradictions generated by language in civil life constitutes "the philosophical problem." Instead of philosophy facilitating the conquest and transformation of civil life as in the Greeks, the existence of civil life—of multiple language regions existing side by side—constitutes the heart of the problematics of philosophy. The resolution of these problematics consists in further development of the resources of language—to use language as a tool for dissolving the congealments of overly extended linguistic usage. There is no escape from the labyrinth of language, except to make it more labyrinthine.

A further implication of the passage that I am analyzing is that a multiplicity of language regions, rather than a plurality of selves, generates the civilizing need for a process of accommodation and adjustment in Wittgenstein. This is another way of saying that his politics (of processes of accommodation and adjustment taking place) is entirely compatible with a denial of ultimate reality to other individuals or to the world. The world has been so thoroughly internalized by Wittgenstein that one can now have a worldly politics taking place without leaving the confines of the individual.

Dualism seems to be an inescapable condition in the history of philosophy. Both empiricism and idealism are dualistic in character, but the dualism is expressed at different points in their respective philosophies. Hobbes, for example, one of the founders of modern empiricism, sets forth a monistic theory of human nature (viewing reason as the "scout," or extension and rationalized version of the passions)[10] while defending a dualistic epistemology. He assigns equal reality to thought and the sense impressions that it absorbs and processes and to the world that provides the stimuli for the exertions engaged in by thought. Plato's and later idealistic philosophies advance a dualistic theory of human nature. We are composed of mind and the passions, or a noumenal self (soul) and a phenomenal self (material body). The epistemology integral to most idealist philosophies, however, is monistic. The world, in a sense, is the product of mind. The intellectual and imaginative capability to fashion the categories by which we organize our experience comes from wellsprings of selfhood lodged within, which are inaccessible to the routine operations of mind.[11] What we thus find in idealism is not the transcendence of dualism, but only, as it were, its internalization—its incorporation into its theory of human nature.

When we apply this schema to Wittgenstein and ask where he fits in, where his dualism is manifested, two responses seem plausible—one focusing on the surface doctrines of his thought, the other attempting to unravel the import of its latent dynamic. On the level of overt doctrine, one might point to his assimilation of both experiences that one might say fall below the linguistic threshold, such as pain, and experiences that one might say exceed the linguistic threshold, such as art and religion, to the level of language. For Wittgenstein, the primary philosophical datum about the experience of pain, and art and religion, is that they belong to different language-games that shape the boundaries of meaningful and communicable experience within their respective spheres. Wittgenstein's emphasizing that it is only language that we work with, that there is no Archimedean point outside of particular language-games through which to legitimize or reject particular forms of experience, appears to be a way of abolishing dualism in philosophy and subsuming all previous philosophical dualisms under a monistic linguistic umbrella. However, I think, such an interpretation would be mistaken. In the *Philosophical Investigations,* the fecundity of language itself becomes a surrogate for such suppressed philosophical dualisms as those between mind and the world, body and soul, and public and private. This fecundity does philosophical dualism's job under a monistic cover. One of the paradoxes of the *Philosophical Investigations* is that Wittgenstein's monism to end all dualisms becomes a multiplication of self-contained monisms (different language-games, different language regions) that far exceeds the ontological extravagance of most dualisms.

The latent dynamic of Wittgenstein's thought also points in the direction of a suppressed—and insurmountable—dualism. Each liberating move that man as an active being (and the philosopher as a reflective, therapeutic being) makes within language becomes a metaphor for the ultimate imprisoning effects of language. As human beings develop new regions of experience in science, art, psychology, religion, philosophy, and everyday life, they evolve vocabularies—public, transpersonal verbal products—that endow their experiences with stability and sense. When philosophical perplexity emerges due to illegitimate extensions of words and concepts that are at home in one region of discourse into other spheres of discourse, the philosopher, through his analysis of terms in their accustomed language regions, calls us back to the original sense of words and concepts and relieves us of our perplexity. Both human beings' vocation as active creatures evolving new vocabularies and the vocation of the philosopher as a reflective creature engaging in his endless corrective tasks—the perpetual oscillation between the twin poles of innovation and recall—suggest an image of human beings as creatures living in time forced by circumstances both to creatively forget and creatively remember.[12] As active creatures responding to new pressures, new challenges, new exigencies, we constantly extend and redraw linguistic boundaries. As reflective personalities who need periodically to establish some distance on what we do (if only for the sake of being able to do it better, with greater fidelity to our original set of purposes), we are puzzled by our own linguistic and conceptual entanglements and feel the need to be called back to the original sense of things.

There is a common pathos surrounding linguistic use and linguistic therapy that grows out of the time-bound nature of human existence. Living in time means that we are doomed to be creatures with an inexact, conceptually overflowing, metaphoric language. We are forced to connect and contrast—indeed, even to locate and identify—activities and experiences with what has gone before and what is likely to come after. There is no ongoing stability, and no permanent human identity, yielded by any one linguistic product connected with any particular activity or experience. Human use of language points beyond itself to a more enduring stability, which language itself constantly undermines. Wittgenstein's preoccupation with questions of language in the *Philosophical Investigations* is perhaps the consummate elaboration in Western philosophy of Locke's designation of man as a "middling creature." Wittgenstein explores more systematically than any Western philosopher before him the metaphysics of the middle. We are fundamentally, crucially in the middle because the very use of language suggests a certain prospect concerning stability and permanence that the use of language also defeats at every turn. The dualism implicit in Wittgenstein's activity of philosophizing in the *Philosophical Investigations* is of human beings poised in two contradictory directions—structure, boundary, stability; collapse of structure, erasing of boundaries, instability—both paradoxically staked out by language. Human beings are creatures in search of a more ultimate reality—whose reality turns out to be language and the limitless, contradictory uses it generates and makes possible.

Applying Wittgenstein's philosophy of language and his concept of action to the study of political-theoretical texts undermines one of the fundamental presuppositions of a historicist position—that a historical actor enjoys a privileged relationship to his or her own actions that it is the job of the historian to re-create. By impugning this privileged relationship, I am by implication attempting to revitalize the concept of tradition as a master category for understanding the literature of political theory.[13] I believe that it is possible to argue that the literature of political theory forms several dominant traditions, constituting relatively self-contained wholes that can be fruitfully studied in at least partial isolation from external context. Regarding the classic texts of Western political thought as constituting a series of traditions and exploring their internal relationships seems capable of yielding unsuspected continuities and discontinuities. The standard division, for example, that more historically inclined commentators have drawn between ancients and moderns (with Plato being the originator of political philosophy in the ancient world and Machiavelli and Hobbes inaugurating the modern period in political thought) might, from a nonhistoricist angle of vision, turn out to be drawn in the wrong places and for the wrong reasons.

In the remaining two sections of this chapter, I shall apply the methodological perspective that I have been defending based upon postmodernist tenets and presuppositions to a classic relationship in the history of Western political thought—that of Hobbes to Plato, and, more specifically, that of Hobbes's text, *Leviathan,* to Plato's text, *The Republic.* In the first of these sections, I explore a psychological basis for regarding Plato and Hobbes as constituting a tradition; in the second, I adduce a linguistic basis for regarding Plato and Hobbes as forming a tradition.

• *Applications (I)*

When confronting a philosophical text like *Leviathan*, one should consider the possibility that there are an independent set of motivations and resources that are annexed to the act of theory construction itself. A mind that sets itself the task of constructing a theory is beset by certain problems, some of which at least have risen to the level of consciousness. What motivates the creation of the theory is an attempt to resolve those problems in a way that will restore satisfaction and repose. "Theory" therefore represents a shorthand term for a series of actions on the part of a theorist as he attempts to deflect and rechannel the sources of tension and conflict within himself into new configurations of meaning and possibility. One can only begin to approximate to the strategic results for a writer in employing "theory" as his mode of literary expression by first exploring the interconnections of the theory—by not stepping outside it, as it were, to gain an external, even biographical, perspective upon it, but by moving more fully within it, attempting to grasp the numerous ways in which it coheres as a unit. In what follows, I hope to provide an analysis of the theory of human nature in *Leviathan* that takes seriously its pretensions to be a philosophical work and to highlight the new possibilities of interconnection that open before us when we approach *Leviathan* from the perspective of theory construction as an activity.

One aspect that this perspective affords us on a theorist's work is the implicit stress it places on his awareness of his predecessors.[14] Such awareness is an essential element of the context of creation and of how the theorist relieves the anxieties pertaining to his relation to his forerunners. Hobbes's statements about his utter break with the ancients are well known[15] and have often been commented upon,[16] but the precise ways in which this self-professed iconoclasm gets expressed in his thought have not been that fully grasped.

One of the anxieties plaguing anyone embarking upon the enterprise of theory construction is the simple awareness that others have been there before him. If the writing of theory generally aims at exploring and evincing the interconnections between human phenomena that on their surface appear to be unrelated (and to exhibit fresh possibilities for thought and action that had not been suspected before),[17] then the mere existence of others in the past who have undertaken the same enterprise—the sheer weight of a tradition of theory and theorizing—must constitute an embarrassment to the current practitioner. The fact that others have existed undermines the credibility of my right to exist. Since they obviously attempted what I am about to do and have failed (the proof of their failure being my trying to do it again), how can I justify to myself embarking upon the same activity?

Hobbes would appear to have a ready answer. He does not seem overawed by the achievements of his predecessors but, if anything, convinced of their inadequacy. He seems to be motivated by an extraordinary competitiveness to outdo his forerunners on their chosen ground of elucidating the nature of human nature and describing the lineaments of the ideal society. What inspires Hobbes with this sense of being able to succeed where he conceives the ancients to have failed is the example of modern science, which has conferred upon human beings unrivaled mastery in the physical world and whose presuppositions and techniques have not yet been applied to politics. It is precisely the transfer of certain key presuppositions and techniques, such as a stress on method, from the study of nature to the analysis of human society that Hobbes regards as his major achievement.

Yet, granting this, it seems to be that even in staunch rejection Hobbes is still grappling with Plato, with what Harold Bloom has called the anxiety of influence. Not only where one acknowledges the relevance, or paradigmatic value, of a predecessor's achievement but (perhaps, especially) when one denies this value to an illustrious precursor can one be said to be working out his anxiety of influence. The act of rejection paradoxically presupposes the continued existence of what is rejected (otherwise there is nothing to reject), unless one is somehow able to overtake the rejected theory from the inside, rewriting it from one's totally altered vantage point.[18] One possible way of reading *Leviathan* is as an elaborate strategy, or series of strategies, designed for coping with the anxiety of influence—of reappropriating Plato's theory from the inside, as it were, and rearticulating a general theory of man and society from Hobbes's vastly altered premises and assumptions. The tenets of Plato's theory that might have appeared most promising to Hobbes for effecting a reinterpretation that would accommodate the principles of modern science are Plato's descriptions of the genesis, and emotional and imaginative capabilities, of the various character types constituting his Republic. Adapting resolutocomposite method and geometric method to the human sciences[19] enabled Hobbes to envisage the transfer to a whole society of possibilities of selfhood that Plato had restricted to a small minority of his population.

It is commonly recognized that one of the most striking expressions in *Leviathan* of the identity of Hobbesian man is contained in the first two paragraphs of chapter 11, where Hobbes speaks about man possessing no *finis ultimus* or *summum bonum:*

> The felicity of this life consisteth not in the repose of a mind satisfied. For there is no such *finis ultimus*, utmost aim, nor *summum bonum*, greatest good, as is spoken of in the books of the old moral philosophers. Nor can a man any more live whose desires are at an end, than he whose senses and imaginations are at a stand. Felicity is a continual progress of the desire, from one object to another; the attaining of the former being still but the way to the latter. The cause whereof is, that the object of man's desire, is not to enjoy once only, and for one instant of time; but to assure forever the way of his future desire. . . .
>
> So that in the first place, I put for a general inclination of all mankind, a perpetual and restless desire of power after power that ceaseth only in death. And the cause of this, is not always that a man hopes for a more intensive delight, than he has already attained to; that he cannot be content with a moderate power; but because he cannot assure the power and means to live well, which he hath present, without the acquisition of more.[20]

I believe that Hobbes's psychological portrait of the average man suggested in these paragraphs contains an implicit extension of certain possibilities of selfhood that Plato restricted to the most exalted and the most abject in his Republic—to philosopher-kings and tyrants. What Plato saw as a possibility of selfhood restricted to a minority among his population, Hobbes recognized as a universal possibility, accessible to the mass of mankind. Even if one identifies the bourgeoisie as the authentic subject of Hobbes's analysis,[21] the bourgeoisie does not represent a closed class in the way that Plato's rational elite does. In fact, what characterizes the early capitalist bourgeois class is precisely its self-definition as an open class opposed to entrenched privilege. This self-image must include widespread upward mobility and large-scale intellectual and technological expansion before the social and economic realities can reflect even that limited degree of "openness" of which C. B. Macpherson speaks. It is the very broadening of the ideological horizons of the nascent middle class that I propose to define in a new way by juxtaposing Hobbes's thought with Plato's.

Before embarking on a detailed description of the points where

Hobbes expands upon and revises Plato's description of human nature, I highlight briefly the structural similarities between Plato's and Hobbes's theories of human nature, in order to bring the differences between the two theories into bolder relief when I introduce them into the discussion later. A central question that one might ask concerning Hobbes's political theory appears to me equally relevant with regard to the political thought of Plato. What must man be like in order for politics to be both a necessary and possible remedy for the human condition? Initially, and in the most general terms, Plato and Hobbes answer this question in the same way. Man must be a bifurcated creature who can yet be held together through some rational organizing principle. In Plato, a hierarchical ordering is established in man according to a vision laid down by the philosopher-king, who is privy to ideal images of the good and the just. This vision requires the subordination of the passionate and spirited elements within individual men (and within human society generally) to more purely rational elements reflecting the eternal order of things. Hobbes agrees with Plato to the extent of saying that a political principle of subordination of certain aspects of self for the sake of giving expression to other aspects of self is necessary in order for man to attain to his full potential as a human being. In Hobbes, the rational organizing principle can be alternatively labeled as one of instrumental rationality or as one of utility.[22] The embodiment of this principle in the lives of ordinary human beings ensures that the passions, in a provisional, temporary sense, will remain subordinate to the dictates of a calculating reason.

In order for their theories of human nature to be persuasive, Plato and Hobbes must show that without implanting a principle of structuring in the very constitution of man he would be at war with himself, capable of only limited and ultimately self-defeating action. Plato identifies a political principle of superordination and subordination in his diagnosis of the just soul. Without this principle, man's internal nature would be a chaos, constantly at war with itself: His baser impulses would overpower his better inclinations. In Hobbes, we have the image of a state of nature, where the life of man is depicted as "solitary, poor, nasty, brutish and short"[23] prior to the achievement of that renovation of self dictated by the principle of instrumental rationality. At this point, however, the comparison between Plato and Hobbes, even on this formal level, breaks down. For Plato, the principle of ordering necessary to constitute the most rational man cannot be fashioned from the unpromising human material that itself gives rise to the problem of the best ordering of man and society. The perspective of the philosopher-king, who is attuned to the ideal forms of the good and the just, is necessary for resolving potential conflicts within the individual, just as his ultimate vantage point is necessary for obviating the potential seeds of discord in the commonwealth. Ordinary citizens need only be inculcated with such medicinal myths as those of the metals in order for those solutions, on both the intrapersonal and interpersonal levels, to be accepted.

The only members of Plato's Republic capable of transformative social action are philosopher-kings and tyrants. For Hobbes, with his universalist moral psychology and his theoretical construct of a state of nature, it is presumably a whole population, or significant segments of it, who are capable of rationalizing for themselves the need for what Hobbes regards as the most creative political act of all—that which institutes and maintains sovereign political authority. What Plato saw as a source of creative anxiety affecting the behavior of an elite of philosopher-kings (namely, the prospect of death), Hobbes generalizes into a universal fear, governing the life-style of a multitude of men. Instead of the aristocratic Platonic notion of death, which leads a restricted class of men to engage in philosophy as a preparation for dying, we find in Hobbes the extension of this anxiety to the mass of mankind, leading them to institute political authority and to structure their lives in such ways as to stave off the possibility of death (and reminders of death) for as long as possible. Hobbes's sense of competitiveness with his predecessors, chiefly Plato, and his inspiration, drawn from the achievements of modern science, converge in his resolving human nature into a fundamental anxiety, the fear of death, as the chief civilizing agency in man. The concept of violent death in Hobbes's thought—its role in his depiction of the state of nature—merely constitutes a heightened, metaphoric expression of the role of death generally in the economy of human motivation.[24] Death, any form of death, including especially natural death, is experienced by Hobbesian men as violent, as a senseless disruption of the pleasures and projects that define human existence for them.

For Hobbes, the basic division in man appears to be between his vanity and his fear of death.[25] Vanity impels man to endeavor to outdistance his fellows and to get them to accept the valuation he places upon himself. Hobbes describes the state of nature as a condition in which the mere presence of other people constitutes a threat to our self-esteem.

> For everyman looketh that his companion should value him at the same rate he sets upon himself; and upon all signs of contempt, or undervaluing, naturally endeavors, as far as he dares, (which amongst them that have no common power to keep them in quiet, is far enough to make them destroy each other), to extort a greater value from his contemners, by damage; and from others by the example.[26]

Counterbalancing man's overweening vanity is his fear of death, which restrains his vanity and leads him to search for ways to make his life less precarious. What is unique to Hobbes—and in sharp contrast to Plato's description of the masses of men—is that he depicts one of the sources of the prime tension in man, his fear of death, as being sufficiently regenerative in character to allow man to reconstitute himself along more rational lines. Hobbes seems to have discovered the dynamic inherent in the idea of one's own dying. He confronts the implications of death as a fully human event, not as a punishment from God, and not as an accidental change in a permanent, ongoing life cycle. Hobbes, I believe, was the first philosopher to become aware of the liberating force of the insight that man owned his own death, as it were, that it was fully as much an event in his life as all the myriad things that occurred in the course of living it. What the perspectives of the Ideal and of God (both extramundane) achieve in Greek and Christian thought, the totally human perspective of death, of mortality, accomplishes in the economy of Hobbes's thought. Death, which is now viewed as a totally human event, replaces as the fundamental organizing principle for one's life the extraterrestrial perspectives emphasized in Greek and Christian thought.[27] The idea of one's own death is functionally equivalent in the economy of Hobbes's thought to the Ideas of the Good and Justice, and of God, in Greek and Christian thought.

I have said that for the majority of men Plato recognizes no sources of energy in the soul that would allow them to transcend their moral corruption of their own volition. The source of redemption, generally speaking, is external to man. There are, however, two main exceptions to this picture of human psychological makeup—

members of the guardian class and tyrants. In order to appreciate that in some sense Plato and Hobbes are really after the same "quarry," that the ends which theory construction are intended to serve are similar for both men—that is, enlargement of the human sense of possibilities by reestablishing for thought its claims to mastery over an internal (psychological) and external (social and political) environment—it will be instructive, I think, to compare Plato's description of the restricted sense of possibilities available to all his character types, except philosopher-kings and tyrants, with Hobbes's description of the psychological makeup and set of motivations governing human nature generally. Plato's insight into the special psychological forces motivating philosopher-kings and tyrants is very instructive of the kind of psychology motivating Hobbesian men generally, who are capable of the kind of self-transcendence that in Plato's thought is reserved for only a tiny minority of the population.

For all the members of Plato's commonwealth, except philosopher-kings and tyrants, limits are set on personal growth and creativity by the sorts of transactions that take place with one's father. In books 8 and 9 of *The Republic*, where Plato speaks about the decline of society and of the soul, he traces the disintegration of the character type of the virtuous man into progressively more corrupt types, corresponding to the various phases of the disintegration of the ideal state. The decline from virtue is depicted in a series of striking psychological vignettes of the tensions surrounding the relationships between fathers and sons, which lead the sons to move away from the models of behavior provided by the fathers. The first phase of the moral deterioration of the virtuous man is marked by the emergence of timocratic man, whose psychogenetic history Plato recounts as follows:

> "He [timocratic man] arises," I said, "in some such way as this. He is the son of a good father, who, as sometimes happens lives in an ill-governed city, and avoids political honours and office and litigation and all those things in which the active politician delights, and who is content to be got the better of if only he is not bothered."
>
> "Then how does the son become what he is?" he said.
>
> "Firstly," I said, "he hears his mother complaining that her husband is not one of the rulers, and that in consequence other women are set above her. Then she sees that her husband does

not trouble himself much about money, and does not fight or wrangle in lawsuits or in the assembly, but takes all these matters very calmly, and she perceives that he is always attending to himself, treating her neither with marked reverence nor marked disrespect. All these things make her angry, and she tells her son that his father is unmanly and utterly casual, and treats him to all the many varied complaints which women love to make on such matters."[28]

Timocratic man's personality emerges as a compromise between his father, "who waters and makes grow the reasoning element in his soul," and the criticisms leveled against the father by his mother and the family's servants, who "nourish the desiring and spirited elements" in him. "In the end," Plato says, "inasmuch as he is not naturally a bad man, but has known bad company, he arrives under the impulsion of these two forces at a middle position, and gives over the rule within him to the middle element, the contentious and spirited, and becomes a lofty-minded and ambitious man."[29]

Oligarchic man emerges from the seeds of the ruin of his timocratic father. After his parent, who has esteemed honor, has fallen from high office, an ambivalent relationship develops between father and son. On the one hand, the son feels emotionally impelled to retain the father as a model. On the other hand, he suffers by extension from the public disgrace of his parent. Again, the son resorts to compromise. He accepts the father's end in life of leaving his mark on the world, but transforms and enlarges upon the means of getting there. He puts the stress on riches, instead of honor, undermining the authority of the spirited elements in his soul and establishing the passions in a position of authority. Plato's almost self-consciously political vocabulary at this point anticipates the image of the proper relationship between reason and the passions advanced by Hobbes, and subsequently endorsed by the whole British empiricist tradition.

> But the reasoning and the spirited elements, I imagine, he makes squat upon the ground beneath it, one here and the other there, and enslaves them. So that the first is allowed to reason of and consider nothing but how money may breed more money, while the second may admire or honour nothing but wealth and the wealthy, and be zealous for nothing but the acquisition of money and anything that may lead thereto.[30]

Democratic man again emerges out of the crucible of his relationship with his oligarchic father. The latter's overly permissive attitude toward him leads democratic man to renounce his father's disciplined and discriminating pursuit of pleasure as a model and to convert the search after pleasure itself into a principle of necessity, granting all pleasures an equal value and establishing no hierarchy between them.[31]

The description of the father-son relationships so far reveals how acutely aware Plato was of the ironic fate of most personal rebellions—of how, even in opposition, the supremacy of the father is, in a sense, reaffirmed. Even when we move to a position directly contrary to that of our fathers, the outer limits of our rebellion, the point of greatest emotional satisfaction, at which we choose to rest, is determined by the starting point that, in effect, they bequeathed to us. The only categories of citizen in the Platonic Republic who are able to escape this dialectical stranglehold are philosopher-kings and tyrants, whose access to their sources of energy is so immediate and intense that they are able to envisage possibilities that are unrelated to the transactional tensions accompanying the paternal relation. Plato discusses the father-son relationship in the context of his psychogenetic account of the rise of the tyrant, hardly mentioning the father at all in his very elaborate discussion of the education of philosopher-kings. If we examine what Plato has to say about the origins of the extraordinarily destructive energies in the tyrant, perhaps we will be able to infer from it something about the roots of the comparably creative sources of energy in the philosopher-king.

Plato prefaces his psychogenetic account of the tyrant's rise with a distinction among unnecessary desires that are lawful and those that are not. The unlawful desires Plato describes as follows:

> Those that are active during sleep. When the rest of the soul, the reasoning, gentle and ruling part of it, is asleep, then the bestial and savage part, when it has had its fill of food and wine, begins to leap about, pushes sleep aside, and tries to go and gratify its instincts. You know how in such a state it will dare everything, as though it were freed and released from all shame or discernment. It does not shrink from attempting incestual intercourse, in its dream, with a mother or with any man or god or beast. It is ready for any deed of blood, and there is no unhallowed food it will not eat. In a word, it falls short of no extreme of folly or shamelessness.[32]

Apparently, at some point in the crumbling positions of moral authority that various types of corrupt fathers are able to assume toward their sons, a qualitative leap (or, more accurately speaking, descent) occurs, so that the father as a source of dialectical tension, controlling even in opposition the distance his son might travel from him, is destroyed. The tyrant, in Plato's piercing phrase, "is a parricide."[33] He summarizes the state of being typical of the tyrant in a formula that grows out of his previous description of the unlawful desires. "He [the tyrant] is surely the man who expresses in waking reality the character we attributed to a man in his dreams."[34] More elaborately, Plato says that

> when Love established his tyranny over him, he [the tyrant] became for always, and in waking reality, the man he used occasionally to be in his dreams. And now he will stick at no frightful murder, no unhallowed food or dreadful deed, but Love swells tyrannically within him in all lawlessness and anarchy. He is sole ruler, and will lead the man in whom he dwells as in a city, into any kind of daring, by which he will support himself and his rabble following, the immigrants whom the man's evil companions have introduced, and the native born whom evil ways of life have released and set free.[35]

The tyrant is able to tap sources of energy lodged in his unconscious that remain forever sealed to those character types formed along the lines of tension and resolution occasioned by their relationships to their families, particularly to their fathers. Traditional patterns of relationship within the family work to inhibit awareness of possibilities of self that are unrelated to the structure of tensions and the system of ego maintenance nurtured within the family. Where the family functions as a viable social unit, whole areas of being remain impenetrable to us. Even our dreams, in the imaginatively impoverished context of the family, refuse to act as gateways and icons of whatever sources of energy might lie hidden in the recesses of our unconscious. It is only when the dialectical stranglehold of the family in general, and the father in particular, is broken that previously unthinkable possibilities begin to dawn upon us. In the case of the tyrant, these possibilities all flow from an extended and deepened imagining of evil. For the philosopher-king, however, a newly appropriated access to internal sources of energy signifies an enhanced capacity to conceive and bring about possibilities for good. I shall indicate briefly how Plato's account of the psychogenetic development of the philosopher-king implicitly follows the scenario laid down in his discussion of the psychological origins of the tyrant.

One of the most striking aspects of the educational scheme that Plato outlines in *The Republic* is its taking place entirely outside of the confines of the family. It seems to me that, bearing in mind Plato's description of the psychogenetic development of the dominant character types corresponding to the various forms of the state, and especially that of the tyrant, we become aware of an essential component of his motivation in placing the raising of children—and of potential philosopher-kings—outside the context of the family. Plato is seeking a functional equivalent to some of the key conditions that made possible the tyrant's access to apparently unlimited internal sources of energy. The son is raised outside the home in Plato's *Republic* not merely, or even primarily, to remove the physical presence of the father, but to obliterate the father as a source of dialectical tension, to allow the son to form possible images of selfhood that are unrelated to his transactional tensions with his parent.

With regard to the content of the philosopher-king's education, one might say that his training in the abstract categories of thought (mathematics, astronomy, and logic) is supposed to wean him away from those styles of thinking that are rooted in an immediate human, material context. The exercises in intellectual self-transcendence that he undergoes are intended ultimately to achieve an overhauling of his whole being, to release sources of energy within his soul that are not moored to any one human, social context. Human social reality reflects what from the perspective of actively pursued, interconnected thought must appear as an arbitrary, refractory quality, which prevents it from assuming those forms that a freely inquiring, roaming reason would dictate. The ultimate aim, perhaps, of the Platonic system of education is to get the philosophical initiate to substitute for a worldly context in his deliberations the context of thought itself—with its implied aspirations toward mastery and completeness. In this way, Plato as theorist strives to create artificially for his future philosopher-king those conditions of access to internal sources of energy that the tyrant achieves effortlessly through the sheer force and perversity of his reigning demon.

In Hobbes, we find a democratization of the Platonic vision. The kind of self-transcendence that Plato attributes to philosopher-kings is ascribed by Hobbes to the class of people who are parties to the original contract—the whole community of citizens.[36] In order to grasp the full metaphysical implications of Hobbes's political atomism—that the parties to the contract are generally conceived as isolated, fatherless individuals—one should read it in the context of Plato's description of the psychological motivations governing each of his major character types. When the context is amplified in this way, we can more fully gauge the revolutionary breakthrough of Hobbes's thought. Not only are the parties to the contract without an official collective past of previous national affiliations, they are also without a significant individual past of family associations. The kinds of projects that large elements of society can now envisage for themselves, and the strategies that they can employ for their attainment, are much more flexible and imaginative than anything conceivable under the Platonic ordering of man and society.

Hobbes's thought records one of the momentous changes in the consciousness of Western man. For Hobbes, previous conceptions had viewed man as entirely too limited a creature, capable of only severely restricted transformations of himself and society. The realm of perfection—where some sort of reality would match man's most grandiose conceptions—was projected either upward into an ideal realm, a vision of which could be attained by a small number of extraordinary individuals in this world, or pushed forward to the end of time and pictured as a reward awaiting the saints. The effect of both these concepts of perfection was to direct man's imaginative energy toward an unknown world, whose existence was accepted by the masses of men purely on faith. What Hobbes sought to do was to redirect this flow of imaginative energy toward the known world, to get the majority of people to see their familiar world as a tissue of possibilities, capable of almost infinite reconstruction.

The implicit argument of *Leviathan* is that the beatific and ideal visions of Christian and Greek thought constitute alienated human possibilities, which a properly grounded moral philosophy must recapture for man. At the beginning of chapter 12 of *Leviathan*, Hobbes diagnoses the origin (what he calls the seed) of religion as being one that is present "only in man, and consisteth in some peculiar quality, or at least in some eminent degree thereof, not to be found in any other living creatures."[37] The seeds of religion, on Hobbes's reading of human nature, turn out to be four: "opinion of ghosts, ignorance of second causes, devotion towards what men fear and taking of things casual for prognostics."[38] Hobbes proceeds to account for the diversity of religious customs and ceremonies by the variegated ways human beings have developed for projecting their fears, ignorance, and superstitions outward upon the world: "which by reason of the different fancies, judgments and passions of several men, [religion] hath given up into ceremonies so different, that those which are used by one man, are for the most part ridiculous to another."[39]

As a counterpart to the understanding of the notion of God as a projection of alienated human possibilities that pervades the second half of *Leviathan*, we are presented in the first half with an implicit rejection of the classic previous understandings of man. These visions converted man into an alienated creature, projecting his own latent possibilities into ideal realms to which he imputed superiority or mastery over human affairs. The movements of thought in the first and second halves of *Leviathan* converge in a demystification of the abstractions of man and God, in an effort to secure a new release of energies for accomplishing specifically human tasks.

We are now in a position to see how the content of Hobbes's theory of human nature, in the general way that I have described it, relates to a specific set of tensions originating in the context of creation. A writer embarking upon the enterprise of theory construction tends to view the mere existence of predecessors motivated by the same quest as an embarrassment and a burden, inhibiting his own ability to create. In order to be able to write at all, let alone attempt to rival the epic pretensions of his predecessors, he must work through the set of anxieties tied to an awareness of previous practitioners of the same craft. Traces of the sort of inner wrestling that I have been describing can be found in the substance of the theory Hobbes has produced. The relationship between the behavior governing the parties to the social contract in Hobbes to the pattern of motivations that Plato attributes to his various classes recapitulates Hobbes's own relationship to Plato. Hobbes, too, in a way is fully usurping the role of the father, relating to the father (Plato) not as a dialectical counterplayer but as someone whose role he has completely absorbed, rewriting Plato's theory for him from his (Hobbes's) own immeasurably altered perspective. Writing under the spell of the first early breakthroughs of modern science, Hobbes discovers a new form of power inherent in scientific method that earlier theorists had left untapped. He sees his vocation as theorist as that of extending the conquests of method—resoluto-composite method and geometric method—to include the human psychological, social, and political realms.

• *Applications (II)*

In order to appreciate the sense in which the extension of a particular metaphor governs the enterprise of political theory from Plato until Rousseau, it is important to bring a particular perspective to bear on the whole body of literature that has traditionally been grouped under the title of "political theory." The political theorist has been driven to create not only a vertically leveled world, without predecessors, in which the anxiety of influence has been overcome, but one that has been horizontally leveled as well, where no voice but that of the theorist himself needs to be listened to. In a dual temporal dimension, the past in terms of influence and the present in terms of competing theorizers, the writing of theory suggests the triumph of the one over the many. Theory construction on an epic scale involves a gigantic act of razing to make the world habitable for the one. The ceaseless pursuit of interconnections is just the other side of the coin of ironing out all contingency, of ferreting out incoherence, by the metaphysical removal of all embodiments of sheer brute otherness, namely, other people. The theorist, in terms of the pretensions of his theory, must strive to eliminate other people, because they serve as the ultimate reminders of the triumph of contingency and are the principle bearers and overcomers of incoherence in human life.

The genesis of the idea of authority seems to me linked with this ambition of the theoretical mind to create a world habitable for itself. At its most fundamental level, the idea of authority simply represents the imperious movement of the theoretical mind seeking to aggrandize all of human reality. The state of total subjectivity, total assimilability, in which human reality appears to a theoretical mind at the moment when its quest seems most fully realized serves as the model for the ideal relationship between sovereign and subject in the more purely political realm.

There is an additional logical factor at work here as well. In order for thought to serve as a metaphor for social reality, one must presuppose the existence of a pretheoretical sovereign self, which does the surveying of the internal (mental) scene and reestablishes order and coherence after periodic breakdown. Without the tacit postulation of such a self as subject confronting the manifold contents of consciousness as its object, an infinite regress would emerge in the task of the crystallization of coherence, since the sorting, judging mechanism establishing the pattern of coherence would itself be called constantly into question. The reigning metaphor constitutive of the activity of political theorizing thus presupposes the existence of a pretheoretical sovereign self that orders the realm of thought, before that in turn serves as a model for organizing social existence.

What I have said so far suggests that the metaphoric extension animating the vocation of political theorizing proceeds in only one direction, from thought to social reality. However, a profounder, more interactionist view of the nature of metaphor should alert us to the possibility that movement is proceeding from two opposing directions simultaneously—from social reality to thought as well as from thought to social reality. According to I. A. Richards, "When we use a metaphor we have two thoughts of different things active together and supported by a single word, or phrase, whose meaning is a resultant of their interaction."[40] In political theorizing as well, the inspiration for the activity does not only come from a unilateral extension of the pursuit of interconnections from the realm of thought to the plane of social reality, but consists in a bilateral movement, where the pursuit of interconnections is also organized along lines suggested by the structure of social reality. The elements going to compose social existence, such as people, territory, conflict, and the like, bear no logical relationship to each other. They constitute a merely fortuitous concatenation of circumstances whose principle of ordering cannot be elicited from any of the elements taken separately or in combination with each other but clearly reflects a direct intervention by man, a relatively arbitrary imposition of will. The pursuit of interconnections in the domain of thought is seen in the image of the ordering principle emerging from an examination of social reality, which is to say that there is a nominalistic bias attached to the idea of theorizing from its inception. According to the interactionist view that I am advancing, political theorizing can most fruitfully be seen as a fusion of the extension to the study of political phenomena of the theoretical impulse to pursue interconnections, and of an extension to an understanding of the theoretical impulse of the political categories of arbitrariness and the sheer imposition of order.

The conception of the activity of political theorizing that I am putting forward here enables us to achieve a more satisfactory interpretation of *The Republic* than is generally available. Most readers of the dialogue would probably agree that Socrates' central antagonist in *The Republic* is the Sophist Thrasymachus. On the surface, no two theories of justice would seem more diametrically opposed than Thrasymachus's conception that justice in any society reflects the interest of the stronger and Socrates' view that justice is to be identified with a particular structuring of society where a rational elite rules over the other members. Yet, when Socrates' theory of justice is placed in the context of the remainder of his argument in *The Republic*, a surprisingly rich and elaborate universe of shared assumptions is revealed between him and Thrasymachus, one that renders Socrates' own positive conception of justice extremely puzzling.

Thrasymachus's definition of "just" or "right" as meaning nothing but "what is to the interest of the stronger"[41] is extremely ambiguous. At first blush, he appears intent on collapsing the level of inquiry from philosophical definition to sociological analysis. Instead of addressing himself to the second-order question of the meaning of the concept of justice as the previous participants in the dialogue (Cephalus, Polemarchus, and Socrates himself) had done, Thrasymachus engages in a first-order sociological investigation of the significance that the term carries in existing societies. He moves from the plane of reasoning about language and concepts to making generalizations about the world, and thus appears guilty of collapsing the second-order nature of the inquiry to a first-order level. How would it be possible to interpret Thrasymachus's statements in such a way that he does not commit this "category mistake?"

One plausible way of accomplishing this is to regard Thrasymachus as making, on the basis of his sociological investigations, a proposal for conceptual revision. He appears to be drawing a distinction between the emotive and the descriptive content of justice.[42] Thrasymachus seems, further, to be suggesting that whereas the descriptive content fluctuates widely, depending on the ascendancy of particular classes within individual societies, the emotive content, which both expresses and attempts to evoke approval for the descriptive content, remains stable. The emotive content always conveys a favorable attitude toward the particular social arrangements described. According to Thrasymachus, therefore, objectively speaking, all so-called instances of justice can be redescribed in terms of the configuration of power within particular communities. He appears to be recommending a banishment of justice from our ontology, for, aside from a stable emotive element that has no external referent whatsoever, all our "justice statements" can be translated without remainder into statements about power.

Taking Thrasymachus to be advocating a skeptical, relativistic metaphysics, it is staggering to contemplate the extent to which his metaphysics dominates the argument in *The Republic* rather than the one that would serve as a natural complement to Socrates' own doctrine of justice. Socrates understands justice as requiring a rigidly hierarchical society where a rational elite rules over the remainder of the population. This stance suggests that there is an objective content to the good and the just that can be perceived by a properly trained intelligence. Yet, when Socrates comes to elaborate and defend his own theory of justice, very little seems to depend on an antiskeptical, objectivist metaphysics, which one would expect to emerge as the contrasting doctrine to Thrasymachus's presentation of his views. Thrasymachus in defeat seems more triumphant than Socrates in victory, for his metaphysics appears to haunt Socrates' presentation of his own argument in numerous ways. Five examples follow.

1. There is an incongruity in *The Republic* between Plato's emphasis on natural-law absolutes—that it is possible to know what the good for human beings is, and to deduce from this the requirements of justice—and his stress on education as total socialization, which seems to suggest that the very concept of humanity (of who human beings are, and what their authentic capacities are) is historically and sociologically determined.

2. Plato's Theory of Ideas, which relegates the facts of the material world to an inferior ontological status, regarding them as mere copies of eternal Forms, can be construed as a metaphoric and picturesque way of stating that so-called facts are theory dependent, that the world of theory is underdetermined by the universe of fact. This is a skeptical view that comports very well with Thrasymachus's concept of justice.

3. Throughout *The Republic*, Plato works with a conception of politics as an omnipresent human phenomenon, one that is not restricted to what takes place in the public sphere. An analogy between the just soul and the just commonwealth dominates *The Republic*. According to Plato, politics does not arise in a determinate historical and social context as a response to a preexisting situation of conflict between men. Instead, it emerges whenever human beings attain to that degree of self-consciousness that allows them to perceive that acting in recognizably human ways nearly always involves the subordination of certain aspects of self to others. Since the very activity

of structuring, divorced from historical or social setting, is regarded as a manifestation of the political, of the exertion of power, politics emerges as a kind of primary datum in human experience. As such, it must be seen from a theoretical perspective that locates its importance and role in some all-embracing vision of human beings and the world. This view is supplied by Plato's theory of justice, which, as a vision of truth, becomes coercive in its own right, without the interposition of a separate theory of political obligation showing why it is in the individual citizen's self-interest to obey the state.

Plato's very broad conception of the political seems to be related to his theory of knowledge generally outlined under (2) above. Plato's stress on the priority of thought over fact predisposes him to become aware of the sheer element of arbitrariness, the factor of personal decision making, involved in the very structure of human personality. This leads him to extend the terms of the political vocabulary—including, especially, its cardinal term, justice—to the private realm as well.

4. By labeling the highest form of knowledge the Good rather than the True—with the True being derived from the Good—Plato perhaps means to suggest the subordination of epistemology to ethics. There is an irreducible contingency in our categories of knowledge that can only be removed by placing them in the perspective afforded by our ethical categories, which decree that the particular ordering of truth and reality made possible and validated by our epistemological categories is good.

5. The Myth of Er, concerning the immortality of the soul, with which Plato concludes *The Republic* depicts human beings as creatures of nearly total self-determination. "But in none of these lives," says Plato, "was there anything to determine the condition of the soul, because the soul must needs change its character accordingly as it chooses one life or another." [43]

Considering the pervasiveness of Thrasymachean metaphysical assumptions and postulates throughout Socrates' presentation of his own argument, how can Socrates' positive theory of justice diverge so sharply from that of Thrasymachus? Considering the evidence I have marshaled, a critical question for interpreting *The Republic* emerges: How does Socrates manage to pull a Socratic rabbit out of a Thrasymachean hat?

Beginning with a roughly similar metaphysics to that of Socrates, Thrasymachus posits a radical disjunction between mind and society, which leads to an extreme relativism and potentially to toleration of diverse political creeds. Socrates, starting with similar skeptical assumptions, extends the architectonic impulse from mind to society. Thought's self-discovered principle of mastery—the discerning of patterns of coherence among the phenomena that confront it—gets extended outward in Plato as the determinative principle of social and political organization. The touchstone here becomes the removal of tension and conflict through the enforcement of patterns of interdependence among the various elements composing Platonic society. On the surface, what do artisans, warriors, and intellectuals have in common? Their coexistence within the same territorial unit seems only to portend tension and conflict within the state. The strategy employed by thought in resolving perplexities in its own domain becomes projected outward in assuring a harmonious life for human society generally.

Viewed from the perspective of theory construction as an activity (and its metaphoric ramifications) that I have been examining so far, an unsuspected continuity emerges between Plato and Hobbes. The vast differences in substantive political doctrine between the two thinkers have obscured the sense in which they entertain similar conceptions of the theoretical vocation. Hobbes, for all his opposition to Plato and to Greek philosophy generally, presupposes a crypto-Platonic conception of a sovereign self. *Leviathan* addresses an extraordinarily heterogeneous range of issues—from the nature of man to the nature of God, the nature of speech and language, the foundations of science and religion, the methodology of Biblical exegesis, justifications for punishment, the concept of law, and principles of dream interpretation, among others—and shows that a correct analysis of any of these topics systematically links up with a true understanding of all the rest. In precisely the same sense that *The Republic* does, *Leviathan* manifests a rigorous pursuit of interconnections. The analogy proceeds even beyond this point. In the political theories of Plato and Hobbes, all voices aside from the theorist's own concerning the ultimate questions of man and society have been stilled. The wrestling with internal perplexity that gives rise to the pursuit of interconnections and that presupposes the idea of authority, of a sovereign self, gets projected outward in both theorists to create a social and political environment safe for the one. On the surface, at least, dissent, opposition, and uncertainty have been as systematically programmed out of Hobbes's

Leviathan-state as they have apparently been from Plato's Republic.

Yet, for all its systematic aspirations and achievement, the argument of *Leviathan* remains strangely silent and incomplete. Plato, at least, refers to a capacity of reason, which he summarizes by the term "dialectic," that might account for the creative, synthesizing activity of mind exhibited in *The Republic*. In his moral psychology, however, Hobbes traces the origins of our ideas to sense experience and provides a generally incremental analysis of how our more abstract concepts and thought processes get built up from an original stock of sense data. His account of the self makes no allowances for the creative, synthesizing functions of mind manifested in *Leviathan* itself.

It seems to me that the economy of the argument of *Leviathan* taken as a whole offers a solution to the problem that I have outlined. Hobbes's idea of authority not only has an external reference, in terms of justifying his concept of political obligation, but it has an internal reference as well. It provides the missing metaphysical underpinning for his conduct of the activity of political theorizing.

Hobbes's radical nominalism, his belief that "truth consisteth in the right ordering of names in our affirmations,"[44] allows him to achieve a kind of "transcendental deduction" of the categories of authority and consent and of the proper relationship that should subsist between them. Since according to Hobbes there is, strictly speaking, no objective external world until we constitute it as such by the act of speech, by the process of naming, he is able to justify philosophically the role of the sovereign. Without the sovereign (who enjoys a monopoly of force and authority within the state) affirming even by his silence the usages current in the society of his time, no stable patterns of communication could exist between men. Also, since the creation of sovereign authority forms a precondition for our world as we know it, people's consent to its formation can be formally, rationally reconstructed.

In demystifying the idea of authority and rooting it in consent, Hobbes accomplishes a reversal in relation to Plato's thought. Instead of having the exercise of political authority depend upon an antecedent cultivation of reason, merging the vocations of philosopher and king, Hobbes shows that one cannot engage in a reasoning process at all without presupposing sovereign authority, which provides us with the stable counters to manipulate in reasoning. Instead of reason serving as the basis for the exercise of political authority as in Plato, Hobbes shows that reason itself is grounded upon an antecedently created authority. The idea of authority, which generates the metaphor that is constitutive of the activity of political theorizing, thus emerges into full self-consciousness only with Hobbes, whereas it is merely presupposed in Plato. Hobbes is able to say outright what Plato's whole theory presupposes but that specific propositions in Plato's thought deny, namely, that reason rests on authority.

As we have seen in Chapter 4, it is the normative status, and indeed even the very intelligibility, of the pretheoretical sovereign self that Rousseau questions in his political writings. He tries to show that the sovereign self, which Plato and Hobbes take so much for granted that they do not even discuss its psychological origins or its philosophical implications, already represents a decadent late flowering in the history of consciousness. Natural man in the earliest phases of his development manifests an almost totally autistic self-involvement or, alternatively, self-forgetfulness. These two states are virtually indistinguishable in Rousseau's description of the early stages of the state of nature. The sovereign self presupposed by Plato and Hobbes represents a futile effort at recovery of mastery, rather than a state so natural and definitive of man that a theorist can afford to leave it out of account in his anthropological investigations. After Rousseau, a major task of the theoretical imagination becomes the reconstitution and legitimation of the theoretical perspective itself, not just a renewed confrontation with its objects.

9 • Thoughts on Lyotard's Postmodernism

Jean-François Lyotard, who has publicly withdrawn from a commitment to Marxism (and in fact has written the essay "A Memorial of Marxism"),[1] might appropriately be regarded as a contemporary spokesman for a politically centrist position. His direct engagement of epistemological and metaphysical issues renders the inadequacy of his thought outside of a generalized-agnostic interpretive framework especially revealing.

Lyotard begins his discussion of justice in *Just Gaming*[2] with what Terry Eagleton has called "a straightforward espousal of intuitionism."[3] We must judge, Lyotard says, "without criteria. . . . It is decided, and that is all that can be said. . . . I mean that in each instance, I have a feeling, that is all. . . . But if I am asked by what criteria do I judge, I will have no answer to give."[4] Eagleton claims that Lyotard buttresses his position by reliance on "a curious amalgam of sophism and Kantianism."[5] The sophism has to do with the sheerly rhetorical import of the arguments that we make; the Kantianism refers to the notion, developed in relation to aesthetic judgement in the *Critique of Judgement*, that moral or political judging too can occur "without going through a conceptual system that could serve as a criterion for practice."[6]

My previously stated objections stemming from the requirement of consistency or reflexivity are applicable to Lyotard's formulations. Is he not advocating a kind of unbounded relativism, what we might call a "relativism of the moment," that remains vulnerable to the charge that it is not reflexively sustainable—that it is relativist about all things but its own relativism? Also, in order for his theory to wield explanatory force in the domains of moral and political decision making, does it not presuppose the continued simultaneous existence of the very position that it negates, namely, the one that holds that there are enduring transcendental norms for judgment, not merely ex post facto immanentist ones? Third, the *distinction* between immanentist and transcendental norms for judgment appears to exceed the content of both conceptual halves introduced by the distinction.

Lyotard holds up for our emulation in *Just Gaming* the narratives of the Cashinahua Indians, where judgment is always rendered "case by case."[7] In his very rejection of principled judgment, Lyotard confronts an acute dilemma. Does not such a rejection itself constitute a new principle—that one is to rely on intuitive delineations of and responses to circumstances rather than on a set of verbal formulations that are more abstract and general? Also, does not the rejection of principled judgments in ethical and political decision making presuppose their continued maintenance in order for his theory of intuitive judgment not to degenerate into a mere tautology? The explanatory force of Lyotard's theory is wielded by the contrast with (and therefore also the simultaneous existence of) what it rejects. Finally, the *distinction* between intuitive and principled judgment cannot be derived from either half of the content introduced by the distinction; it is therefore also in this additional sense not reflexively sustainable.

In *Peregrinations*, published three years after *Just Gaming*, Lyotard picks up the intimations of his own position and begins to gesture toward the generalized agnosticism that I am advocating in this book:

> Presumably there are no more criteria in politics than in esthetics. We have to "listen" here and there to the manifold contingency of data, be it chromatic or anthropological. It is not a matter of how numerous, small, or unstable the clouds of colors or motivations are, nor how overwhelmed thinking is amidst thoughts. No, the point is that a painter does not have as his goal to know the essential definition of colors, either per se or as they are compounded in the landscape in which he is going to be emerged. Nor does the politician try to have as complete knowledge as possible, the knowledge a scientist could have, of the situation in which he is implicated. The knowledge he needs is nothing but a part, a moment in a process of action. The stakes of politics are definitely not to know something but to change something, and the stakes of art are to make something that has been given to one's sensi-

bility and is transferred to others. I am merely arguing that both art and politics are excepted, although in different ways, from the hegemony of the genre of discourse called cognitive.[8]

Lyotard's formulation as it stands confronts an acute dilemma of reflexivity. Is not disowning the hegemony of "cognitive discourse" over the practices of art and politics itself a move in a cognitivity game? Is not noncognitivism itself a cognitivist position—just one possibility among the broad spectrum of positions one could occupy in playing the cognitivity game?[9] The other two dimensions of the problem of reflexivity are also present in Lyotard's formulation. In order for his noncognitive aesthetic and political theory to harbor any explanatory force, it is parasitic upon the continued maintenance of the cognitivist theories it rejects. In addition, the *distinction* between cognitive and noncognitive is not derivable from the content introduced by either half of the distinction, and it is therefore also in that sense not reflexively sustainable.

As a way out of these dilemmas, perhaps Lyotard would want us to interpret release from "the hegemony of the genre of discourse called cognitive" along the lines of the generalized agnosticism I have been defending in this book. Even a reader as critical of Lyotard as Terry Eagleton acknowledges that while "Lyotard is out to sever the connections between truth and justice . . . he does not deny that truth is possible."[10] A generalized agnosticism that integrates into its position our incomplete knowledge of objective reality is suggestive of the possibility that the way the world actually functions might be most accurately captured by a multivalued logic that maps the suspension of the law of excluded middle. Our alternatives are then increased beyond A and not-A. The extension of alternatives beyond A and not-A and the dissociation of language and concepts from secure contact with reality that a generalized agnosticism affords lets Lyotard off the hook in relation to all three dimensions of the problem of reflexivity previously discussed. We are also enabled to glimpse the kind of politics he would prefer in a new light. Instead of the deductivist politics that characterizes liberal-democratic and authoritarian regimes being regarded as the norm (where both state action and the permissible spheres of individual initiative can be subsumed under a parsimonious set of interrelated principles), Lyotard would like to replace a deductivist politics by what we might call an inductivist politics— where the implications and presuppositions of different spheres of activity do not necessarily have to cohere with one another and articulate a restrictive canon of legitimate explanation and justification. Lyotard might want us to envision a politics where individuals and groups discover (or rediscover) what they have done only after they have done it—politics as persistent refusal of incipient explanation, politics as involving a continual gesturing toward the unknown.

This sort of reading receives support from what Lyotard says later on in *Peregrinations* in explicating Shusaku Arakawa's concept of the "blank":

> It's the emptiness, the nothingness in which the universe presented by a phrase is exposed and which explodes at the moment the phrase occurs and then disappears with it. The gap separating one phrase from another is the "condition" of both presentation and occurrences, but such a "condition" remains ungraspable in itself except by a new phrase, which in its turn presupposes the first phrase. This is something like the condition of Being, as it is always escaping determination and arriving both too soon and too late.[11]

The rhythms of sentential and paragraph formation that Lyotard theorizes in his explication of the "blank" cohere with the generalized agnosticism I have depicted, where no affirmation is so complete as to rule out its own denial and no denial is so extreme as to preclude a possible affirmation. Being, thereby, "is always escaping determination and arriving both too soon and too late."

PART TWO ·

BETWEEN HOBBES AND PLATO: ENVISIONING THE TRANSITION BETWEEN MODERNIST AND POSTMODERNIST DEMOCRATIC SOCIETY

10 · Power and the Political and the Roles of "Distance" and Leadership in Plato

Terry Eagleton argues that postmodernist civilization is defined by a tension between capitalist economy and bourgeois culture.[1] The latter favors tradition and hierarchy, whereas the logic of late capitalism converges with the subversive cultural energies of the avant-garde. He refers to the culture of late capitalism as being saturated with a "fetishism of style and surface, its cult of hedonism and technique, its reifying of the signifier and displacement of discursive meaning with random intensities."[2] The most significant historical precursor of postmodernism is fascism, with its interpenetration of the economic and the symbolic.[3] The invocation of fascism in this context is suggestive of a common underlying factor leading to the "wholesale aestheticization of society"—a stagnating economy. Prospects of limited economic growth and curtailed social mobility make investment less important than consumption in the capitalist scheme of things. The values of self-abnegation and self-sacrifice (which are primarily investors' values) are demoted in favor of the efflorescence of an aestheticized general and economic culture, which in postmodernist society encourages consumer appetites and splurges and diverts attention from harsh economic realities. The logic of scarcity, as Fred Hirsch has reminded us, is built into the structure of capitalist civilization even prior to the advent (or widespread acknowledgment) of concrete resource scarcities, enduring ecological constraints upon economic growth, and huge budget and international-trade deficits.[4] Competition for material goods in the history of capitalist development becomes secondary to competition for positional goods as the urge to outshine one's fellows gets shifted in a climate of economic success from a concrete material arena to a less tangible positional arena. Material needs and appetites get subtly transmuted into socially designed and induced appetites by way of both whetting and satisfying human strivings toward vainglory and competitive advantage. Social scarcity, we might say, is thus an integral part of the individualist metaphysics of capitalism even before scarcity emerges as a concrete, worldly, historical factor to haunt the fate of the late stages of the system.

The generalized agnosticism that I have been arguing for throughout this book—with its continual openness to the future and its potential for continual interlocking reorderings of past and present—might, in the current historical moment, be suggestive of a coalescence (or merging) between liberalism and at least some forms of communitarianism. Specifically, it might suggest a participatory democratic society.

In this section of the argument, I attempt to assess theoretically the significance of the emergence of an epoch of diminished national and global economic growth since the mid-1970s. Every new perception of the present helps to order an appropriate set of images of the past that serves as a fitting complement to our awareness of the present. In this era of problematic liberalism, both Hobbes and Plato as the putative intellectual originators of the voluntaristically organized and the rationalistically inspired state, respectively, can be read in ways that help to clarify the nature of our predicaments and to delineate possible approaches for extricating ourselves from them. They can, in short, be appropriated as pathbreakers to postmodernist society.

What follows is an attempt to rearticulate some key understandings and concepts of the traditions of Western political theorizing for purposes of orienting us in relation to a specific problem—the emergence of a national and worldwide society of limited growth. All theorists of the future, from the most pessimistic to the most optimistic, suggest the existence of limits to our planet's tolerance of continuous economic growth. Even if one accepts as the most enduring constraint on limitless growth the ability of the ecosphere to absorb heat (which gives humanity a margin of safety for about 250 years)[5] many people recognize that the pattern of growth that has characterized our immediate past cannot extend into the indefinite future. In point of fact, most of the optimistic opponents of the no-growth theorists see the limit as occurring much earlier—generally sometime at the end of the twenty-first century.[6] Fundamental to my discussion of the future shape of society will be an analysis of the vicissitudes that the concept of the political has enjoyed within and between key political theorists in Western history. Initially, I shall focus on the concept of power and its relationship to the understanding of the political in the thought of Plato and Hobbes—and the implications of both constellations of views for the concept of political participation.

Throughout *The Republic*, Plato works with a conception of politics as an omnipresent human phenomenon, one that is not restricted to what takes place in a public sphere. An analogy between the just soul and the just commonwealth dominates the dialogue.[7] According to Plato, politics does not arise in a determinate historical and social context as a response to preexisting conflict between people. Instead, it emerges whenever human beings attain to that degree of self-consciousness about themselves which allows them to perceive that acting in recognizably human ways nearly always involves the subordination of certain aspects of self to others. Since the very activity of structuring, divorced from a historical or a social setting, is regarded as a manifestation of the political—of the exertion of power—politics emerges as a kind of primary datum in human experience.

Plato's very broad conception of the political, as we have seen, seems related to his theory of knowledge generally.[8] Plato's Theory of Ideas, which relegates the facts of the material world to an inferior ontological status, regarding them as mere copies of eternal Forms, can be construed as a metaphoric and picturesque way of stating that so-called facts are theory dependent, that the world of theory is underdetermined by the universe of fact. One might say that Plato's stress on the priority of thought over fact predisposes him to become aware of the sheer element of arbitrariness, the factor of personal decision making, involved in the very structure of human personality. This leads him to extend the terms of the political vocabulary—including, especially, its cardinal term, justice—to the private realm.

Plato's denial, in the senses just described, of given rational essences—his recognition of the assertion of power in the creation of human personality implied by his epistemology and his political theory—suggests that it is only through doing that we become. First one acts—with others, in the presence of others—and then one is. Participation becomes a major precondition for the formation of human personality. It is a necessity if a proper human self is to be formed.

The fact that the self is in many ways a creation, a posit, means that a self that does not actively participate with others regarding matters of common concern is literally impoverished and stunted. In the process of self-creation, which is the only true conception of the formation of the self, large-scale interaction with others enables one to flex and extend one's sense of self—to fashion a sense of personal identity that is at once resilient, imaginative, and reliable. One might say that according to Plato we are rescued from inconsequence by constant interaction with others, which provides us with a common framework by which to test capabilities and ambitions. An isolated self—one that has shunned the possibility of sustained interaction with others—has denied itself the best opportunity to unravel its contradictory potential in ways that will be both personally satisfying and externally rewarded. An isolated self is one in the process of endless becoming, because there is no external mooring through which it can be, rather than incessantly become.

We should recognize that participation with others regarding matters of common concern is an important feature of Plato's Republic. It is not just the ruling philosophical elite who are required to participate with their fellow philosophers in considering public matters, and then to do the actual governing in the light of their deliberations.[9] The rigid class hierarchy in The Republic—the fashioning of separate living arrangements and life-styles for the Guardians and Auxiliaries on the one hand and the Artisans on the other, with minimal circulation of personnel and ideas between the classes—means that, in effect, Platonic society is composed of at least two separate, relatively self-contained minisocieties,[10] with participation being a major societal good at each level.

Platonic society appears as a tightly coordinated, cohesive unit only when viewed from the outside. Perceived from the point of view of the members of such a society, what must seem of overriding importance is the insulated and disjointed nature of class relationships, which only come together to present a united front and then slip into mutual metaphysical nonrecognition pacts. Plato recognizes how, in his ideal state, the structure of disjointedness is working against the ideology of cohesiveness and unity. He attempts to resolve this tension through perpetrating the myth of the metals. That Plato has to resort to this device suggests that there are other features of this society undermining his professed ideals of unity and class integration.

The very insulated and disjointed nature of the class structure suggests that within the confines of their own classes individuals will be thrown on each other to achieve whatever degree of social expressiveness and interaction they can muster. But "participation" is not just an adventitious sociological consequence flowing from Plato's structuring of his various classes. Participation at the organizational level of the class constitutes, I think, an integral part of Plato's design for his just society. He accepts Thrasymachus's challenge of showing the good of justice—how justice is an instrumental as well as an intrinsic good. The good of justice is happiness, which Plato defines in much more long-range terms than does Thrasymachus. Happiness for Plato consists in abolishing the tension between ambition and ability, where each person is doing that for which he is ideally suited—tapping internal stores of energy that are most truly expressive of the self. The abolition of this tension—the achievement of happiness—means discovering that optimal structuring of self that would make possible the release of a person's deepest drives and energies. Since the activity of structuring a self involves a residual element of arbitrariness that can never be totally factored out, the process of discovering the optimal structuring of the self involves participation with others for purposes of fashioning and perfecting one's own sense of being. The artisans and warriors in their way, just like the intellectuals at the top, are provided by Plato with an ideal class context to participate with others for purposes of mutual self-discovery and the reinforcement of their most creative selves.

From the perspective that I am advancing here, Plato's understanding of how selves get formed remains continuous throughout *The Republic*. Participation forms as much a need of the Auxiliary and Artisan classes as it does of the Guardian class. Their fixed structuring is only evident to the philosopher-shaper from the outside. From within each class, the specific structures of being defining each class [11] have to be arduously appropriated by each of its members.

In amplifying the Platonic argument that I have just presented, I think that one can make the case that the concepts of distance and of leadership are ontological categories to the same extent, and for analogous reasons, that the political is an ontological category. One might say that leadership constitutes an intrapersonal psychic phenomenon—the result of that internal conversation that never ceases as long as we live. When one part of ourselves addresses other aspects of ourselves, strategies of leadership are already being manifested. In the course of fashioning a coherent self poised on the brink of action, leadership is being exercised. Since the possibilities and opportunities available to a self are constantly in flux (and need to be continually reassessed and reappropriated), internal leadership functions never lapse, but form an integral part of a viable concept of self. In contrast to the category of the political, which calls attention to the exertion of power by one component of self against others, the notion of leadership highlights the other modes of relating, such as persuading, cajoling, and compromising, that can subsist between the various aspects of a self in the course of assuming and constantly reassuming a normal human identity capable of making decisions and acting upon them.

There are three aspects of the manifestation of distance in the intellectual life, which constitute more heightened, self-conscious expressions of distance than are present in the lives of ordinary individuals. The three manifestations of distance are as follows: between theory and tradition; on the level of theoretical formulation proper, between an idiom of truth and an idiom of approximation; and, in the process of thinking itself, between discourse and silence.

Throughout Western history, the intellectual has served as social and political innovator, fashioning new intellectual and political structures and helping to destroy old ones as they failed to meet his standards of coherence. Who is the intellectual? What lies at the root of his dual identity as creator and destroyer? A persuasive answer, it seems to me, comes from a description of the intellectual vocation in an essay by Edward Shils:

> In every society there are some persons with an unusual sensitivity to the sacred, an uncommon reflectiveness about the nature of their universe and the rules which govern their society. There is in every society a minority of persons who, more than the ordinary run of their fellow men, are inquiring, and desirous of being in frequent communion with symbols which are more general than the immediate concrete situations of everyday life and remote in their reference in both time and space. In this minority there is a need to externalize this quest in oral and written discourse, in poetic or plastic expression, in historical reminiscence or writing, in ritual performance and acts of worship. This interior need to penetrate beyond the screen of immediate experience marks the existence of the intellectuals in every society.[12]

According to Shils, what chiefly characterizes the intellectual is his approaching reality from the perspective of the sacred. What this means, I think, is a refusal to treat any aspect of existence as isolated, searching out instead the implications and interconnections of whatever discrete aspects of existence lie immediately before one. What defines the divine perspective on reality is precisely that there are no anomalous aspects of existence for it, no loose ends that somehow fail to link up to larger patterns of meaning. Evil and suffering, for example, which constitute the most glaring forms of human anomaly, are seen from the perspective of the sacred as merely abbreviated moments of some larger excellence.

The intellectual's proclivity to pierce beyond appearance and to pursue the interconnections of things leads to the formation of a special style in written and spoken discourse. The theoretical mode of apprehending and describing reality seems uniquely appropriate to a sensibility bent on subsuming discrete phenomena within larger frameworks of intelligibility and coherence.

The sacralization of existence that the intellectual achieves on the plane of thought by cultivating a theoretical perspective also has its counterpart in the sphere of action. Traditions, I believe, form the counterpart in the real world to theories. Both theories and traditions involve creating a fabric of at-homeness for human beings in the world. Theories accomplish this by locating isolated, discrete phenomena in some overall pattern of significance. Analogously, traditions are conducive to the same result in the real world by erecting a network of metaphysical assumptions, ethical imperatives, and approved ways of perceiving and acting within the world that link individual responses to some overall pattern of permanent significance. If the identity of the intellectual is as Shils describes it, then the intellectual needs traditions as desperately as he does theories to accord relevance and value to individual thoughts and actions. For an intellectual, it would appear, it is usually a question of substitution of traditions. Rarely, if ever, is it a question of their abandonment altogether. The ideology of the New Left in the nineteen sixties, for example, insinuated the contours of a new tradition—one that was radically at variance with ongoing institutions and structures, to be sure, but a tradition nonetheless. No important area of life lay beyond the pale of its ideology. Prescriptions regarding food, sleep, and dress were all incorporated as elements in the altered life-style advocated by the New Left.

The intellectual thus emerges in this analysis as the possessor of a dual identity, as both creator and subverter of traditions. His basic need, apparently, is to fashion ever-more accommodating structures of coherence with which to make sense of the manifold phenomena within and around him. Initially, this takes the form of the elaboration of theories, some of which in turn serve as a basis for organizing social and political life. When thought is translated into action, the real world inevitably gives rise to anomalies and unplanned consequences that seriously call into question the aspirations toward comprehensiveness and coherence animating the original theory. At this point, the intellectual in the guise of subverter of tradition seeks again, initially on the plane of thought, to fashion a more accommodating structure of coherence and then to translate it into reality. The constant dialectical tension between tradition and thought seems to be a recurring feature of the intellectual life, one that is destined to endure as long as the time-bound nature of human existence is not totally superseded.

One can sketch in broad outline the intellectual history of the modern world through this dual identity of the intellectual, who fashions new intellectual and political structures and helps to destroy old ones as they fail to meet his standards of coherence. Lionel Trilling, in his book *Sincerity and Authenticity*,[13] sees authenticity as emerging into prominence at the turn of the nineteenth century with the advent of romanticism. Broadening the scope of Trilling's analysis, one might say that sincerity emerges as a cardinal virtue with the collapse of traditional (i.e., medieval) society.[14] The movement from the moral, social, ethical, political, and even aesthetic ideal of "tradition" to "sincerity" and then to "authenticity" represents the emerging into a fuller self-consciousness of the goals and methods of the intellectual life. In the ideal of authenticity, we have the closest possible approximation on the level of content to the enduring form that the intellectual life has taken. What is now certified substantively under the label of authenticity as the highest moral and aesthetic ideal is nothing else but the attaining of the greatest possible degree of coherence about oneself and the world, which has served as the impetus behind the intellectual quest from its inception.

The revolt of "sincerity" against "tradition" consists in its (i.e., the intellectuals' advocating it) advancing the notion that one cannot merely do things like praying to God and relating to other people by just going through the motions. The authority of one's whole being, of the self that one recognizes himself to be, must be brought to bear in one's relationships to God and to his fellow man. It is the isolated, organically severed individual who must now testify out of the resources of his own being to the truthfulness of his multiple relations with God and man. Instead of an externally sanctioned morality, the rise of the virtue of sincerity heralds a displacement of external sources of authority and value by the individual, who serves as the sole guarantor of the genuineness and seriousness of his commitments.

However, the centrality of the virtue of sincerity from the seventeenth to the nineteenth centuries should not delude us into thinking that a fully autonomous basis for morality had emerged during this period. Stress on the virtue of sincerity could still coexist with (in fact, the precise connotations of the term in some sense required) a heteronomous basis for morality. The norms to which one gave one's allegiance were still regarded as emanating from outside. Emphasis on "sincerity" merely placed a qualitative demand on the conformity that one was supposed to grant to norms antecedently regarded as binding. With the opening up of a metaphysical gulf between the concept of the individual and such corporatist structures as national churches and the state, the proper relationship between the individual and those structures was projected in the virtue of sincerity.

Amplifying the Marxian idea of praxis, one might construe the historical shift from sincerity to authenticity in terms of Western man's eliciting the theoretical kernel from, and expanding to other fields, the lessons learned from engagement in a great historical event—the French Revolution. The value of authenticity represents an extension into the realms of art and morality of the notions of self-creation and self-transformation that in retrospect were seen to inform the actions of the men who made the revolution. "Authenticity," which initially summarized human beings' awareness that in making the revolution they had created a new form of social action where they had remade themselves in the course of ostensibly waging war against their oppressors, was elevated by the generation of romantic writers and their successors into an independent value, serving as the new norm for human beings to aspire to in the realms of morality and art.

The intellectuals who carried the banner of "authenticity" against "sincerity" were reverting in a sense to a traditional life-style. A pristine follower of tradition is not conscious of pursuing any end not dictated by the self; he is not conscious of any competition between alternative and incompatible ends. What stamps someone as a pure follower of tradition, and not a mere traditionalist, is just this lack of awareness of a distinction between self and other in relation to the norms that govern one's existence. Likewise, the advocates of "authenticity" sought to recapture the sense of self-rootedness that prevailed when tradition governed peoples' lives. The ideal of "authenticity" betokens a revolt against the separation of self (felt experience) and other (moral imperatives) that opens up when the requirements of "sincerity" form the highest moral ideals of a society. By contrast, "authenticity" places the notion of the individual as the legislator of the norms governing his own life at the very heart of the moral enterprise. Those who revolted against sincerity in the name of authenticity, however, still sought to preserve the critique of the moral life incorporated in the ideal of sincerity—namely, that the level of integration achieved in living a life according to tradition is spurious, that the gulf between self and other remains, even where traditional norms paper it over and pretend that it does not exist. "Authenticity" heralds a return to the form of the older ideal of tradition, whose content has now been transformed by fusion with the intermediate ideal of sincerity.

Sincerity and authenticity have their matching epistemologies in empiricism and idealism, respectively. An analogue to the gap between avowal and actual feeling that forms the basis of the moral tension experienced by the sincere individual is built into the very structure of empiricist epistemology. The building blocks for statements about the world and oneself—including moral statements, such as "This is good" and "This is evil"—are always sensations. The task of the epistemologist or psychologist (the two enterprises are usually not distinguished in the early modern period) is to embody the ideal of sincerity by collapsing the distance between statements and their roots in sensations and establishing legitimate psychologistic patterns of derivation between the two. In idealist epistemology, on the other hand, the very fundamental categories by which we perceive and organize experience (e.g., time, space, causality, and substance) are themselves regarded as legislated by human beings.

There are tensions defining the intellectual life on the levels of theoretical formulation proper and of the process of thinking itself that are analogous to those that I have described between tradition and thought. On the level of theoretical formulation proper, one might describe the dominant tension as that between pursuit of an idiom of truth and an idiom of approximation. If, as Shils describes him, the intellectual is initially motivated to view reality from the perspective of the sacred, why is it that there are so few intellectual products in any sphere of discourse in the arts and sciences that purport to define reality in an unmediated, wholesale fashion? How does one explain the proliferation of work by intellectuals scrupulously concerned with one particular sector of reality that has been methodically detached from any organic connection with the whole? What inherent dynamic is there in the intellectual life that can account for the devolution of statements uttered by the great innovators of modern science or modern historical method—which are, after all, statements about the world, purporting to answer some basic questions about man and reality—to the statements uttered by most contemporary practitioners in either area that have become utterances in the world, yielding their cautious, provisional truths?

It seems to me that these paradoxes can be resolved if we recall one fundamental datum about ourselves, that we are creatures living in time. This means that the moments of glaring insight when we indeed perceive interconnections to which we were previously impervious become vitiated just by virtue of the fact that we go on living, encountering new things, items of experience that are potentially discordant in a variety of ways with our original formulations. What happens in science and history, and possibly even in art, is that the perspective of the innovator gives way to that of members of a tradition, of people who see their tasks as reconciling the unifying vision of the founder with other elements of reality that were either ignored or slighted in the original formulation. Traditionalists, working in an idiom of approximation, spring up about innovators, writing in the idiom of truth, as a manifestation of a kind of compensatory mechanism, whereby the initial burst of concentrated energy expressed by the original formulation can be reconnected with a multifarious reality that refuses to be contained by even the most sustained and leaping vision.

In the process of thinking itself, one can discern a dialectical movement parallel to that which takes place on the level of theoretical formulation and on the level of practice. One might say that the movement here is from silence to discourse and back again. Silence, the vast internal silence that renders us surprising even to ourselves, serves simultaneously as the great reservoir from which discourse flows and as a check upon it. By silence, I mean our sense of ineffableness about ourselves, the feeling that we have at particular moments that we are experiencing much more than we are capable of putting into words, or articulating even emotionally. All our discourse represents quarryings from the silence, a continual but ultimately fruitless attempt to permanently reduce the gap between feeling and discourse, between our nascent sense of wholeness and self-possession and the words or whatever other medium we use to stake out our sense of the communicable and the knowable. Living in time again means that silence will eventually overwhelm discourse, that the vicissitudes of our lives will be such that on particular occasions our given stock of words, concepts, *and* feelings will seem inappropriate to orient us in the situations that confront us, or that in our intellectual explorations or moments of introspection we will feel the need on some inchoate level to say something for which everything that we already know how to say seems inadequate. Silence within the confines of our selves thus serves as a check on the overweening aggrandizement of discourse in much the same way that traditionalistic elaboration clips the wings of theoretical formulation and, on the level of practice, traditions represent a falling away from the original theories that inspired them.

11 • Moral Psychology, Power, and the Political in Hobbes

Regarding Hobbes as the philosophical founder of modern liberalism, one can point to a theoretical connection in his thought between his moral psychology, his conception of power and the political, and the absence of a concept of political participation. Hobbes's notion of reason as being subservient to the passions rests upon an understanding of reason as being incapable of discerning any substantive truths about man and the world. Reason's role in the economy of the human person is sheerly instrumental; it exists to enable the passions to attain their ends more expeditiously. There is thus no sharp caesura, no large qualitative distinction, between reason and the passions as pictured in ancient and medieval thought, but simply a difference of degree between them. Reason and passion exist along the same continuum, with reason emerging as a kind of self-conscious passion, knowing more effectively how to achieve its ends than a randomly directed passion would.[1]

On the level of substantive content, Hobbes's delineation of the relationship between reason and the passions suggests a jettisoning of the concept of power. The idea of power connotes an element of arbitrariness, that things could be other than what they are. We typically employ the idea of power with regard to political matters, for example, because decision making in politics takes place in a context of at least a partial vacuum of rationality. We can usually adduce rational arguments in support of conflicting sides of political issues, so that the reference to power is meant to indicate that from a sheerly rational perspective the eventual outcome could have been other than what it was. If, however, one regards a particular state of affairs as being purely a matter of conditioning—that there is no element of choice present in its formation—then one is unlikely to think or speak in terms of power. This is exactly the case with Hobbes's doctrine of the relationship between reason and the passions. The subordination of reason to the passions—the birth of instrumental, calculating reason— coincides with a societywide emergence from the dire conditions of the state-of-nature society into the more peaceful world of civil society. The passions (i.e., the pleasure-pain apparatus that governs their operation) manage to bring forth in the course of time a calculating mechanism, instrumental reason, that helps to ensure the creation of a more stable context for the realization of the ends that they dictate. But Hobbes conceives the whole process of the creation (and the eventual triumph) of instrumental reason as being a gradual one— the result of the conditioning effects of the pleasure-pain apparatus lodged within each of us. The unpromising human materials that give rise to the problem of human insecurity—the centrality of the passions—are themselves the source of salvation. The vast conditioning effects of the pleasure-pain apparatus shield the human exertion of power from view until a relatively late stage in social evolution, when the state has already been formed and certain significant intermediate choices, such as that between a monarchy and a parliamentary form of government, have to be made. Until that point, everything appears to be conditioned by the laws of human nature, the laws of moral psychology.

Aside from the specific intellectual content of Hobbes's notion of reason serving as a "scout" for the passions, an additional perspective that might be brought to bear on his moral-psychological schema is not to analyze what it *says* but what it *does*—its role as a speech act, what it enables Hobbes and his readers to accomplish. Viewed in this light, what the subordination of reason to the passions facilitates is the masking of the human exercise of power in creating a world characterized by the pursuit of "commodious living." Hobbes's moral psychology also shields his readers from an awareness of their responsibility for fashioning such a world. The creation of the totally secular, this-worldly mode of existence described in *Leviathan* is not the result of any deliberate exertion of power. It represents the working out of the implications of our being the captives, the playthings, of our passions. They drive us onward in the formation of a Hobbesian world, rendering us, in a sense, powerless in its creation.

It seems to me plausible to suggest that the avoidance of power that so many commentators have remarked upon in the conduct of politics in liberal states (e.g., bursts of moralism in foreign policy, tremendous ambivalence in contemplating military responses to threatening international situations, the recurring appeal of isolationism, etc.) is not just an accidental accretion that has happened to affect the history of particular liberal states. Rather, avoidance of power might be integral to the whole complex of ideas that goes to make up classical liberalism, which would be unintelligible without this concept. It might very well be that from the perspective of the intellectual founders and political innovators of modern liberalism an avoidance of power is requisite to the psychological and political tasks they had set for themselves. It might be that liberalism took the specific theoretical forms with which we are familiar in the works of Hobbes and Locke and the U.S. Founding Fathers because it enabled them to remove their gaze from certain power transactions and to effect psychological and social transformations in a power-neutral environment.

Liberalism evolved as the first mass-based form of political rhetoric, thought, and action. Even if from a twentieth-century perspective early liberalism as an ideology seems to crystallize around the aspirations and interests of restricted segments of an emerging middle class,[2] in relation to what came before liberalism represents a significant broadening of the sphere of effective action. From the perspective of early liberalism, the actions of more and more people were beginning to count in a metaphysical, psychological, and political sense. It may be that only an intellectual elite can refer to and deliberate about power in its own terms; the masses require an abrogation of self-consciousness in order to act effectively. The new modes of relationship that are being established in liberal society have to be conceptualized without making any overt reference to power. New possibilities for including a section of the mass in politics have to be developed that will obfuscate any direct link with the exercise of power. In order to confer legitimacy on emerging social and political arrangements, the political ideology of classical liberalism masks the presence of power in the organization of human personality and society.

What we might therefore regard as a manifestation of false consciousness in liberalism's conceptualization of the role of power in the human economy was experienced by its founders as a liberation, making possible a vast reorganization of men's internal energies and of the societies they inhabited.

Hobbes's conception of the political that masks the exercise of power can also be inferred from his discussion of the state of nature and of the social contract. Conceptually, there are at least two aspects to power—as releasing mechanism and as restraining mechanism. One connotation of the term "power" is what the person mobilizing or exerting it is enabled to do. Another connotation is the restraining effects of such exertions on the will or freedom of other people. The myth of the state of nature (prior to its debilitating effects becoming apparent and the necessity for establishing the state becoming broadly perceived) is one of uncoordinated, spontaneous aggrandizement that emphasizes the releasing aspect of power to the exclusion of the restraining aspect. The state of nature in its early and middle phases represents a utopian myth of innocent power—power as releasing mechanism (enabling people to go on getting things), minus the restraining aspect (preventing others, and, ultimately, oneself from doing so).

Entering into the social contract signifies the emergence of a new realm, the public or governmental, that enjoys a monopoly of force and authority within the community and is thus able to wield effective sanctions against recalcitrants who trespass upon others' possessions. Hobbes's concept of the political is linked with the public realm, with the activities (mainly of security and protection) that it was created to advance. For Hobbes, the public realm posits no independent set of ends of its own. The ends that it seeks to further—the pursuit of "felicity," of "commodious living"—are those of the private realm itself. The public realm merely provides a secure context for realizing these private ends. The subordination of the public realm to the private realm within Hobbes's political philosophy—coupled with a tacit premise of potential abundance—suggests that the ideal of the state of nature, of the possibility of achieving an innocent use of power that would not require extensive mobilization of its restraining aspects, remains present even within the context of liberal civil society. In the fully articulated political theory, innocent power—power as releasing mechanism—is accorded a preeminent position above power as restraining mechanism.

The stress on releasing rather than restraining power in classic liberal thought also relates to the denigration of participation as a political value. Emphasis on power as releasing mechanism suggests an environment in which a relatively isolated, highly motivated individual can realize his goals without unduly interfering with (or involving) his fellows. For Hobbes and liberalism, self-realization means the attainment of egoistic passion, while, in nonliberal democratic theory, political action—participation in community with others—is integral to self-realization. The functional equivalent for participation with others in classic liberal thought is the passions. Personality definition comes internally from the passions instead of externally through interaction with other people. Who we are can be accounted for, according to classic liberal theory, internally and monolithically (by rooting all our motivations in the passions) instead of externally and pluralistically (by interacting with diverse people). In liberal thought, it is always a question of interaction with others as mediated by the passions, instead of the dictates of the passions as mediated by interaction with others (as in Platonic thought).

In the popular liberal imagination of the eighteenth century, which to some extent builds upon the Hobbesian family of notions we have been examining, popular consent is viewed as an alternative to power. Consider the following almost parenthetical statement by the American Whig pamphleteer Stephen Hopkins: "If the House of Commons did not receive this authority from their constituents, it will be difficult to tell by what means they obtained it, except it be vested in them by mere superiority and power."[3] This passage points to a dichotomy between consent and the exercise of power. Consent, in this view, represents a manifestation of natural necessity—people simply desiring something and moving along on that basis—rather than a fully self-conscious human intervention. Instead of viewing consent, as Machiavelli would have suggested, as the most economical expression of power (which does not have to be physically deployed because it is already present), consent, from the classic liberal perspective (drawing upon Hobbes's moral psychology) is viewed as an alternative to power, as something purer and more innocent than the raw exercise of power. Consent in classic liberal thought is seen as the political translation of desire, or passion, which involves bypassing power.

The subtle modifications that Locke introduces into the Hobbesian motivational pattern we have been considering are twofold. First, in the *Second Treatise* Locke calls attention to two major exemplifications of power in a pure form—the penal power and military power. Yet the motivational apparatus through which the implications of these overt applications of power are grasped by individual consciousness promotes the invisibility of power through consent. In Locke, the overt forms of the penal power possessed by the state in domestic affairs and in international relations take on a kind of admonitory quality, inducing human beings to play off prospects of pain against possibilities of pleasure in such a way that they "consent" to the ordering directives of the state. There is perhaps a more detailed appreciation in Locke than there is in Hobbes of the interplay between the power that is officially sanctioned and the power that is being diluted and made to appear invisible in the form of citizen consent—of how the latter arises through confronting the implications inherent in the former.[4]

Second, the category of "inconvenience" in Locke represents a kind of domestication of the more blatant forms of anxiety found in Hobbes. For the latter, the anxiety attendant to the perpetuation of the state of nature—striving to sustain the possibility of totally innocent power against its palpably destructive consequences—is nearly paralyzing in its effects. Only a step as drastic as the creation of indivisible sovereign authority can relieve one of the gnawing anxiety of the state of nature. For Locke, the inconveniences surrounding the state of nature serve to prompt thinking concerning how one might remedy the deficiencies of that state. The proliferation of interpreters of the law of nature in the state of nature introduces a manageable anxiety in which one seeks to temper the excesses of democracy without destroying the possibility of formulating diverse points of view within governmental forums.

Perhaps the secret of the success of liberal ideology in America has been the paradoxical result of the geographic size and diversity of the country. The liberal doctrine of limited, divided government has actually worked to increase the fund of power generally available to government in such a context rather than to diminish it. Multiple foci of authority have only provided additional channels through which power could flow when the incentives seemed especially compelling.

The Framers appear to have had a Newtonian understanding of governmental institutions. They perceived them as played off against each other in a state of equilibrium, in much the same way that planets circle each other in their orbits while the pull of gravitation keeps them intact. Interaction affects the movements of a body, its velocity or orbit, but not its internal makeup. Analogously, executive, legislature, and judiciary check each other by the way they are positioned, but no traces are left affecting the internal structure or power of the interacting institutions. The official theories of separation of powers and checks and balances of the Framers, for example, deliberately set up an adversarial relationship between the president and Congress where neither is envisaged as being able to mobilize power that cannot be countered by the intervention of the other. Historically, one of the first things that happened in working out this adversarial relationship was for Alexander Hamilton, as secretary of the treasury, to suggest that the executive bring to Congress proposals for policy. The very stress on balance, on perfect equipoise, means that someone has to initiate policy, and Hamilton seized the opportunity to have the executive do it. A whole world of politics grows up around executive initiative in policy formulation, which results from Hamilton's adroit manipulation of the tension between the ideology of balance and the institutional working out of balance. In the early years of American government, the Treasury Department under Hamilton becomes the main center of initiative in the executive branch, not only in domestic affairs but in foreign affairs as well. The very ideology of balance ensures that no alarm bells will go off when Hamilton makes his proposal concerning executive initiatives. The genius of the ideology is precisely that it remains indifferent to maneuvers of this sort.

Bringing my thesis concerning the connection between avoidance of power and legitimacy to bear as an organizing perspective on the Constitution, one might say that the animating purpose behind such doctrines as separation of powers and checks and balances, which officially limit power, is to further the corrective, centralizing federalism manifested directly in some sections of the Constitution itself. Just as the federalism of the Constitution—as opposed to the confederalism of the Articles of Confederation—facilitates centralized control over local authorities, so too are separation of powers and checks and balances conducive to the same result. One of the major manifestations of checks and balances within the Constitution is assigning to the president veto power over acts of Congress. The positive, enhancing aspect of this short-circuiting of congressional power is that it enables the president to overturn legislation that too directly reflects local interests to the detriment of what the president would regard as the national interest. The "interstate commerce" clause, lodging supervisory control over the economy in Congress, is intended to remedy the defects of extreme localism. Giving the president veto power provides an additional check along the same lines—to prevent the pursuit of parochial advantage and trade-offs between the states from reasserting themselves within the confines of Congress.

The stiff two-thirds constitutional requirement for overriding a presidential veto might also derive from an analogous concern. The Framers sanctioned Congress's holding sway over the president only when it functioned in a presidential role—that is, when its will represented an overwhelming majority sentiment which indicated that more than purely local advantage was at stake. Only under these circumstances, when Congress itself was achieving the dominant end of corrective federalism—to exercise a check over rampant localism—could it be entrusted with supreme power under the Constitution.

The Anti-Federalists, who opposed the adoption of the Constitution, were more sensitive to the power realities camouflaged by its official language than were the Federalists themselves. They perceived that the rhetoric of separation of powers and checks and balances really masked new opportunities for the aggrandizement of centralized governmental power. This is why someone like George Mason could state, "This government will commence in a moderate aristocracy; it is at present impossible to foresee whether it will, in its operation, produce a monarchy, or a corrupt oppressive aristocracy; it will most probably vibrate some years between the two, and then terminate in the one or the other." [5]

12 · *Abundance and Scarcity: Spatial and Temporal Politics*

Just as we have seen that the concept of the political animating liberal thought is flawed and inadequate with regard to a climate of scarcity, so too the notion of leadership deriving from liberal theory seems unsatisfactory with regard to the requirements of a society of scarcity. A good recent statement of a liberal theory of political leadership is *The Presidential Character* by James David Barber.[1] Barber employs two variables in analyzing presidential performance. The first is a president's enjoyment level—his attitude toward what he does, whether positive or negative—his self-image. The second is a president's activity level—whether he is active or passive in the conduct of his office.[2] It should be fairly evident what Barber has done, and what makes his paradigm of analysis of presidential leadership so quintessentially liberal. He has highlighted those characteristics that have historically contributed to successful entrepreneurial performance in the private realm and has used them as the basic criteria to evaluate presidential performance in the public realm. The quality that we remarked upon in our discussion of Hobbes's political philosophy—how within the context of a fairly rigid distinction between the public and the private realm, it was the values of the private realm that triumphed in the very conceptualization of the public realm—is duplicated in Barber with regard to a specific issue, that of democratic political leadership.

In order to diagnose more clearly the built-in limitations, as it were, of Barber's analysis of presidential leadership, let us raise some questions in relation to it. How valid is his analysis of political leadership outside the American context? Are the qualities and possibilities of political leadership in developing countries, for example, captured by his categories of analysis? What does Barber's framework of analysis presuppose about America? Answering the third question first will provide us with a key for dealing with the other two.

Barber's scheme of analysis assumes that activity matters—that as long as a president is temperamentally predisposed toward being active and has positive emotional affects associated with that activity, that it contributes to raising his self-esteem—then presidential greatness is virtually assured. Barber is basically presupposing an economy of continuing abundance—that the resources are there to support presidential initiative. The only thing that matters is the mobilization of that initiative. Once it is mobilized, the success of presidential endeavors is virtually guaranteed in advance. Barber leaves theoretically unilluminated the problem of those parts of the world that cannot count on abundance—or, in some cases, even on the availability of resources. He also leaves unconfronted the question of what the prospects for leadership in America become as we move into an era of declining (and stabilizing) resources.

Barber's conception of leadership sees it as a purely interpersonal, public phenomenon, rather than as something that is manifested in relation to ourselves. His notion goes bankrupt in a context of scarcity, where the external environment does not seem likely to reward the kinds of exertions he favors.

The alternative concept of leadership discussed previously, which views it as an intrapersonal, psychic phenomenon, gains plausibility to the extent that it illuminates the sense in which "leadership" will still be going on in an environment that will not respond to activist initiative alone. Where limits on the sorts of lives we might lead become more severe than they are today, we shall especially need leadership in the alternative sense that I am proposing of structuring and restructuring of self to help us fashion viable concepts of personal identity, and viable projects in life, that will enable us to deepen our sense of personal integrity and coherence in a dramatically transformed economic and social environment.

Leadership in a context of scarcity duplicates to some extent the conditions of leadership in a context of modernization. Both involve fashioning a satisfactory sense of personal identity in an environment where one has to make do with little. One has to become that sort of self that can maximize the opportunities of a resource-deficient environment. The leader, in contexts of modernization and of scarcity, through precept and example aids in the restructuring process whereby human personality is enabled to adapt to the stringencies of an especially oppressive environment. In a setting of relative abundance, on the other hand—where people have greater access to goods and status—leadership is more typically perceived, not as a mode of relationship having natural roots in individual psychology, but as something artificial (an exclusively social phenomenon) having to do with the superintending of conflict over and between large groups. Barber's activity-oriented categories of analysis represent a late flowering of perceptions and priorities that are inherent in the native American liberal tradition, rather than an attempt to revise them in response to prospects of continuing scarcity.

The relationships between the concept of power and the political—and the role of participation—in Hobbesian and Platonic thought suggest the rudiments of two contrasting ideal types of politics: what one might call, respectively, a spatial and a temporal politics. The first regards the sources of conflict as social, rooted in such factors as the coexistence of large numbers of people within a limited geographic area, the finiteness of resources, and the assertions of multiple claims upon those limited resources. A temporal politics, by contrast, views the major sources of conflict in human life as being personal rather than social, rooted in the time-bound nature of human existence itself, which means that channeling and mediating processes must always be invoked in order for us to realize our aims and projects in life. No matter how intense our feelings on a given occasion, there is a radical nonimmediacy attached to the context of our lives because of the progressive, evolving nature of our time-bound existence. Our thoughts and feelings of a moment get modified just by virtue of the fact that we go on living—remaining susceptible to new intrusions of feeling and experience that alter the immediately urgent and "permanent" of a moment before. To live is always to abstract from a broader context of thinking and feeling whose outward contours and trajectory we are never able to grasp completely, even on a conceptual level. A temporal politics is concerned to reconcile our transitoriness with our urge toward completeness—to evolve a modus vivendi between our doing and our being. Plato is the philosopher par excellence of a temporal politics, which attempts to annul the external, spatial dimension of human life for the sake of exclusive focusing on those internal transactions that would allow human beings to realize their highest selves. Hobbes is the philosophical innovator who perceived in a context of growing material advance that it would be possible to find a spatial analogue for every temporal anxiety and deflection (and also analogues to the strategies of overcoming) that Plato restricted to the intrapersonal, psychic sphere.

The famous passage on felicity at the beginning of chapter 11 of *Leviathan* can be construed along these lines:

> The felicity of this life consisteth not in the repose of a mind satisfied. For there is no such *finis ultimus*, utmost aim, nor *summum bonum*, greatest good, as is spoken of in the books of the old moral philosophers. Nor can a man any more live whose desires are at an end, than he whose senses and imaginations are at a stand. Felicity is a continual progress of the desire, from one object to another; the attaining of the former being still but the way to the latter. The cause whereof is, that the object of man's desire, is not to enjoy once only, and for one instant of time; but to assure forever the way of his future desire. . . .
>
> So that in the first place, I put for a general inclination of all mankind, a perpetual and restless desire of power after power that ceaseth only in death. And the cause of this, is not always that a man hopes for a more intensive delight, than he has already attained to; that he cannot be content with a moderate power; but because he cannot assure the power and means to live well, which he hath present, without the acquisition of more.[3]

Hobbes perceives that in an expanding economy the tension between doing and being would get played out against the background of man's relation to things rather than his relation to himself. The tensions of a temporal politics addressed by Plato in the context of what in many respects appears to be a steady-state society would get resolved in a certain sense by being reenacted in an external, spatial sphere. The world was now seen as rich enough to reward the pursuit of "power after power that ceaseth only in death." At the deepest level, the conundrums of reason do not get resolved. They simply get duplicated in spheres other than their first appearance. This is what the prospect of abundance will have wrought with the Platonic dilemmas.

On the level of latent philosophical content, it might be that this is what is encoded in Hobbes's telling of the myth of the social contract (which can be viewed as a myth about thought itself). The only way that thought can resolve internal perplexities is by pulling back, as it were, and postulating additional entities. The myth of the social contract tells the story of how the chaos of the state of nature, reflecting the paramountcy of the passions within humanity, gets remedied through the creation of another faculty out of the womb of (i.e., a conditioning process working its effects on) the passions themselves—namely, instrumental reason. The tale of the social contract can thus be viewed as a myth concerning the strategies of thought itself as it goes about evolving counterstructures to those requiring explanation and resolution in order to dissolve internal perplexity. The solution to the dilemmas of temporal politics symbolized by the social contract seems to be that only by the articulation of a counterentity (the "immanentizing" of time into space, as it were) can thought achieve its greatest repose.

The organizing category of a temporal politics is justice—construed as the optimal ordering of human energies, and also as the optimal ordering of relationships between human beings to maximize the potential of all. The organizing category of a spatial politics is political obligation—which takes profitable individual interaction with the world for granted and merely raises the question of how the curbing of such an irresistible individualism can be justified. Let us focus on the logical structure of the commitment to the priority of justice in Platonic theory and, correspondingly, on the logical structure of the commitment to the priority of political obligation in Hobbesian theory. We can then explore what implications follow for theoretical dilemmas likely to arise in an age of scarcity.

For purposes of my analysis, I will set out two abstract schemata, culled from the writings of Hobbes and Plato, to clarify interconnections between theories of politics, justice, and political obligation. The Priority of Political Obligation Schema locates the unique character of political activity in a distinction between a private and a public realm; politics emerges as a kind of second-order human activity, concerned with reconciling competing claims of private interest. Political activity arises only under a determinate set of historical circumstances, where territorial cohesiveness and the extent of interdependence among a population have become sophisticated enough to warrant the institution of regularized procedures for containing conflict. Politics addresses itself initially to procedural questions, staking out certain ground rules for mitigating conflict, while leaving untouched the whole range of substantive questions having to do with the inherent justness of the claims that clamor for resolution in the first place. Political activity appears on the human scene to facilitate the pursuit of private interest, not to institute a regime of truth.[4]

Under this conception of politics, the imposition of political obligation has to be justified through those first-order interests whose competing claims pose the problem of politics. Thus, we could expect theories of obligation arising under this conception to be individualist, seeking to justify political obligation in terms of the furtherance of individual interest. The theory of justice, in this view, remains subordinate to the theory of political obligation. For, once it can be shown that a particular political order fully recognizes those first-order claims that give rise to sovereign political institutions, that political order is ipso facto just. Hobbes was merely spelling this relationship out when he equated justice with the performance of covenants, with men's fulfilling what their rational recognition of their own interest dictates.[5]

The second schema, which I am calling the Priority of Justice Schema, states that political activity is present wherever structuring—the subordination of some elements to others—takes place. Under this conception, politics does not arise in a determinate historical and social context as a response to preexistent conflict between men. Instead, it emerges whenever human beings attain to that degree of self-consciousness about themselves which allows them to perceive that acting in recognizably human ways nearly always involves the subordination of certain aspects of self to other aspects.

To use a more modern idiom to elucidate this understanding of politics: This tradition of Western speculation, whose votaries have extended beyond Plato to include Rousseau, Hegel, and Marx,[6] focuses on the conceptual link between action and repression. To act meaningfully and responsibly in the world is to suppress certain aspects of self in order to realize others. Refusal to engage in an internal strategy of suppression incapacitates one for action. Since the very activity of structuring, divorced from historical or social setting, is regarded as a manifestation of the political, of the exertion of power, politics emerges as a kind of primary datum in human experience. It follows that politics cannot be justified in terms antecedent to itself. Not an actual historical context (a particular state in the evolution of society), but a larger theoretical construct (a vision of the truth) forms the appropriate setting for grasping the nature of political activity. Therefore politics, as a primordial human phenomenon, must be seen from a theoretical perspective that locates its importance and role in some all-embracing vision of human beings and the world.

The definition of justice—which phenomena relating to humanity's personal, social, and political life need to be theoretically justified and explained—will vary according to these alternative conceptions. Insofar as politics, as in the second understanding of it, emerges as a first-order human activity, the theory of politics will determine at the very outset what sorts of lives people should lead and, consequently, what claims to satisfaction they might legitimately make. For this conception of politics, rooted as it is in the theoretical imagination rather than in any particular historical setting, there is nothing more basic than the image of a just ordering of human society. Recourse to private interest in justifying political obligation would at best appear redundant and, at worst, positively immoral. An image of a true ordering of human society possesses its own intrinsic claim to being fulfilled, and is primary over individual interest. Once the pretensions of the theory of justice allied to this second understanding of politics are taken seriously, the ground of political obligation is established automatically. In diametrical opposition to the relationship between the theory of justice and the theory of political obligation under the first schema, here the theory of political obligation is subsidiary to and derivative from the theory of justice.

I wish to argue that the schema which emphasizes the Priority of Political Obligation has become increasingly irrelevant, while the Priority of Justice Schema appears to provide much more appropriate theoretical underpinnings for speculation concerning the future.

We are witnessing today, I believe, in the controversy over the nature and extent of global resource scarcities, a kind of factual translation of the idea of a necessarily just ordering of human life emphasized by the second schema. The objective facts of the human situation are such, many theorists of the future appear to be telling us, that only a particular ordering of human society—one that drastically restricts social mobility and the life prospects of individuals—can accommodate human needs within a world economy of dwindling resources.

It would appear that theoretical justifications appropriate for any deprivations that are instituted during the intervening stages in a global declension through states of increasing scarcity (i.e., before a fully stabilized no-growth society is reached) would differ substantially from justifications suitable to the end stage, when a stationary state has actually come into existence. What needs to be accounted for by theories of justice and political obligation during the earlier phases is taking away from people what they already have, not merely preventing them from getting more. One might call the first "compulsory deprivation" and the second "preventive deprivation." It might well be that theories conforming to the Priority of Political Obligation Schema can only justify deprivations of the first sort, where such notions as private interest still retain a modicum of intelligibility in a fluid, but still recognizably capitalistic, society.

It is also conceivable that where individual deprivations are linked to the stabilization of resources of a whole society at a level significantly below the status quo, the individualistic theories of political obligation enshrined in my first schema fail to work completely. In the classic social-contract theorists, deprivations are tied to increases in the life prospects of individuals. Man is pictured as an endlessly aggrandizing creature, who can legitimately be induced at least partially to forego the satisfaction of his ravenous impulses by the institution of a structure of political obligation within society only where the resulting containment of his desires can be shown to lead to more enduring satisfactions later on. But where self-restraint can only lead to a peaceful allotment of the shrinking resources of society, it might be that the classic theories of the social contract fail to justify the institution of political obligation altogether.

Peace and social stability are viewed in classical social-contract theory as necessary preconditions for the enhancement of individual life prospects. Peace carries no intrinsic justification. So in an economy where the two goals, peace and the improvement of individual life prospects, conflict, the classic social-contract theorists might well permit war with one's fellows, with the possibility of improving one's material situation, rather than advocate a peace that will necessarily shrink the life prospects of all members of society. In a world economic context of growing scarcity, parties to the original contract may choose the state of nature or lone defiance over the status quo—anarchism, in effect, over the institution and maintenance of political authority.[7]

Hume might have been making explicit a major presupposition of social-contract theory when he wrote about the circumstances of justice.[8] For him, the economic base of society must be poised between total abundance and absolute scarcity in order for "justice" to become operative.[9] Where the economy leans too heavily in the direction of scarcity, justice might no longer appear as the relevant virtue. In a situation where the principled renunciations embodied in rules of justice seem to place ludicrous overreliance on human generosity, human beings, if indeed they retain a moral sense at all, might need other guidelines, perhaps of a more subjectivist sort, such as the injunction to show compassion to others in distress. Thus, on a general societal level, in a context of resource scarcity, the alternatives might appear to be anarchism or collectivism, with collectivism triumphing. Where the end stage of a fully stationary society is reached, and purely private interest (understood in the conventional sense of the possibility of upward mobility) has been all but obliterated, I think it evident that theories which emphasize political obligation would no longer be serviceable. We would then require theories exemplifying the priority of justice, to orient us in a radically transformed social and economic environment.

The two schemata carry profound implications for some of the major issues that have exercised the imaginations of political theorists. In hierarchical order, these issues might be formulated as follows: (1) Politics and eschatology, (2) Human nature, (3) The ideology of growth, (4) Nature and scope of individual rights, (5) Theory of sovereignty.

1. The theory of politics enshrined in the Priority of Political Obligation Schema divorces politics from eschatology—the doctrine of the last things, or matters of ultimate concern. Under this theory, the authentic allocation of values, moral and spiritual as well as material, takes place initially in the private sphere, with political activity entering the picture only to obviate or contain situations of conflict. Therefore, politics is viewed as an enterprise that restores or creates temporary equilibriums between opposing forces, while itself taking no stand on the more ultimate substantive issues of value giving rise to conflict in the first place. Both the sources and resolution of conflict are regarded as temporary.

In the Priority of Justice Schema, on the other hand, a much closer connection is presumed to exist between politics and eschatology. The true ordering of human society that politics in the narrow sense is meant to serve also offers answers to the more ultimate, metaphysical questions humanity has raised about itself and the universe. In a world where declining energy sources have immediate repercussions for population and economic growth, for the curve of technological expansion, and for the whole question of the obligations of the rich to the poor (both internationally and nationally), the very structure of the world seems to accord with the one predicated by theorists who have argued the priority of questions of justice over those of political obligation. A connection between politics and eschatology, which earlier generations of theorists and practitioners of politics could either make or refuse to make at will, seems to have been irretrievably supplied by events. The curtailed options and the policies of overall retrenchment that today characterize most industrial societies suggest an image of a world in which what is—the hard facts of human reality—secrete a particular set of norms as being most conducive to the ultimate survival of human beings on this planet. The rootedness of political decisions in ultimate issues affecting the quality and style of life is becoming apparent to almost everyone.

From a more positive perspective, in a society such as that projected by theorists of impending global resource scarcities, in which the opportunities to engage in the practice of politics in the narrow sense of compromise and conciliation are severely limited by the reality of universal shortages, politics in the more grandiose sense envisioned by the theorists represented in my second schema—politics in the service of truth—appears to have an opportunity finally to come into its own. In a no-growth society, matters that were previously regarded as being of ultimate concern (e.g., those pertaining to the quality and meaning of life) are metamorphosed into bread-and-butter political issues.[10]

2. Moreover, theorists who have linked politics with eschatology have usually revealed a more imaginative grasp of human nature than those who have not sought to draw connections between the two. The theorists who emphasized the priority of justice have generally had a more protean image of man, asserting that human nature was not exhausted in the limited set of roles regarded as paradigmatic by Hobbes and his liberal successors. In an era when the roles pre-eminently identified with the pursuit of material progress and the extension of technological civilization are becoming more difficult to actualize, the repertoire of possible images of selfhood suggested in the writings of Plato, Rousseau, and Marx opens new vistas for us.

Such fundamental metaphysical questions as Who is man? What sorts of activities are characteristically human? are beginning to take on a new urgency. The theorists who have exemplified the Priority of Political Obligation Schema have identified "human nature" with the kinds of pursuits that have come to typify the private realm in Western civilization, activities such as seeking personal wealth and status. By contrast, Priority of Justice theorists have stressed that human beings are capable of diverse paths toward self-realization, including ones that have been obscured in our culture by a too-narrow understanding of the political. Such a conception, exemplified in the Priority of Political Obligation Schema, has identified the coercive element in human affairs with what transpires in the public realm rather than with what happens within the confines of the person himself as he chooses to give expression to certain aspects of self at the expense of others.

3. Flowing from their alternative conceptions of human nature, the two schemata suggest two incompatible ideologies of growth, two mutually exclusive answers to the question of what constitutes "progress." A theoretical stress on the primacy of the private sphere insinuates a conception of progress that is radically at odds with a no-growth society, and is in any case probably not sustainable in a world of scarcity. As long as the possibility of increased material progress remains, the network of concepts and the justificatory structure of the Priority of Political Obligation Schema continue to generate for their adherents a feeling of at-homeness in the world. The brakes on individual aggrandizement that the schema recognizes can be accepted with relative equanimity, so long as the possibility for future material improvement remains. But the schema breaks down completely at the prospect of freezing the material well-being of whole societies at particular levels.

Plato, Rousseau, and Marx, by contrast with theorists representative of the first schema, were extraordinarily ambivalent in their attitude toward material progress. In fact, working with a much broader conception of the political, of where precisely in human relationships power is being exercised, such theorists have helped to make Western man excruciatingly aware of the costs of progress, of what he has had to sacrifice in terms of perhaps more valid conceptions of well-being in order to achieve his phenomenal material growth. The possibility of growth involving nonmaterial dimensions constitutes a central theme in the work of theorists exemplifying the Priority of Justice Schema.

Perhaps an expanding technology will be able at least temporarily to fill the breach created by extraordinary demographic and resource pressures on individual life prospects. Perhaps the visions of doom are premature, a hasty extrapolation from current demographic and resource trends into the immediate future. What the prophets of scarcity overlook, one might claim, is the historical resiliency of the scientific and business communities in developing new sources of energy as old sources get depleted or become uneconomical. Technology, the bugbear of romantics bent on preserving the individual from being swallowed up by mass society, might yet prove to be our salvation by restoring individual life prospects as the prevailing energy sources of a mass consumer society are used up.

But the remedy might prove worse than the disease. With the continued application of technology to the problems of excessive population growth and a dwindling resource base, the individual who is ostensibly being saved by modern science might be further reduced to a nullity as the potential for manipulation inherent in modern technological progress assumes unprecedented proportions. At this point, the advantages of the Priority of Justice Schema become evident. The structure of justification enshrined in the Priority of Political Obligation Schema makes us aware of the problem of restoring individual freedom and initiative in a situation of growing resource scarcity. However, this paradigm offers us no guidance once we attempt to grapple with resource scarcity by the application of technology. Here the schema that asserts the primacy of justice can prove helpful. The categories of thought that are central to it can in effect help us post warnings in the face of an advancing technology. An ambivalent attitude toward material progress and the advances of modern civilization—as well as the importance attached in the Priority of Justice Schema to the concept of alienation—make it useful as a guide in helping us to achieve a proper balance between the application of advanced technology and the preservation of a viable concept of the individual.

4. The two schemata also reflect very different conceptions of the nature and scope of individual rights. The Priority of Political Obligation Schema implies a negative understanding of such rights, one that seems in many ways antithetical to the way of life likely in a no-growth society, and even during some of the intervening stages leading to it. This schema, presupposing as it does the inherent legitimacy of most individual wants and desires, seeks to justify infringements in terms of the safeguarding of a more ultimate self-interest. Not only the psychological but the theoretical paramountcy of an egoistic self is taken for granted. Restrictions placed on the unbridled assertion of self are justified as contributing to the enduring realization of the dictates of the ego. The appeal in political theories exemplifying the

Priority of Political Obligation Schema is usually from a cruder to a more enlightened and sophisticated understanding of self-interest.[11]

Theories of justification falling under this schema obviously work best in an expanding material and technological environment, where payoffs for the imposition of fundamental restraints on individual aggrandizement are most evident. But such significant restrictions on the exercise of ego as instituting a permanent structure of political authority within society can be accepted only when an abundant natural environment supports the link between restraint and improved chances for material progress for everyone. Where this link breaks down—when people's aspirations vis-à-vis the state are transformed from a negative one, simply being left alone to pursue what their conception of their self-interest dictates, to a positive one, whereby the state should guarantee a minimum level below which people's standards of living will not be allowed to fall—the stresses implicit in the Priority of Political Obligation Schema render it unable to provide one with neutral, principled grounds from which to voice demands against the state.

Historically, the notion of self-interest has been understood in too narrowly egoistic terms to allow the state much latitude in effecting redistributive schemes that would permit it to meet people's positive demands. It is here that the Priority of Justice Schema evinces its superiority. By displacing the individual as the "lever" that makes possible the moves from one stratum of theoretical argument to another, and starting instead with the requirements of theory and of truth, the Priority of Justice Schema seems eminently suitable for a time in which the constraints exerted by certain hard facts about the physical universe again make human beings subservient to structures of necessity in which they must find their appropriate niche.[12]

In a world where the possibility for upward mobility is drastically curtailed, and where the state's monopolization of control over available resources may be much greater than is the case at present, the needs of citizens for guarantees of certain positive rights will loom more important than ever. Rights to a minimum standard of living, to meaningful use of leisure time, to travel, to learn, grow, and enjoy certain of the civilized amenities of life might be among those rights that citizens of a future society will expect the state to support.[13] The Priority of Justice Schema enjoys the distinct advantage in not having to follow the "justificatory detour" of the alternative approach by showing how fundamental state institutions and practices accord with individual self-interest. The notion of positive rights accords well with the presuppositions, stresses, and omissions of the Priority of Justice Schema. In elaborating their argument, theorists who emphasize the priority of justice can proceed directly from their statement of perceived basic truths concerning human nature and society to the imperatives that follow, regardless of how well these conform to people's conventional assessment of their evolving and expanding self-interest.

In a no-growth world, not only will the obligations of the richer to the poorer classes within a single nation need reconsideration, but, on an international level, the obligations of richer countries toward poorer ones will pose novel practical and theoretical dilemmas. As is already well recognized,[14] in order for rich nations to achieve a stabilized state, poor countries will have to make conscious decisions to adopt certain policies, such as encouraging extensive birth-control measures, which rich countries appear much better able to afford than poor ones. In order for the poor to undertake the requisite changes in social and economic policy, inducements will have to be proffered by the rich, translating into workable policies that ideal of interdependence of which the wealthy have so far been the most vocal proponents.

On the agenda for innovative policymakers, then, is the drawing up of a list of positive rights of poor countries against rich countries, which will require extending the Priority of Justice Schema to encompass the international community.

5. The issue of the obligations of the rich to the poor borders on a fifth area where my two schemata have contradictory implications—the theory of sovereignty. The Priority of Political Obligation Schema appears wedded to a conception of sovereignty that an emerging international community characterized by resource scarcity will render increasingly obsolete. Viewing politics as a particular form of human organization that arose when societies reached a certain degree of differentiation and complexity, this theory of politics implies the limited utility of political procedures for territorial units beyond the nation-state. By contrast, the notion of politics referred to in the Priority of Justice Schema, by not associating political activity with any particular form of human social organization, does not by implication underwrite a conception of sovereignty that is being eroded by events.

It has become a staple of contemporary discussion that advancing technology creates its own imperatives; that multinational corporations, unencumbered by the constraints of national political life, are able to follow these imperatives more fully than sovereign states themselves.[15] Multinational corporations, which enjoy greater flexibility than nation-states, can take immediate advantage of, and even deliberately foster, an explosive technology in ways that wreak havoc with the chains of accountability that link governments to their citizens and vice versa, as well as with the scheme of obligations and rights reciprocally binding governments to each other.

A whole cluster of theoretical questions opens before us that can be more easily accommodated under the Priority of Justice Schema than under the Priority of Political Obligation Schema. In a depersonalized global technological environment, are the authentic units of governance to be equally depersonalized—the faceless, computer-controlled apparatuses of multinational corporations, which must tax the furthest reaches of ingenuity in order to achieve an acceptable level of accountability? Must nation-states gradually relinquish aspects of their sovereignty to larger governing units in order to achieve an end that sovereignty has historically achieved—a mutual relationship of accountability between governors and governed within a particular territorial unit? The Priority of Justice Schema affords us the conceptual tools with which to imaginatively grasp governmental units that are both smaller and larger than the nation-state. This schema allows us to articulate and work toward the goal of a restructured world political environment more in consonance with the movement toward unity implicit both in advanced technological development and in a shrunken world material and resource base.

Just as the organizing political metaphor of a temporal politics is participation (as the dominant means of overcoming the distances and healing the arbitrariness of being), so too the organizing political metaphor of a spatial politics is representation—which enables the relatively self-sufficient, spatially anchored individual to attain his diverse ends without forfeiting his freedom or his individuality. A narrow doctrine of political authorization and representation is central to the political teaching of *Leviathan*.[16] What has not been that often remarked upon is the pervasiveness of a concept of representation in most key aspects of Hobbes's philosophizing and the concept's relationship to his positivistic theory of law and to a tacit background assumption concerning abundance. We now turn to an examination of these issues.

The notions of law and representation lying at the foundation of

the modern liberal-democratic state—indeed, the very close conceptual link between them, legitimizing and properly denominating as
law only what can be clearly shown to follow from an adequate scheme
of representation—have their intellectual origins in Hobbes. *Leviathan*
forms the locus classicus in which our modern understandings of the
nature and role of law in human society and of its intimate connection
with representation find their first systematic expression. If we today
in American society are experiencing a crisis of law and legitimacy—
where the Hobbesian equation between law and representation is still
acknowledged on one level of public awareness, but where his infer-
ence concerning legitimacy is denied on another, deeper level—it be-
hooves us to pause and reassess the Hobbesian legacy of ideas and to
consider the background assumptions that might have conditioned or
influenced their emergence. We must ask whether such assumptions
are still operative today and, if not, what new understandings are developing to replace them. The argument of this section of the chapter
therefore proceeds in three stages: an analysis of Hobbes's concepts
of law and representation, and the strategic role of these ideas in the
larger design of the argument in *Leviathan;* an exploration of the tacit
background assumptions facilitating the emergence of Hobbes's system of ideas; and a consideration of the fundamental alterations in the
background conditions that have taken place which call into question
the Hobbesian network of ideas, together with an overview of what a
more compelling theoretical alternative might be.

One might say that a notion of acting for (as opposed to merely
standing for)[17] provides a unifying perspective on several of Hobbes's
key formulations in *Leviathan.* An official doctrine of representation
as authorization is presented in the final chapter of part one: "A
person," he says, "is he whose words or actions are considered, either
as his own, or as representing the words or actions of another man,
or of any other thing, to whom they are attributed, whether truly or
by fiction."[18] The sovereign, whether a single individual or a group of
men, such as a parliament, can thus be said to constitute a person because what he or they do represents the actions of the body of citizens.
What is conspicuously lacking in Hobbes's concept of representation,
and what thus makes it sound ominously archaic and authoritarian to
modern liberal ears, is any doctrine of accountability.[19] Representation
in Hobbes is defined statically, as a once-and-for-all authorization; it
requires no continual checking mechanism in order to be legitimate.
Hobbes's concept of law follows as a close corollary from this idea of

representation. "Law," in his view, "is not counsel, but command; nor a command of any man to any man; but only of him, whose command is addressed to one obliged to obey him. And as for civil law, it addeth only the name of the person commanding, which is *persona civitatis,* the person of the commonwealth." [20]

The office of the sovereign representative can be rationally reconstructed as following upon the consent of the governed. There is a very tight conceptual connection between authority and consent that results from Hobbes's radically nominalistic epistemology and metaphysics. He says that "there is nothing in the world universal but names; for the things named are every one of them individual and singular." Two pages later, Hobbes adds that "truth consisteth in the right ordering of names in our affirmations." [21] The radical nominalism expressed in these passages suggests that for Hobbes what there is depends in a crucial sense on our naming of it. Before our naming of things, there exists only an indeterminate flux of experience. There is, strictly speaking, no objective external world by which individual statements about experience can be either verified or falsified until we constitute this "objective world" in the act of speech—of naming.

Hobbes's nominalistic epistemology enables him to achieve two objectives that are fundamental to his concepts of representation and law: to justify on philosophical grounds the role of the sovereign, without whom no stable patterns of meaning would emerge between men; and to show that since, without the creation of sovereign authority, no ordered communication between men would be possible, then the basis of sovereign authority is consent. The existence of such authority forms a precondition for our world as we know it, and therefore consent in the formation of sovereignty can be formally, rationally reconstructed.

Hobbes's elucidation of the relationship between authority and consent, showing them to be two sides of the same coin—the idea of consent presupposing the idea of authority, and the most persuasive analysis of "authority" being one that shows it to be rooted in consent —is a classic instance of Hobbes's resoluto-composite method at work. Once the ostensibly antithetical concepts of "authority" and "consent" are decomposed into their most fundamental elements and reconstituted on that basis, a dialectical relationship is disclosed, and, instead of being seen as antagonistic, they are revealed as being almost mutually supportive.

With his radically nominalistic metaphysics and his elaboration of its implications for the ideas of authority and consent, Hobbes lays the foundation for modern liberalism. What is needed in order to yield the full-dress modern liberal version of these ideas is a dynamic concept of accountability, which recognizes the relationship between authority and consent as an ongoing institutional problem, not just as a theoretical conundrum that can be resolved once and for all. From Locke onward, important thinkers in the liberal tradition have sought to provide the institutional refinements and justifications that would permit "authority" and "consent" to contribute effectively to the actual workings of government. One possible way of viewing Hobbes's relationship to his liberal successors would be to regard him, with his extreme nominalism and the political-theoretical innovations to which it leads, as the paradigm creator, and to see Locke and James Mill, Jeremy Bentham, and a number of other liberal theorists as paradigm workers, extending and deepening the original formulation in a more liberal direction than its creator would have approved, thoroughly "operationalizing" it with this liberal gloss.

Running parallel to the formal-philosophical argument for Hobbes's concepts of representation and law is an argument based upon his reading of human nature, centering upon the notion of "interest." In his depiction of the state of nature, Hobbes seeks to show that qualitative distinctions between human beings based upon their own estimates of superior intelligence or strength are nothing but an expression of their vanity, since in the uncoordinated environment of the state of nature all displays of superiority are soon undermined by an equality of vulnerability. "When all is reckoned together," Hobbes says, the "difference between man and man, is not so considerable, as that one man can thereupon claim to himself any benefit, to which another may not pretend, as well as he. For as to the strength of body, the weakest has strength enough to kill the strongest, either by secret machination, or by confederacy with others, that are in the same danger with himself."[22]

The myth of the social contract is intended to symbolize a movement of recoil of the passions, which impel us toward limitless self-aggrandizement. Paradoxically, in order to achieve their fullest possible realization, the passions must be coaxed into a movement of withdrawal. Only by human beings withdrawing their total claims against each other and agreeing to carry on the normal transactions of daily life against the backdrop of a coordinated environment where one agency within the community enjoys a monopoly of force and authority and can enforce compliance among lone defiers can the ends of life to which our passions impel us be most fully realized. Thus, establishing the sovereign representative—the agency within the state that facilitates coordinated interaction between human beings—and agreeing to be bound by all his decrees as law are the major lessons that an enlightened self-interest dictates. Hobbes's authoritarianism rests upon an extreme individualism.

So far I have considered representation, and the concept of law to which it leads, in their confined, literal senses. It is important to recognize, however, the pervasiveness of some form of the concept of representation throughout much of Hobbes's argument in *Leviathan* in order to gain greater insight into its underlying design and unity, and to appreciate more fully the sense in which his overall political theory is in crisis and the directions in which it might have to be superseded. One might say that the concept of "representation" as acting for someone or something else summarizes Hobbes's strategy for overcoming distance in the manifold senses in which the awareness of distance haunts his argument in *Leviathan*. This awareness takes several forms: (1) between man and man, (2) between reason and the passions, (3) between God and man, (4) between life and death, and (5) between thought and action. I shall briefly indicate how distance is manifested in each of these areas, and how a strategy of representation (in contrast to participation) helps Hobbes to overcome distance.

1. Between man and man. The state of nature—where, in Hobbes's classic phrase, the life of man is "solitary, poor, nasty, brutish, and short"[23]—is characterized by physical proximity and insurmountable psychological distance between human beings. Though the next person might be geographically close, psychologically (working out the logic of the moral psychology that Hobbes attributes to the character type inhabiting the state of nature) people have no choice but to regard their neighbors as their enemies. The very existence of others constitutes a threat to me, because they embody other centers of passion bent on the same limitless aggrandizement of all the goods of the world that I am driven to. The menacing distance of the state of nature is overcome through creating the sovereign representative, who, by facilitating a universal movement of recoil of the passions, paradoxically enables the individual members of society to pursue their passionately motivated goals in the most effective manner possible.

2. Between reason and the passions. In his moral psychology, Hobbes employs the vocabulary of dualism to support a monistic position. In the state of nature, man is motivated almost totally by his passions—which create a sense of menacing distance between one human being and the next. With entrance into the social contract, a new faculty is born in man, something to be contrasted with passion, which might loosely be called reason. But Hobbesian reason is a sheerly calculating instrument—serving as a "scout" for the passions.[24] He downgrades the intimative role of reason, its intimating to us a world that is more coherent and satisfactory than the one immediately available in experience. In Hobbes's reading of human nature, the intimative role of reason, such as one finds exemplified in Plato's *Republic*, merely represents a projection of our passions and has no independent validity. A concept of reason purged of its self-delusions would see it as a calculating phenomenon—delineating more clearly than the passions themselves what the ends of action are to which our passions impel us and, most important, helping us to determine the most expeditious means for attaining those ends. In Hobbes's ultimately monistic account of human nature, then, reason emerges as a species of rationalized passion. Calculating reason serves as a representative of the passions—acting on their behalf, and guiding men to the most expeditious means for attaining their passionately rooted ends.

3. Between God and man. Hobbes advances a radically austere, monotheistic conception of God: "When we say anything is infinite, we signify only that we are not able to conceive the ends, and bounds of the things named; having no conception of the thing, but of our own inability. And therefore the name of God is used, not to make us conceive him, for he is incomprehensible; and his greatness, and power are inconceivable; but that we may honor him."[25] The only bridge between such a God and man is the sovereign representative who authoritatively interprets the divine Word just as he authoritatively ordains human law.

4. Between life and death. This, the ultimate distance affecting human life, is also mitigated through the institutionalization of the sovereign representative. Through his monopolization of force and authority within the community (all lesser exercises of these within the commonwealth being manifested by his grace), he provides the necessary precondition for the coordinated social environment that

enables human beings to stave off the prospects of violence and of death for as long as their physical constitutions will hold out.

5. Between thought and action. "A good and orderly method in proceeding from the elements, which are names, to assertions made by connection of one of them to another; and so to syllogisms, which are the connections of one assertion to another, till we come to a knowledge of all the consequences of names appertaining to the subject in hand" is, according to Hobbes, the hallmark of science.[26] "Science is the *knowledge* of consequences, and dependence of one fact upon another: by which, out of that we can presently *do*, we know how to *do* something else when we will, or the like another time; because when we *see* how any thing comes about, upon what causes, and by what manner; when the like causes come into our *power*, we *see* how to make it *produce* the effects."[27] Correct scientific method mediates between the teachings of thought and the exigencies of successful action. The idea of method suggests a relationship between thought and action in which the former is subservient—representing and acting for "action," condensing and adjusting itself to accommodate the requirements of action. Right method codifies the rules for translating thought into successful action.

Why are literal and metaphoric structures of representation so central to the argument of *Leviathan?* One factor to take into account is the nature of Hobbes's audience. Who is he trying to convince? Whose influence is he trying to counteract? The prime subverters of political order during Hobbes's revolutionary generation are the Puritans—with their rehabilitation of a purified, remote Old Testament conception of God, purged to a large extent of paganistic influences found in the New Testament.[28] The paradox lying at the foundation of Puritan theology was that this Wholly Other God was yet in intimate dialogue with individual believers, in which he counseled radical political action. Part of the rhetorical strategy of *Leviathan* is to convince the Puritans and their sympathizers—on Puritan grounds—that it is wrong to be a Puritan. Hobbes seeks to accomplish this by unraveling once and for all the theological mystery of how God is both totally distant and utterly near. From this vantage point, we can appreciate the strategic rhetorical and political uses of the concept of representation, which allows Hobbes to perform an ultimate act of demystification on Puritan theology. The capacity of being both distant and near is not a mysterious divine attribute but a human power. Through representation, a process of acting for, a human being can be distant in a physical, geographic sense and yet make his will felt in Parliament. Properly construed, what the Puritans regarded as a mysterious attribute of the Divine—which, from Hobbes's perspective, had such catastrophic political consequences in his time—could more correctly be seen as an authentic human power, enabling people to extend their mastery over the human realm to a much greater extent than would otherwise be possible. Wherever one turns in *Leviathan*, the distances that threaten man and jeopardize his aspirations toward mastery are mitigated through mechanisms of representation.

The literal doctrine of representation in which Hobbes's positivistic conception of law is grounded is a response to distance as a primary defining characteristic of the human condition. He is not alone in his perception of distance as an important qualitative feature of the newly emerging seventeenth-century environment. Pascal, Hobbes's contemporary, remarks in the *Pensées* that "the eternal silence of these infinite spaces casts me into dread." [29] Part of the reason that distance constitutes such a persuasive metaphor for the human condition for Hobbes and Pascal and for their audience is a tacit background economic assumption—namely, the possibility of abundance. Isolation, distance, space affect men's self-image in the seventeenth century because the world they are inhabiting is perceived at some level of consciousness as harboring the prospect of abundance, which drastically limits the sense of individual implication in the destiny of the collective. With proper cultivation of internal and external sources of energy, the world can be made to yield enough to satisfy individual demands without particular members of society having to devote specific attention to collective tasks and collective responsibilities. The economy will reward a constriction of the focus of consciousness to questions of individual exertion and control. Hobbesian political theory is predicated upon the assumption that a relatively narrow egoistic focus is enough to sustain society. Humans can institute and maintain society while never abandoning the perspective of the individual. The prospect of economic abundance forms a major tacit assumption of *Leviathan*, which enables its key concepts and metaphors, such as distance, representation, and law, to emerge and cohere as a persuasive family of notions.

The concept of distance functions in at least two ways in the argument of *Leviathan:* normatively and descriptively. Because abundance and distance are not yet full-fledged givens in Hobbes's environment but mainly potential features of it that need to be cultivated, there is a dynamic, dialectical relationship between the normative and descriptive elements of "distance" in *Leviathan*—with adherence to "distance" as norm making possible the emergence of "distance" as fact. Hobbes not only sees "distance" as a potential sociological and economic fact. He also views it as a necessary precondition for the process of individuation, of the formation of individual personality, to take place. His first law of nature enjoins "that everyman, ought to endeavor peace, as far as he has hope of obtaining it," or, more succinctly, "to seek peace and follow it."³⁰ In this law, Hobbes is seeking a secular, rationalist surrogate for the concept of God. The notion of peace summarizes his hermeneutical work on the concept of God—the strategic metaphysical/psychological role performed by the concept of God that becomes evident from a reading of the Old Testament. Primitive animistic religion, which is the historical alternative opposed by Biblical monotheism, posits a multiplicity of demons and deities haunting human life at every turn. This has the effect of abrogating a free, unperturbed space around human beings, thereby inhibiting any tendencies toward individuation. Biblical religion, by attempting to rationalize the set of prohibitions and commandments governing human life—excising as far as possible the element of caprice—facilitates the emergence of a protective distance between one human being and the next and thereby enables individual personality to emerge.³¹ Its strategy for accomplishing this is to posit an all-knowing, all-powerful God, who is the ultimate source of the commandments and prohibitions affecting human life and wields sanctions against recalcitrants. In Hobbes, the secular concept of the pursuit of peace replaces the theological notion of God as the epitome of that factor which creates indispensable, salutary distance between men.

In contrast to Hobbes, a dominant metaphor of our evolving postindustrial civilization is congestion, the shrinkage of space. The substitution of organizing metaphors has profound implications for political theory, particularly for the concepts of representation and law that I have been considering in this section of the chapter. It is not a notion of action at a distance (and its corollary for Hobbes of legal positivism) that will enable a secure sense of the whole to emerge out of the radically atomized parts of society. Hobbes's positivist conception of law, his equation of law with justice—"The definition of injustice is no other than the not performance of covenant. And whatsoever is not unjust is just"[32]—makes sense where the very establishment of the sovereign representative constitutes a moral/prudential victory in the face of the temptation to lone defiance and the preservation of an anomic context that a potentially abundant society offers. Where it is scarcity and not abundance that becomes an overriding concern for society, we need to move beyond formal, procedural justice to some articulation and defense of a substantive theory of justice that can form the basis of a public philosophy for the allocation of scarce resources.[33]

If we consider the other strand of argumentation that Hobbes employs to support the identification of law with justice—the argument from self-interest—the supersession of his whole frame of reference under current historical pressures becomes equally evident. Hobbes's legal positivism, and its corollary of the primacy of procedural justice and the dispensability of substantive visions of justice, might seem morally persuasive and function as the bedrock of American legal philosophy until the last third of the twentieth century because a tacit premise of economic abundance has been serving as a moral leaven on legal positivism from its inception. Individual pursuit of self-interest was compatible with the attainment of justice throughout society because the economy was rich enough to tolerate the articulation of all reasonably legitimate interests within society and to reward them if only they would agree to be bound by rules of procedural justice—by principles of fairness. A tolerable justice in a substantive sense (the long-range interests of society) would prevail simply through the determined pursuit of individual interest. Today's economic constraints are becoming such, however, that no automatic balancing mechanism can be presumed to operate in favor of long-range interests. If they are not specifically taken into account and legislated for in advance, they are sure to fail.

A crisis of law and legitimacy that developed in the great flowering of capitalism between 1945 and 1973 introduces an intricate pattern of transition to the changes that will be required to preserve the rule of law in an age of diminishing resources. The growth in technological sophistication and the expansion of society and government over the past two generations have meant that legislative mandates have had to be articulated very broadly, with vast bureaucracies remote from voter accountability charged with the task of investing a precise content into the legislative will.[34] The resultant blurring of lines of responsibility has led to a weakening of confidence in the democratic process. Paradoxically, the erosion of mechanisms of law that was symptomatic of the high tide of capitalism foreshadows further erosions of law that seem likely in an era of scarcity. The legal process serves as a brake on processes of social and economic change. Pressures for change have to be translated into legal form—into some semblance of an adversarial proceeding—before they can be accommodated by the legal process. This process itself, through its hierarchical mode of conflict resolution, represents a conservatizing influence on the development of society. During an age of scarcity, where responses to problems might have to be more immediate and direct than is currently the case—and where supervision of results might have to be more continuous and intense than the normal operations of the judicial process would allow—we may find a further downgrading of the role of law in the liberal political culture of the West.

In order to relate to the new world in which we are all just beginning to live, political philosophy might have to begin, as Hobbes began in *Leviathan*, with an exploration of the organizing myths and metaphors that register our current sense of reality. Instead of grappling with infinite distance and space and resorting to a scheme of representation and a positivistic conception of law to overcome the yawning distances affecting human life, we shall have to confront the shrinkage of space and the closing of distances. We shall need to develop schemata stressing political immediacy, rather than displacement—organic involvement with others, rather than atomistic pursuit of self. In such a metaphysical seedbed, perhaps the concept of law itself will come to be redesigned to play a more secondary role in the organization of society. It might very well be that the radical nominalism upon which Hobbes's psychological and political concepts are built is itself a historically conditioned phenomenon.[35] Making will central to one's understanding of human life, and emphasizing the continual mobilization of energies of will in response to the multifarious projects of living, might be functionally related to an expanding economy. A contracting economy might not be able to afford such a luxury and might have to evolve a more realist metaphysics. What the role of law becomes in such a realist metaphysics appears as one of the great, vexing questions confronting theorists of a society of scarcity.

By way of applying my theoretical discussion of the altered role of the concept of law in a society of scarcity, I will focus briefly on the dominant legal institution in American society—the Supreme Court—

and consider the transformations that it is likely to experience under conditions of scarcity. The ongoing debate in the legal community between judicial activists and judicial conservatives might be superseded in an age of scarcity. With resources shrinking, the locus of authority in American society might shift to experts, claiming on the basis of mastery of various technical fields to know how to maximize wealth and the distribution of whatever resources are in fact available. The Supreme Court, whose pretensions to authority rest upon mastery of nontechnological legal materials and traditions, would be thrust into the role of acquiescing in whatever the experts decided. Even if arbiters were needed to judge between conflicting recommendations of the experts, the role of the Court as mediator between these opposing views might be suspect because of the traditionalist basis of its claim to authority.

Max Weber spoke of the evolution of Western society as proceeding from charismatic rule to the routinization of charisma exemplified by bureaucracy. It might very well be that in an era of scarcity we will come to draw a distinction between two different sorts of bureaucracies: the routinized bureaucracies that Weber spoke about and the re-charismatized bureaucracies that might become the focus of much public expectation and concern during a time of scarcity. Routinized bureaucracies function well when the problems of the present seem to emerge in a straight line from the problems and solutions of the past. Where a large-scale discontinuity takes place, such as the one ushered in by an age of scarcity, it might be that only re-charismatized bureaucracies—those held to have abundant powers of knowledge, insight, and renewal, which would enable them to grapple successfully with the unprecedented problems coming to the fore—could serve as the focus of public loyalty and confidence.[36]

Law becomes a significant agency for social amelioration and control when routinized bureaucracies predominate. In an era of intense boundary management,[37] such as that connoted by the supremacy of routinized organizations, the mechanism of law is needed to adjudicate conflicts between competing and overlapping bureaucracies and to protect individuals against too-rampant incursions into their rights. In an age where overriding problems of survival and security lead to a re-charismatization of bureaucracy, the role of law as a supervisory adjunct of such structures might be correspondingly diminished.

In the classic period of American industrial expansion, from the middle to the late nineteenth century (and during the first third of the twentieth century, as well), the Court played a passive role, giving free rein to the inherent dynamic of the private realm. Ironically, in an age of scarcity the Court might again be passive, allowing the expanding imperatives of a re-charismatized public realm to be played out to the full.

The prospect of an age of scarcity provides us with an unusual organizing perspective on the history of the Supreme Court. The period in the twentieth century when it most actively promoted civil liberties corresponds to the time when economic growth could be taken for granted and when the narrow supervisory problems of boundary management between various governmental and private bureaucracies and the protection of individual rights against bureaucracy could be safely left to the Court. From the perspective afforded by hindsight during an era of increasing scarcity, it appears that the role of the Court, from the inception of American history, has been much more continuous than those who have examined its history from the perspective of 1937[38] or the mid-1960s have led us to believe. Even during the period of its greatest activism in civil liberties—from the late 1930s to the late 1960s (with periods of quiescence in between)[39]— the Supreme Court was performing in a much more peripheral role in relation to American society and government than its vociferous defenders at the time would have us believe. During this activist period (an age of great economic expansion in American history), the Court helped work out the implications of abundance in ways that were more fully in consonance with the imperatives of routinized bureaucratic organization than would have been the case without its intervention. The Supreme Court (and the legal process generally during this time) enabled the vast bureaucracies of American society to function more smoothly, containing conflict between them. Furthermore, and most important from the perspective of the Court's vaunted role as the promoter of civil liberties, it helped to enfranchise previously disadvantaged groups within American society. The Supreme Court thus extended the reach and scope of American bureaucratic organization and provided it with more personnel who could be usefully employed in its ever-expanding networks. Where the means of bureaucracy (a rigid and self-serving interpretation of the rules) got in the way of the ends of bureaucracy (the expansion of a mode of governance over more and more people and things), the Court in its adjunct role as supervisor of bureaucracy intervened to bring means and ends into closer alignment. Through this structuralist reading of the role of the

Supreme Court in American history that I am propounding, we are enabled to perceive an underlying continuity of passivity defining its function in American history, which persists beneath the more superficial fluctuations between "activism" and "passivity."

From my historical perspective, the most creative period in the Supreme Court's history would be at its inception. During the tenure of Chief Justice John Marshall, the Court did not merely serve as the adjunct of bureaucracy in the senses described above but actually furnished American bureaucracy itself with the legal and constitutional tools that enabled it to expand to its twentieth-century proportions. The extending and enabling function that the Court performed for the objects of American bureaucracy after 1937 it also performed for American bureaucracy itself at the turn of the nineteenth century.

Our excursus into the history of the Supreme Court—and our discussion of the fate of the Court and of the role of law generally in an age of scarcity—should warn us to be especially mindful of hidden premises concerning scarcity and abundance in discussions and critiques of contemporary liberal politics. One surprising area where not enough attention has been paid to the roles of abundance and scarcity in influencing and shaping argument is in the critique of the pluralist model of politics (and its aftermath) that originated in the 1960s.[40]

Consider, for example, Steven Lukes's three-dimensional delineation of power,[41] and why it misfires when applied to American society and politics. In contrast to Robert Dahl and Peter Bachrach, Lukes offers a view of power that proposes to deal with latent as well as observable conflict, and with real and not merely subjectively defined interests. The burden of Lukes's neo-Marxist critique of liberal society is that such a society's typical ways of conducting political business work to repress certain conflicts rather than allowing them to become overt and to encourage certain strata of the population to lose track of their real interests and to subjectively define those interests so as to enhance the power of the already powerful within society.

However, in order for Lukes's radical critique of liberal society to work, he must presuppose the economic abundance that is a key factor in enabling liberalism's masked deployment of power to succeed. The very possibility of a gap between observable and latent conflict—and between subjective interests and real interests—seems to be predicated upon the existence of certain objective economic conditions (such as an expanding economy) that prevent people from identifying and acting upon their real interests and thus renders social conflict latent. Lukes's argument appears to be conditioned by the same set of political and economic factors that were crucial in forming the theories that he criticizes. If Dahl's (and even Bachrach's) frameworks of analysis work to reinforce the very values of liberal society that they claim to be studying dispassionately, Lukes's critique of these writers, and of liberal society, would also be impossible without presupposing the continuation of key background economic factors—expansion and abundance—that enabled liberal society to give rise to the distorted replication found in their theories. A central irony that emerges in confronting Lukes is that liberalism, in masking the exercise of power, and his radical view, which tries to expose the most insidious manifestations of liberalism's masking function, both presuppose the same thing—an economy of abundance.[42]

What might occur in an age of scarcity is more graphically illuminated by Machiavelli's notion of *opportunità* than by Lukes's vocabulary of latent versus observable conflict and objectively versus subjectively defined interests. Lukes's radicalism presupposes the continuation of a key background assumption that he shares with those views that he criticizes—namely, the prospect of continued economic growth. A radicalizing of mass consciousness, however, will not occur in a context of elitist theoretical innovation unmediated by actual changes in the world. Machiavelli, with his highly paradoxical notion of *opportunità*, might have been the first modern theorist to be aware of the structural detour that needs to be taken to close the gap between consciousness and action. Here is the relevant passage from *The Prince*:

> And when we come to examine their actions and lives, they do not seem to have had from fortune anything other than opportunity. Fortune, as it were, provided the matter but they gave it its form; without opportunity their prowess would have been extinguished, and without such prowess the opportunity would have come in vain.
>
> Thus for the Israelites to be ready to follow Moses, in order to escape from servitude, it was necessary for him to find them, in Egypt, enslaved and oppressed by the Egyptians. For Romulus to become king of Rome and founder of his country, he had to have left Alba and been exposed to die when he was born. Cyrus needed to find the Persians rebellious against the empire of the Medes, and the Medes grown soft and effeminate through the long years of peace. Theseus could not have demonstrated his prowess had he not found the Athenians dispersed. The oppor-

tunities given them enabled these men to succeed, and their own exceptional prowess enabled them to seize their opportunities; in consequence their countries were renowned and enjoyed great prosperity.[43]

Machiavelli's highly paradoxical notion of opportunity—identifying it with danger and adversity—constitutes a theoretical refinement over Lukes's approach in terms of achieving a radical politics in an age of scarcity. With the shrinkage of the resource base of society, the masses will know on a visceral level what radically inclined theorists have been telling them for some time, namely, that the theoretical priorities of liberalism—for example, its concern with "political obligation" over "justice"; its emphasis on representative as opposed to participatory political structures—could seem persuasive and efficacious only in a context of economic abundance, and are unmasked as spurious ideological camouflages when there are not enough economic "crumbs" to share with the less-well-off members of society. The very extremity of our situation in a climate of scarcity constitutes a veiled opportunity for bringing political action into harmony with vanguard political consciousness, by facilitating, through the spreading of participatory networks, a fundamental reordering of power relations within society.

13 • Hobbes's Metaphysics, Participation, and Scarcity

There is a subversive underside to Hobbesian thought, which carries over to liberalism as well, that is in tension with the understandings of politics, representation, and the priority assigned to political obligation that we have been examining in this part of the book. The liberal articulation of the nature of politics as an external, social phenomenon—the stress laid on mechanisms of representation in both theory and practice—and the priority assigned to the concept of political obligation over justice all lead to a rejection of participation as a principal organizing category for responding to human needs in politics. However, certain key metaphysical elements upon which liberalism has been historically grounded since the time of Hobbes point to "participation" as an appropriate complement to the tendencies implicit in these metaphysical ideas. It is to an exploration of these tensions within liberalism that we now turn.

Hobbes's rooting of the very possibility of rational argument in the existence of authority—and the resolution of the metaphysical problem of where the theorizing activity exhibited in *Leviathan* comes from, and how it can be justified, discussed in Chapter 8—issues forth in the thesis of what we might call "power as rationality." If the ultimate foundation for the exercise of human reason rests upon what, from an absolutist philosophical perspective, can only appear as an arbitrary allocation of words and their significations, then the paradox emerges that instead of "power" and "rationality" being antithetical concepts, as our conventional discourse would have it, power emerges as the distinct form of human rationality—the very syntax, as it were—through which rationality gets expressed. Hobbes's setting forth of the relationship between reason and political authority leads to an understanding of human nature as being radically discontinuous, with the conceptual frameworks employed for interpretation having epistemological priority over the events, ideas, feelings, volitions, and so on being interpreted. We Are What We Choose to Read Ourselves to Be might serve as the motto for the understanding of human nature implicit in Hobbes's theorizing of the foundations of reason. This understanding of human nature establishes the basis for a reversal of our ordinary grasp of the nature of power. Instead of power being viewed as an irrationalist intrusion into a rationally connecting network of understandings and relationships (the exertion of power as overturning norms of involvement and relationship between individuals and between nations), power is seen from this perspective as a dominant mode for establishing continuity itself. According to this view, it is only through the exertion of power that we have an enduring presence even to ourselves.

The idea of power as the distinct mode of human rationality carries momentous consequences for the theory and practice of political participation. The greatest ontological burden that human beings shoulder, according to the subversive underside of liberalism and the overt doctrine of Platonism, is that it is power which holds us together—that gives us our recognizable human identity. The only thing that can redeem this insight, and confer a certain amount of grace on human living, is to share this insight with others in participatory frameworks. Participation, as it were, takes the sting out of being human.

The metaphysics of representation needs to be sharply distinguished from the metaphysics of participation. The concept of representation as historically justified and implemented in liberal societies rests upon an understanding of power that sees it as opposed to rationality. Beneficiaries of the status quo view power as an irrational intrusion by political actors bent upon upsetting previously stable arrangements in order to enhance their individual positions. Where power is seen as contrasting with rationality, the problem of co-optation looms as insurmountable. All situations of stability in politics, where rationality is prevailing against power, are also occasions in which the already strong (or, from James Madison's perspective in Federalist Number Ten, the debtor class aspiring to a position of political strength comparable to its numerical majority) might be using current stability as a "cover" to further augment their power positions. The problem described by Madison in Federalist Number Ten of achieving a genuine, as opposed to a spurious, stability between contending forces that would not be upset by the co-optative strategies of the parties remains insurmountable within the inherited framework of liberal ideas that he is working with.

The solution to the Madisonian dilemma of establishing power arrangements within society that do not succumb to the degenerative, destabilizing tendencies present in what he takes to be all historically known examples of structured relationships of power is, in the first instance, to recognize that there is a conceptual alternative to the power-rationality dichotomy. It is possible to conceptualize power so that the operative contrasting term is not rationality, but discontinuity. Under the auspices of this revised conceptualization, the exercise of power ceases to be a zero-sum game and becomes instead a universal enterprise in which one person's access to the experience of full being does not require the exclusion or suppression of others but is, rather, predicated upon their more intense involvement.[1] In order for a theory of political participation to reach its highest level of coherence, it must take the offensive on the issue of co-optation and show how the pervasiveness of this problem is locked into the conceptual net of liberalism. The false consciousness about power that I suggested earlier was built into the warp and woof of classic formulations of liberal theory leads to a sealing off of the connotations of power so that the operative contrast is between power and rationality. With liberal terminology and strategies of argument diminishing the visibility of the operations of power, the extent to which it is manifested internally in relation to the self will obviously be lost sight of, and the efficaciousness of the contrasting term, discontinuity, will be nowhere apparent. Once the concept of power is disentangled from the liberal conceptual net, the possibility of theoretically articulating—and realizing in practice—a sum-sum concept of power that would not be vulnerable to the degenerative dynamic of co-optation becomes possible for the first time.

Carole Pateman's formulation of the whole participation issue in her classic work, *Participation and Democratic Theory*, might be skewed in such a way as to make it irrelevant for a society of scarcity.[2] Pateman's stress on personal efficacy as a facilitator and extender of participation presupposes a society in which large bureaucratic structures predominate and where increased involvement in decision-making processes by the masses would foster a sense of efficacy and serve as an impetus to increased political participation. What happens when, in a contracting economy, large-scale industrial bureaucratic structures begin to decrease and opportunities for forging Pateman's empirical link between efficacy and participation also correspondingly diminish? In a situation of economic helplessness and social immobility, the external structures in Pateman's scheme conferring a sense of efficacy leading to increased participation also decline. Participation, then, as a political value would appear to lose all relevance with the supersession of the prospect of an affluent society.

It seems, then, that precisely at the moment when people are most in need of the restoration of a sense of self-worth and personal efficacy—in an environment of scarcity—Pateman's theory breaks down. At this point we shall need a rehabilitation of the classic priorities of Platonic theory, where the stress falls on participation itself as filling a metaphysical void. To rearticulate the coherence and integrity of the self in a radically transformed external environment, we might need to design new forums in which involvement with others can take place. Not efficacy as leading to participation, but participation itself as leading to a sense of efficacy and self-worth—this is the Platonic route that we shall need to retraverse in an age of scarcity.

In an age of scarcity, the process and method of participation would not only have to be constantly reinvoked to ward off the specter of co-optation and the emergence of re-charismatized bureaucracies but also to ward off an even more dangerous possibility—that human beings might cease to be history-making creatures altogether. With the entrenchment of worldwide resource scarcities, we might see the path described by the trajectory of the modernization process during the nineteenth and twentieth centuries move the other way. Instead of modernization being equivalent to establishing the desiderata of a spatial politics, it will become synonymous, in an age of scarcity, with the successful negotiation of the transition from a spatial to a temporal politics entirely unrelated to prospects of economic growth. Not reindustrialization—but deindustrialization—and the establishment of stable patterns of living centered around a diminished resource base of society might become the watchwords of the day.

In such a context of deceleration of life-styles to accord with a scaling down of basic resources, participation might loom as important to ward off a new danger emerging on the horizon. What might be at stake is nothing less than the preservation of that residuum of human identity that would allow human beings to continue to function as history-making creatures even in an age of scarcity. Western man has been a history-making creature since the Renaissance because the conquering of external worlds—the presence of an apparently unlimited field of action—has ensured that the distance between who man is (what he perceives himself to be from moment to moment) and what he does to live out his life in time would continue to widen, thereby goading man to fashion ever-more grandiose structures in the world, to forge a permanent coincidence between his being and his doing.

With the shrinking of an external sphere of action in an age of stable scarcity, the essential tension between being and doing that forms the precondition of human beings' identity as history-making creatures might collapse. In an important sense, if human beings do not make history, they no longer have a history. One can argue that human beings can understand only what they themselves have fashioned.[3] The generation of the tension between being and doing that is essential for human beings to function as history-making (and therefore also as historically reflecting) creatures might be sapped by an external environment of scarcity. Human beings would be poised on the threshold of returning to a state of metaphysical thinghood and losing their identity once and for all. In order to ward off the prospect of what, from our current perspective, must appear as a horrible mutation in human identity and consciousness—signaling nothing less than the end of human beings, as well as the supersession of history—the creation of participatory networks throughout society will be especially crucial. Creating the infrastructure of a temporal politics would help foster the notion that human beings could go on doing, investing their energies in creative ways, even where the prospects of material advance had been removed. A participatory praxis would help lend substance to the notion of a human world outside a context of material investment and technological improvement. We could perhaps lay claim to our humanity just by virtue of willing it into existence through participatory involvements with others, divorced from concerted exploitative interaction with the world.

14 • Justification of Basic Premises in Plato and Hobbes

Even though Plato's political philosophy and my decoding of the subversive underside of Hobbes's thought point toward participation as the appropriate supreme political value, other factors coexisting with these tendencies of thought introduce elements of tension that lead Plato and Hobbes to resolve the problem of justification in an ironic way. The thesis of power as the distinct form of human rationality that is suggested by Plato's understanding of the nature of the political is obscured to some extent by his taking a stand in overt opposition to Thrasymachus. With regard to Hobbes, even though the thesis of "power as rationality" can be seen as embedded in his rooting of rational argument in the existence of authority, this thesis is obscured by Hobbes's narrow conception of the political and his stress on representation as opposed to participation. I shall sketch three mutually exclusive approaches adopted by Plato and Hobbes with regard to the challenge of justification.

If, as I argue in Chapter 8, a large proportion of Plato's considered theory of justice is taken from Thrasymachus—with the major point of difference between them revolving around the question of whether there is a skeptical response to skepticism that can yet yield some positive content concerning justice—then it becomes intensely revealing of Plato's own position concerning justice to be able to point to three mutually exclusive attitudes toward it present in Thrasymachus's formulation of his position. The most straightforward approach to the status of justice is contained in Thrasymachus's first formulation of his own position, when he says that " 'just' or 'right' means nothing but what is to the interest of the stronger party."[1] This suggests a conception of justice as a conspiracy of the strong against the weak. Overtaking the vocabulary of justice to promote their own interests provides the already powerful with the shortest route for entrenching those interests. Thrasymachus's formulation implies an understanding of morality, construed as the institution of a fundamental system of restraints on the untrammeled exercise of human impulses, as resting upon the freezing of the status quo in favor of the ascendant class's interest(s).

A second foundation for morality and justice is suggested by Thrasymachus's statement later on in *The Republic* that "when people denounce injustice, it is because they are afraid of suffering wrong, not of doing it."[2] The emphasis on "suffering wrong" suggests the abandonment of the conspiracy view altogether in favor of an ineradicable human reality—a universal vulnerability outside a framework of external, coordinated control of human interaction to the aggressive exploits of others. Thrasymachus's formulation of the basis of justice in the passage just cited does not seem that far removed from the more avowedly contractarian understanding of the nature of justice advanced a little later in the dialogue by Glaucon and Adeimantus:

> That is what right and justice is and how it comes into existence; it stands half-way between the best thing of all—to do wrong with impunity—and the worst, which is to suffer wrong without the power to retaliate. So justice is accepted as a compromise, and valued, not as good in itself, but for lack of power to do wrong; no man worthy of the name, who had that power, would ever enter into such a compact with anyone; he would be mad if he did.[3]

A third contradictory understanding of the foundations of justice and morality is suggested by the following passage:

> Do you think the unjust are positively superior in character and intelligence, Thrasymachus?
> Yes, if they are the sort that can carry injustice to perfection and make themselves masters of whole cities and nations. Perhaps you think I was talking of pickpockets. There is profit even

in that trade, if you can escape detection; but it doesn't come to
much as compared with the gains I was describing.[4]

These words suggest that morality and justice represent a conspiracy by the weak against the strong. The unjust, left to their own
devices, have characters and intelligences powerful enough to "carry
injustice to perfection and make themselves masters of whole cities
and nations." What holds them in check, keeping the native power of
the unjust from getting expressed to the full, are the rules of justice,
which therefore from this perspective might be viewed as a conspiracy
wrought by the weak against the strong to create a society that will be
safe for themselves.

This ironic stance toward the foundations of justice has parallels in Hobbes. The most straightforward understanding of what he
perceives those foundations to be would link them with the basic concepts of his version of social-contract theory—of "the war of all against
all," of a universal human vulnerability—that is present in the state-
of-nature society before the institution of political obligation and the
rules of justice. There are intimations within Hobbes's political philosophy, however, of the other two contradictory understandings of
the foundations of justice that we have discussed in Plato—of justice as a conspiracy engaged in by the strong against the weak and of
justice as a conspiracy wrought by the weak against the strong.

With regard to the first conspiratorial view of justice, Hobbes is
confronted with a dilemma in his adaptation of what he takes to be
scientific method to politics. One of the two dominant scientific methods he follows in pursuing a scientific approach to political questions
is a deductive, geometric one that involves working out the implications and interconnections of his basic axioms. However, the status
of these principles themselves is not resolved by geometric method.
Hobbes is therefore faced with the problem of justifying his basic axioms and proving them worthy of the privileged epistemological status
they enjoy within his system.

There are at least two references in *Leviathan* that can be construed as responses to this basic question. One occurs near the end of
the introduction, where Hobbes says that

he that is to govern a whole nation, must read in himself, not
this or that particular man; but mankind: which though it be hard
to do, harder than to learn any language or science; yet when I

shall have set down my own reading orderly, and perspicuously, the pains left another, will be only to consider, if he also find not the same in himself. For this kind of doctrine admitteth no other demonstration.[5]

Another possible attempt to resolve the basic question concerning the status of the initial axioms of *Leviathan* can be found in Hobbes's discussion of the role of universities.

> For seeing the Universities are the fountains of civil and moral doctrine, from where the preachers, and the gentry, drawing such water as they find, use to sprinkle the same (both from the pulpit and in their conversation), upon the people, there ought certainly to be great care taken, to have it pure, both from the venom of heathen politicians, and the incantation of deceiving spirits. And by that means the most men, knowing their duties, will be the less subject to serve the ambition of a few discontented persons, in their purposes against the state; and be the less grieved with the contributions necessary for their peace, and defence; and the governors themselves have the less cause, to maintain at the common charge any greater army, than is necessary to make good the public liberty, against the invasions and encroachments of foreign enemies.[6]

The suggestion contained in these two passages is that the basic axioms concerning man and society leading to the promulgation of the rules of justice in Hobbesian society, if they do not exactly represent a conspiracy perpetrated by the strong against the weak, at least constitute an assertion of power by the strong against the weak. In the end, Hobbes seems to recognize, you either evoke intuitive acknowledgment of your basic principles or you control the seats of learning disseminating the first principles of your society. There is no third practical alternative.

A third contradictory approach to the problem of justification can be inferred from Hobbes's nominalism and his conception of the role of intellectuals within society. Since "there is nothing in the world universal but names; for the things named are every one of them individual and singular" and "truth consisteth in the right ordering of names in our affirmations," inquiry after truth (and the propounding of truth) will always have to remain a discursive activity. The articulation of truth involves the systematic manipulation of names and is therefore always at least at one remove from "reality." One major function of the intellectuals within society, as the earlier passage concerning universities makes clear, is to be the formulators and preservers of the traditions of rational discourse and to communicate them to the opinion makers within society in such a way that they percolate downward and become the settled opinions of the masses. It is also true that Hobbes would like to see his civil teaching contained in *Leviathan* form the basis for the organization of an actual society. Like Plato, he harbors ambitions for the yoking of philosophy with power. But the very conception of philosophical activity as involving the nominalistic tasks described above already introduces a conservatizing influence on the role of philosophers within society. With the imposition, sorting out, and systematizing of names constituting the major burden of their theoretical role, one might say that they bear a defensive, reactive relation to reality. Their vocation has been defined in such a way that it subsists on a secondary level of classification and reflection, rather than on a primary level of intervention and action.[7] This set of implications of Hobbes's nominalism is politically disarming. Intellectuals, as the codifiers of names, are likely to become the permanent apologists—instead of the permanent revolutionaries—of society. This understanding of their role forms the counterpart to the Platonic "conspiracy of the weak against the strong."

15 · Conversation: The Ethics of Participation

The ethics informing the activity of participation has been nowhere better captured than in the following famous description by Michael Oakeshott of the nature of conversation:

> In a conversation the participants are not engaged in an inquiry or a debate; there is no "truth" to be discovered, no proposition to be proved, no conclusion sought. They are not concerned to inform, to persuade, or to refute one another, and therefore the cogency of their utterances does not depend upon their all speaking in the same idiom; they may differ without disagreeing. Of course, a conversation may have passages of argument and a speaker is not forbidden to be demonstrative; but reasoning is neither sovereign nor alone, and the conversation itself does not compose an argument. A girl, in order to escape a conclusion, may utter what appears to be an outrageously irrelevant remark, but what in fact she is doing is turning an argument she finds tiresome into a conversation she is more at home in. In conversation, "facts" appear only to be resolved once more into the possibilities from which they were made; "certainties" are shown to be combustible, not by being brought in contact with other "certainties" or with doubts, but by being kindled by the presence of ideas of another order; approximations are revealed between notions normally remote from one another. Thoughts of different species take wing and play round one another, responding to each other's movements and provoking one another to fresh exertions. Nobody asks where they have come from or on what authority they are present; nobody cares

what will become of them when they have played their part. There
is no symposiarch or arbiter; not even a doorkeeper to examine
credentials. Every entrant is taken at its face-value and everything
is permitted which can get itself accepted into the flow of speculation. And voices which speak in conversation do not compose a
hierarchy. Conversation is not an enterprise designed to yield an
extrinsic profit, a contest where a winner gets a prize, nor is it an
activity of exegesis; it is an unrehearsed intellectual adventure. It
is with conversation as with gambling, its significance lies neither
in winning nor in losing, but in wagering. Properly speaking, it
is impossible in the absence of a diversity of voices: in it different
universes of discourse meet, acknowledge each other and enjoy
an oblique relationship which neither requires nor forecasts their
being assimilated to one another.[1]

Conversation, in Oakeshott's sense, can be viewed as the culmi-
nation of the traditions of modernity. The project of modernity can, I
think, be most succinctly arrived at by way of exegesis of one of the
most famous prophetic passages in the Bible. Isaiah, speaking of the
Messianic age, describes it as one in which "the wolf shall dwell with
the lamb, and the leopard shall lie down with the kid; and the calf
and the young lion and the fatling together; and a little child shall lead
them. And the cow and the bear shall feed; their young ones shall
lie down together; and the lion shall eat straw like the ox."[2] Piercing
beyond the literal, obviously pacific intentions of this passage, one
might say that it envisages the Messianic age as one in which the historicization of nature shall have taken place. Human beings will no
longer experience a dichotomy between "history" and "nature"—between what they do and make and an external order that is set over
and above them and whose outline and limits are fixed in advance. In
the Messianic age, "nature" itself shall evolve from being a fixed category to becoming a fluid category whose very mainsprings of behavior
shall be amenable to human design and control: "The wolf shall dwell
with the lamb . . . and a little child shall lead them."

Hovering at the interface between "nature" and "history" is the
whole phenomenon of war and violence, which from earliest times
has posed an obdurate problem of classification. Is physical conflict
the result of evil designs among people, representing a perversion of
the constructive tasks of history, or are violence and war events that
can be more accurately subsumed under the natural order, captured
by such metaphors as an overflowing river and an ever-recurring cycli-

cal flow of time? Are violence and war species of misconceived history or inevitable natural occurrences before which historical intervention remains helpless? The true triumph of history over nature therefore cannot take place until war itself has been overcome, wrenched from "nature" and challenged, disciplined, and defeated by "history." This is why Isaiah includes in his vision of the Messianic age an image of the abolition of war—the authentic triumph of history over nature: "nation shall not lift up sword against nation, neither shall they learn war any more."[3]

I do not think that it is farfetched to view the intellectual and scientific achievements of the nineteenth and twentieth centuries as approximating to this interpretation of Isaiah's vision of the Messianic age as representing the metamorphosis of "nature" into "history." Working in the shadow of Marx and Freud, contemporary social science has sought to remove all traces of "reified external structure" from its understanding of human beings and society and to see in their place deposits of previous human efforts that in the course of time assume an independent, alienating presence. The implicit message of Marx and Freud is that what has been made by human beings can be changed by them. Our psychological and social ontologies need only consist of ourselves and the provisional structures that we have fashioned in the course of engaging in multiple relationships with others and with ourselves. All the rest is myth and ideology that needs to be demystified and subverted.

Some of the most outstanding achievements of modern physical science, from quantum physics to molecular biology, also exemplify this larger theme of the relativization and historicization of nature—extending the empire of "history" to transform our understanding of "nature."

The appropriate vocabulary for articulating our sense of being in an age in which both external and human nature are in the process of being thoroughly historicized is a participationist one suffused with the understandings of Oakeshott's "conversation." One orients oneself in a universe thoroughly impregnated by historical categories by relating to others in a participatory manner and learning to converse in Oakeshott's sense—by recognizing the provisionalness, one might almost say the playfulness, of one's intellectual constructs. The world and ourselves are both in the process of creation. There is no basis for sanctifying one perspective above the rest and imputing to it a higher reality.

Our nature is such that at the same time that new opportunities for gaining freedom and autonomy are becoming available to us in the age of the historicization of nature, the prospects of destruction—and, more poignantly, of self-destruction—are also correspondingly increasing. If the transformation of nature into history heralded by advancing physical and social science seems to broaden our options almost limitlessly, the entrenchment of an era of scarcity appears to curtail them drastically, beyond recognition. The promise that the creation of a participatory society governed by the ethics of conversation has to offer is that, if we pursue it, we shall remain in self-conscious confrontation with our humanity, regardless of the extraordinary vicissitudes of historical fortune.

•

NOTES, BIBLIOGRAPHY, AND INDEX

Notes

Preface

1. The denial of the law of excluded middle is not contradictory. It does not constitute a violation of the law of contradiction.

Chapter 1

1. Thomas Nagel, *The View from Nowhere* (Oxford: Oxford University Press, 1986), 25.

2. Hannah Arendt, *The Origins of Totalitarianism* (New York: Harcourt, Brace, 1951); J. L. Talmon, *The Origins of Totalitarian Democracy* (London: Secker and Warburg, 1952).

3. Joseph R. Levenson, *Confucian China and Its Modern Fate*, 3 vols. (Berkeley: University of California Press, 1958–65).

4. When I speak about democratic tradition superseding such traditionalistic alternatives as communism, I am using the terms "tradition" and "traditionalism" to denote collective historical entities ("democracy" and "communism" respectively) and do not intend to prejudge the question of whether "tradition" itself can be broken down to disclose a multiplicity of traditionalistic acts of acceptance. I answer this question in the affirmative in Chapter 3.

5. Charles Taylor, *Sources of the Self: The Making of the Modern Identity* (Cambridge, Mass.: Harvard University Press, 1989), 159–76.

6. Seyla Benhabib, "Lyotard, Democracy, and Difference: Reflections on Rationality, Democracy, and Postmodernism." Paper presented at the 1992 annual meeting of the American Political Science Association, Chicago, Illinois, September 3–6, 1992.

7. Claus Offe, "Capitalism by Democratic Design? Democratic Theory Facing the Triple Transition in East Central Europe," *Social Research* 58 (1991): 864–92.

8. Peter Bachrach and Aryeh Botwinick, *Power and Empowerment: A Radical Theory of Participatory Democracy* (Philadelphia: Temple University Press, 1992).

9. Offe, "Capitalism by Democratic Design?" 872; cited in Benhabib, "Lyotard, Democracy, and Difference," 3.

10. William Pfaff argues that historical factors, such as Woodrow Wilson's intervention in the immediate aftermath of World War I, are responsible for a conceptually distinct notion of citizenship emerging in eastern Europe and the Balkan states from what prevailed elsewhere in Europe and North America. Outside of eastern Europe and the Balkans, the concept of citizenship had undergone a long evolution from the earliest forms of sociopolitical organization, which were pastoral and agricultural settlements, until the emergence of the modern nation state in the nineteenth century. Therefore, the idea of a unique people occupying a specific territory was only one strand in a complex and differentiated notion of citizenship. In eastern Europe and the Bal-

kans, on the other hand, where states and hence "citizens" were deliberately fashioned after World War I, citizenship was—and remains—much more emphatically ethnic and therefore exclusive in character. "It cannot be acquired in any way except by having been born into it—it is compromised if equal standing is accorded other nationalities within a country's borders." (William Pfaff, "The Absence of Empire," *New Yorker* 68 (August 10, 1992): 59–69. The quotation occurs at page 68.)

Pfaff's argument suggests that modifying this ethnically grounded concept of citizenship will be an uphill battle. Paradoxically, it might be the lesson imbibed from waging democratic revolution and enacting the participatory roles in the workplace suggested in the text that might in the course of time wean denizens of eastern Europe and the Balkans away from the excesses of ethnic overidentification that have been nurtured by their history.

11. Stanley Hoffmann, "Delusions of World Order," *New York Review of Books* 39 (April 9, 1992): 37–43, at page 38.

12. Hoffmann, "Delusions of World Order," 41.

13. Robert Reich's views are cited in Thomas L. Friedman, "As Some Nations Build, the Past Devours Others," *New York Times,* July 12, 1992, 4-1. The distinction between "McWorld" and "Jihad" is found in Benjamin R. Barber, "Jihad vs. McWorld," *Atlantic Monthly* 269 (March 1992): 53–65. I am indebted to Bruce Jennings for calling my attention to both articles.

14. Barber, "Jihad vs. McWorld," 65.

15. Ernesto Laclau, "Interview," *Strategies* 1 (Fall 1988): 25.

16. Richard J. Bernstein, "Fred Dallmayr's Critique of Habermas," *Political Theory* 16 (1988): 583.

17. Claude Lefort, *Democracy and Political Theory,* trans. David Macey (Minneapolis: University of Minnesota Press, 1988), 17–19; cited in Fred Dallmayr, "Post-Metaphysics and Democracy." Paper delivered at the 1990 Annual Meeting of the American Political Science Association, San Francisco, August 30–September 2, 1990, 20.

18. Dallmayr, "Post-Metaphysics and Democracy," 22.

19. Lefort, cited in Dallmayr, "Post-Metaphysics and Democracy," 24.

20. Charles Taylor, "Legitimation Crisis?" in Charles Taylor, *Philosophy and the Human Sciences: Philosophical Papers 2* (Cambridge: Cambridge University Press, 1985), 288.

21. Mickey Kaus, "For a New Equality," *New Republic,* May 7, 1990, 20.

22. Compare Bachrach and Botwinick, *Power and Empowerment.*

23. Laclau, "Interview," 13.

24. Cited in Bradley J. MacDonald, "Toward a Redemption of Politics: An Introduction to the Political Theory of Ernesto Laclau," *Strategies* 1 (Fall 1988): 8.

25. Laclau, "Interview," 25.

26. Ibid., 24.

27. Ibid., 25.

28. Cited in Patrick Riley, "The Voice of Michael Oakeshott in the Conversation of Mankind," *Political Theory* 19 (1991): 335; emphasis in original.

Chapter 2

1. W.V.O. Quine, *The Ways of Paradox and Other Essays* (New York: Random House, 1966), 8.

2. Benson Mates, *Skeptical Essays* (Chicago: University of Chicago Press, 1981), 16.

3. John M. Cooper, *Reason and Human Good in Aristotle* (Cambridge, Mass.: Harvard University Press, 1975), 51; cited in Alasdair MacIntyre, *Whose Justice? Which Rationality?* (Notre Dame, Ind.: University of Notre Dame Press, 1988), 138.

4. MacIntyre, *Justice,* 139.

5. In the case of (extreme) skepticism, what I am calling the conclusion might more appropriately be labeled the continuation of the argument.

6. Stanley Fish, *Self-Consuming Artifacts: The Experience of Seventeenth-Century Literature* (Berkeley: University of California Press, 1972).

7. Fred Dallmayr, "Habermas and Rationality," *Political Theory* 16 (1988): 553–79.

8. Ibid., 559.

9. The distinctions in all three cases are rather presupposed by the content of both halves introduced by the various distinctions. This will be true mutatis mutandis for all other manifestations of this dilemma that I am considering in this chapter.

10. Richard J. Bernstein, "Fred Dallmayr's Critique of Habermas," *Political Theory* 16 (1988): 580–93.

11. Ibid., 583.

12. Thomas Nagel, *The View from Nowhere* (Oxford: Oxford University Press, 1986).

13. I have pursued the implications of enactment, tacit knowledge, and dialectical-historical approaches to issues of skepticism in *Skepticism and Political Participation* (Philadelphia: Temple University Press, 1990), chapters 3–6.

14. W.V.O. Quine, *Ontological Relativity and Other Essays* (New York: Columbia University Press, 1969), 26–68.

15. Donald Davidson, *Inquiries into Truth and Interpretation* (Oxford: Clarendon Press, 1984), 183–98.

Chapter 3

1. Thomas Nagel, *The View from Nowhere* (Oxford: Oxford University Press, 1986).

2. Thomas Nagel, "Moral Conflicts and Political Legitimacy," *Philosophy and Public Affairs* 16 (1987): 216; emphasis in original.

3. John Rawls, *A Theory of Justice* (Cambridge, Mass.: Harvard University Press, 1971).

4. John Rawls, "The Independence of Moral Theory," presidential address delivered before the Seventy-First Annual Eastern Meeting of the American Philosophical Association, Washington, D.C., December 28, 1974; "Fairness to Goodness," *Philosophical Review* 84 (1975): 536–54; "The Basic Structure as Subject," in *Values and Morals,* ed. A. I. Goldman and J. Kim (Dordrecht: D. Reidel, 1978), 47–71; "Kantian Constructivism in Moral Theory," *Journal of Philosophy* 77 (1980): 515–72; "Justice as Fairness: Political, not Metaphysical," *Philosophy and Public Affairs* 14 (1985): 223–51; "The Idea of an Overlapping Consensus," *Oxford Journal of Legal Studies* 7 (1987): 1–25; "On the Idea of Free Public Reason," paper delivered under the auspices of the Conference for the Study of Political Thought, New York, May 1988; "The Priority of Right and Ideas of the Good," *Philosophy and Public Affairs* 17 (1988): 251–76.

5. Ronald Dworkin, *Taking Rights Seriously* (Cambridge, Mass.: Harvard University Press, 1977), 182.

6. Adina Schwartz, "Moral Neutrality and Primary Goods," *Ethics* 83 (July 1973): 298.

7. Rawls, "Constructivism."

8. Rawls: "Justice"; "Consensus"; "Public Reason."

9. Rawls, *Theory*, 263.

10. Robert Nozick, *Anarchy, State, and Utopia* (New York: Basic Books, 1974).

11. Michael J. Sandel, *Liberalism and the Limits of Justice* (Cambridge: Cambridge University Press, 1982), 66–77.

12. Rawls, *Theory*, 179.

13. Nozick, *Anarchy*, 228; emphasis in original.

14. Thomas Nagel, "Review of John Rawls, *A Theory of Justice*," *Philosophical Review* 82 (1973): 220–34.

15. Ibid., 227; emphasis added.

16. Ibid., 228–29.

17. Ibid., 230.

18. Ibid.

19. Rawls, *Theory*, 178; cited in Nagel, "Review," 232.

20. Nagel, "Review," 232.

21. Ibid., 233; emphasis added.

22. R. Dworkin, *Rights*, 152.

23. Rawls, *Theory*, 433.

24. Schwartz, "Moral," 297.

25. Ibid., 302.

26. Rawls, "Fairness to Goodness."

27. Gerald Dworkin, "Non-neutral Principles," *Journal of Philosophy* 71 (1974): 491–506.

28. Ibid., 503.

29. Rawls, *Theory*, 19–21, 48–51.

30. Rawls, *Theory*, 587; cited in William A. Galston, "Moral Personality and Liberal Theory: John Rawls's 'Dewey Lectures,'" *Political Theory* 10 (1982): 510.

31. Norman Daniels, "Wide Reflective Equilibrium and Theory Acceptance in Ethics," *Journal of Philosophy* 76 (1979): 258–59.

32. Schwartz, "Moral," 298.

33. Rawls, "Independence," 8.

34. W.V.O. Quine, *From a Logical Point of View* (New York: Harper Torchbooks, 1961), 42–43.

35. Rawls, "Constructivism."

36. Ibid., 518; cited in Galston, "Moral," 510–11; emphasis added.

37. Rawls, "Justice," 230 and 231ff.

38. Rawls, "Consensus," 1.

39. Rawls, "Public Reason," 1.

40. Michael Walzer, *Spheres of Justice* (New York: Basic Books, 1983).

41. Michael Walzer, *Interpretation and Social Criticism* (Cambridge, Mass.: Harvard University Press, 1987); Joshua Cohen, "Review of Michael Walzer, *Spheres of Justice*," *Journal of Philosophy* 83 (1986): 457–68.

42. Walzer, *Spheres*, 313; cited in Cohen, "Review," 466.

43. Cohen, "Review," 466.

44. Alasdair MacIntyre, *After Virtue*, 2d ed. (Notre Dame, Ind.: University of Notre Dame Press, 1984); Alasdair MacIntyre, *Whose Justice? Which Rationality?* (Notre Dame, Ind.: University of Notre Dame Press, 1988). Sandel, *Liberalism*.

45. Bernard Williams, "Persons, Character, and Morality," in *The Identities of Persons*,

ed. Amelie Oksenberg Rorty (Berkeley: University of California Press, 1976); cited in Galston, "Moral," 502–3.

46. Galston, "Moral," 502–3.

47. MacIntyre, *Justice*, chapter 17.

48. Rawls, "Constructivism," 545, cited in Galston, "Moral," 503.

49. Charles E. Larmore, *Patterns of Moral Complexity* (Cambridge: Cambridge University Press, 1987).

50. Ibid., 70.

51. Richard Rorty, *Contingency, Irony, and Solidarity* (Cambridge: Cambridge University Press, 1989), 65; emphasis in original.

52. Ibid., 92.

53. Nagel, *View*.

54. Ibid., 26.

55. This formulation presupposes the validity of Quine's argument in "Two Dogmas of Empiricism" (Quine, *Logical*, 20–46) that it is the totality of the statements that we take to be true that is hauled before the bar of experience in the face of any given adverse experience, and that therefore the line demarcating analytic and synthetic statements is shifting and pragmatic—ultimately (but not immediately) rectifiable in the light of experience.

56. Jean-François Lyotard, *The Postmodern Condition: A Report on Knowledge*, trans. Geoff Bennington and Brian Massumi (Minneapolis: University of Minnesota Press, 1984), 54.

Chapter 4

1. Jean-Jacques Rousseau, *The First and Second Discourses*, trans. Roger D. Masters and Judith R. Masters, ed. Roger D. Masters (New York: St. Martin's Press, 1964), 127.

2. Jean-Jacques Rousseau, *Emile; or, On Education*, trans. Allan Bloom (New York: Basic Books, 1979), 95.

3. Ibid., 89.

4. Ibid., 266–313.

5. Jean-Jacques Rousseau, *On the Social Contract*, trans. Judith R. Masters, ed. Roger D. Masters (New York: St. Martin's Press, 1978), 68.

6. There is an important exception to this in the case where the sovereign asks the citizen to serve in the military and defend the state. Where the citizen's life is jeopardized, he is permitted to place his own interest in staying alive above the sovereign's interest in protecting the state. "No law," says Hobbes, "can oblige a man to abandon his own preservation" (*Leviathan*, chapter 27).

7. Rousseau, *Social Contract*, 66.

Chapter 5

1. Jürgen Habermas, *Moral Consciousness and Communicative Action*, trans. Christian Lenhardt and Shierry Weber Nicholsen (Cambridge, Mass.: MIT Press, 1990), 43–45; Peter F. Strawson, *Freedom and Resentment and Other Essays* (London: Methuen, 1974), cited in Seyla Benhabib and Fred Dallmayr, eds., *The Communicative Ethics Controversy* (Cambridge, Mass.: MIT Press, 1990), 7.

2. Habermas, *Moral Consciousness*, 45.

3. Even though in Chapter 3 I cited with approval Nagel's "rezoning" of an agent's formulation of his reasons for action under the rubric of an objective account of his action (which seems to be evocative of the position of moral phenomenology), I interpret Nagel so that his position can most fruitfully be seen as endorsing a generalized agnosticism. I criticize other versions of moral phenomenology to the extent that they lay claim to a larger degree of objectivity than that allowed for by Nagel.

4. Jacques Derrida, in Richard Macksey and Eugenio Donato, eds., *The Structuralist Controversy* (Baltimore, Md.: Johns Hopkins University Press, 1972), 264–65.

5. Charles Taylor, *Human Agency and Language: Philosophical Papers I* (Cambridge: Cambridge University Press, 1985), 75.

6. William E. Connolly, "Taylor, Foucault, and Otherness," *Political Theory* 13 (1985): 366–67.

7. Charles Taylor, *Sources of the Self: The Making of the Modern Identity* (Cambridge, Mass.: Harvard University Press, 1989), 31.

8. Fred Dallmayr, *Margins of Political Discourse* (Albany: State University of New York Press, 1989), 57.

9. Friedrich Nietzsche, *On the Advantage and Disadvantage of History for Life*, trans. Peter Preuss (Indianapolis, Ind.: Hackett, 1980), 38.

10. The subjectivization is not transcended or ameliorated by invoking criteria of intersubjectivity as a basis for validating epistemological and moral judgments. The notion of intersubjectivity forms part of a surrogate vocabulary reflecting the absence of more objectivist canons of judgment. Intersubjectivity constitutes a second level in an argument whose first tier involves the radical subjectivization of judgment achieved through the historicizing and relativizing of epistemological concerns and perspectives. This second level of moral-phenomenological argument presupposes the validity of the first tier, which attempts, through historicizing techniques, to keep epistemology in its place. It is precisely the efficacy of these initial, facilitating moves that I am trying to call into question by the arguments adduced in the text.

The upshot of the generalized-agnostic approach that I pursue in the text is that theoretical space is cleared for such a doctrine as intersubjectivity (since our knowledge of objective reality remains incomplete, the idea of intersubjectivity might appropriately capture how our perceptions and judgments get built up without falling prey to the Scylla of an unbridled subjectivism or the Charybdis of an unattainable objectivism) while remaining faithful to the challenge of skepticism. Heidegger and the moral phenomenologist dismiss skepticism and relativism prematurely in carving out the primacy of ontology over epistemology. As I have indicated in the text, they are presupposing their theoretical efficacy in the course of "transcending" them, which is why their arguments remain viciously circular. The virtue of my generalized-agnostic approach to issues of skepticism and relativism is that it unflinchingly acknowledges their pervasiveness in argument (and shows how they are only sustainable as a generalized agnosticism) and, only after enabling them to run their course, illustrates how the counterchallenges of common sense, practical life, and moral deliberation can be met.

11. Jürgen Habermas, "Toward a Theory of Communicative Competence," in *Recent Sociology* 2, ed. Hans Peter Dreitzel (New York: Macmillan, 1970), 114–48; "Vorbereitende Bemerkungen Zu Einer Theorie der Kommunikativen Kompetenz," in Jürgen

Habermas and Niklas Luhmann, *Theorie der Gesellschaft oder Sozialtechnologie—Was Leister die Systemforschung?* (Frankfurt: Suhrkamp, 1971), 101–41; "Wahrheitstheorien," in *Wirklichkeit und Reflexion: Walter Schulz zum 60, Geburtstag,* ed. Helmut Fahrenbach (Pfullingen: Neske, 1973), 211–65; "Some Distinctions in Universal Pragmatics," *Theory and Society* 3 (1976): 55–67; "Was heisst Universalpragmatik?" in *Sprachpragmatik und Philosophie,* ed. Karl-Otto Appel (Frankfurt: Suhrkamp, 1976): 174–272; *Communication and the Evolution of Society,* trans. Thomas McCarthy (Boston: Beacon Press, 1979); *The Theory of Communicative Action, vol. 1, Reason and the Rationalization of Society,* trans. Thomas McCarthy (Boston: Beacon Press, 1984); *The Theory of Communicative Action, vol. 2, Lifeworld and System: A Critique of Functionalist Reason,* trans. Thomas McCarthy (Boston: Beacon Press, 1987); John B. Thompson, "Universal Pragmatics," in *Habermas: Critical Debates,* ed. John B. Thompson and David Held (Cambridge, Mass.: MIT Press, 1982), 116–33; Richard Rorty, "Habermas and Lyotard on Postmodernity," in *Habermas and Modernity,* ed. Richard J. Bernstein, (Cambridge: Polity Press, 1985), 161–75; Stephen K. White, *The Recent Work of Jürgen Habermas: Reason, Justice, and Modernity* (Cambridge: Cambridge University Press, 1988).

12. J. L. Austin, *Philosophical Papers* (Oxford: Oxford University Press, 1961); *How to Do Things with Words* (Oxford: Oxford University Press, 1962); John R. Searle, *Speech Acts: An Essay in the Philosophy of Language* (Cambridge: Cambridge University Press, 1970).

13. Habermas wants to build his case for a beachhead of rationality especially on what he calls "institutionally unbound speech-acts," but the criticisms that I direct against his positions in this chapter remain unaffected by this special emphasis.

14. Ludwig Wittgenstein, *Philosophical Investigations,* 3d ed., trans. G.E.M. Anscombe (New York: Macmillan, 1969).

15. Ronald Dworkin, *Taking Rights Seriously* (Cambridge, Mass.: Harvard University Press, 1977), 152.

16. Wittgenstein, *Investigations.*

17. Saul Kripke, *Wittgenstein on Rules and Private Language* (Oxford: Basil Blackwell, 1982).

18. Ibid., 7–8.

19. Ibid., 68–69.

20. Ibid., 73.

21. David Pears, *Ludwig Wittgenstein* (New York: Viking Press, 1970), 179.

22. Wittgenstein, *Investigations,* part I, 654–55.

23. Ibid., 109.

24. Ibid., 124.

25. The relationship between "language regions" and "language-games" can be formulated as follows: There is usually a plurality of language-games within particular language regions.

26. One cannot defend Wittgenstein at this point by saying that philosophy as a second-order discipline is necessarily parasitic upon other regions of discourse for its exercise, and that this extrapolation therefore does not constitute an illegitimate extension of philosophical method to other domains. Many other distinctive language regions, like the sciences (as analyzed in the *Tractatus* and the *Investigations,* for example), have features that can be transferred—legitimately or illegitimately—to other regions and have the potential for remaking them in their own image. It is the very

conceptualization of philosophy as a parasitic, second-order discipline that licenses the spread of philosophical terminology and techniques to all other regions of discourse that is at issue in the argument in the text.

27. Jürgen Habermas, "A Review of Gadamer's *Truth and Method*," in *Understanding and Social Inquiry*, ed. Fred Dallmayr and Thomas McCarthy (Notre Dame, Ind.: University of Notre Dame Press, 1977), 335–63.

28. It accommodates it only up to a certain point—but not completely. For if to believe that one can validate the critiques and self-critiques of reason is modernism, then to renounce such belief is postmodernism. From this perspective, one would have to say that Habermas and I are modernists. Habermas's modernism consists in his efforts to justify a minimalist infrastructure of rationality based upon the speech-act vocabulary. My modernism is more formal and procedural still—since it consists in arguing in defense of a generalized agnosticism as the most appropriate and revealing argumentative structure for capturing our foundationless theoretical plight.

29. Jürgen Habermas, "Philosophy as Stand-In and Interpreter," in *After Philosophy: End or Transformation?* ed. Kenneth Baynes, James Bohman, and Thomas McCarthy (Cambridge, Mass.: MIT Press, 1987), 296–315.

30. Ibid., 310.

31. Ibid., 311.

32. Habermas, "Gadamer."

33. Arthur C. Danto, *Analytical Philosophy of History* (Cambridge: Cambridge University Press, 1965), 17f.; cited in Habermas, "Gadamer," 349.

34. Jürgen Habermas, *The Philosophical Discourse of Modernity: Twelve Lectures*, trans. Frederick Lawrence (Cambridge, Mass.: MIT Press, 1987), 10–16.

35. Ibid., 10.

36. Walter Benjamin, *Illuminations*, ed. Hannah Arendt, trans. Harry Zohn (New York: Schocken Books, 1969), 261; cited in Habermas, *Discourse*, 10.

37. See chapter 8 of my book *Skepticism and Political Participation* (Philadelphia: Temple University Press, 1990) for an analysis of Maimonides as a precursor for this Benjaminite messianic conception.

38. Habermas, "Gadamer"; Hans-Georg Gadamer, *Philosophical Hermeneutics*, trans. and ed. David E. Linge (Berkeley: University of California Press, 1976), 26–36.

39. Habermas, "Gadamer," 361.

40. In the cases of Gadamer and Habermas, the skepticism is more inclusive than that suggested in the text. Mental concepts in the work of Gadamer and material concepts in the work of Habermas have a largely instrumental, pragmatic status.

Chapter 6

1. Leo Strauss, "The Mutual Influence of Theology and Philosophy," *Independent Journal of Philosophy/Unabhängige Zeitschrift fur Philosophie* 3 (1979): 117.

2. Leo Strauss, *The Rebirth of Classical Political Rationalism*, selected and introduced by Thomas L. Pangle (Chicago: University of Chicago Press, 1989), 169; emphasis in original.

3. Ibid., 142.

4. Moses Maimonides, *The Guide of the Perplexed*, trans. Shlomo Pines, introductory essay by Leo Strauss (Chicago: University of Chicago Press, 1963), xvi.

5. Ibid., xvi–xvii.

6. Ibid., liii.

7. Ibid., I:35:80. References throughout are to part, chapter, and page of the *Guide*.

8. Even though aderence to a multivalued logic violates Maimonides' own strictures concerning the implacableness of (Aristotelian) logical necessity—"the impossible has a stable nature, one whose stability is constant and is not made by a maker[—]it is impossible to change it in any way. Hence the power over the maker of the impossible is not attributed to the deity" (*Guide:* III:15:459)—the negative theological arguments that Maimonides makes insinuate a metatheory that is at odds with the one he officially endorses. This would not be the first time in the history of philosophy where the official theory espoused by a philosopher is in conflict with the metatheoretical conceptions he or she supports. One of the most instructive examples occurs in Hume's *Treatise* where his theory of personal identity is in sharp tension with the tenets of empiricism he has previously mentioned. Hume's case is remarkable on two counts: First, the suppressed tension comes to the surface and is acknowledged in the Appendix to the *Treatise;* and second, the most cogent strategy of resolution of the incoherence in Hume's argument seems to me remarkably isomorphic—if not directly continuous—with the most persuasive approach to take with regard to Maimonides' argument.

To illustrate: Hume in his theorizing of personal identity ends up with a self-referentialist dilemma that he is not able to overcome. If the self is a bundle of perceptions, and all our distinct perceptions are "distinct existences," and the mind never perceives any real connexion among "distinct existences" (David Hume, *A Treatise of Human Nature*, 2d ed., ed. L. A. Selby-Bigge and rev. P. H. Nidditch [Oxford: Oxford University Press, 1978], 636), then what is the status of the self that pronounces this judgment about the utter severability of the components of the self? Hume's theory of personal identity self-referentially collapses because it is not able to account for itself. A theoretical vantage point that notices that the self consists of nothing more than a bundle of perceptions has to itself consist of more than a bundle of perceptions. In the Appendix to the *Treatise*, Hume confesses that he is unable to fill in the gap in his argument. This gap can be overcome by attributing to Hume a generalized agnostic version of skepticism that leaves the door open for the possibility that a multivalued logic that maps the suspension of the law of excluded middle more accurately encodes reality than the traditional Aristotelian logic does. In that case our alternatives are increased beyond *A* and not-*A* and Hume could affirm that the self both does and does not consist in a bundle of perceptions. It does for all purposes except the occasion of theorizing this very position itself.

9. Maimonides, *Guide*, I:35:80.

10. Moses Maimonides, *Code, vol. 1, The Book of Knowledge*, trans. Moses Hyamson (New York: Feldheim Publishers, 1974), 66a–b, 67a.

11. As Josef Stern has pointed out to me, my construal of Maimonides in the text renders him vulnerable to David Hume's criticism in the *Dialogues concerning Natural Religion* that, since we have no conceptual or empirical grip on the concept of God, Maimonides has explained nothing by his invocation of him. Given my generalized-agnostic reading of Maimonides' negative theology, I would defend him at this point by saying that Hume's critique highlights how we need to scale down our expectations of what explanations in all spheres can achieve. Since our theoretical formulations cannot neutrally attest to their intersection with a reality outside themselves and the implicit circularity of all our arguments follows, there is at most only a difference in degree—but not one of kind—between our theological formulations and our scientific ones. In

both cases, the returns are not yet in—and we have only interim reports and interim hypotheses and speculations that at best only tenuously hook up with a not fully known reality. As I indicated in Chapter 2, as long as scientific and theological communities, as well as other bodies of inquirers and speculators, continue to provide us with interim and evolving notions of reality (which my generalized agnosticism is able to uphold), we have a notion of an "outside" (our theoretical formulations) that is stable enough to make sense of the enterprise of explanation.

12. Maimonides, *Guide*, xiv; Introduction: 6–7.

13. Jacques Derrida, *Writing and Difference*, trans. Alan Bass (Chicago: University of Chicago Press, 1978).

14. I am indebted to Josef Stern for pointing out to me that, for Maimonides, "first cause" and "necessarily existent" do not mean—or refer to—the same things (see *Guide*, II: 4: 258f.). Nevertheless, for purposes of the point that I am making in the text, their content is closely enough related for me to bracket them together.

15. Maimonides, *Guide*, II:13:282; II:28:334.

16. Leo Strauss, *Persecution and the Art of Writing* (Glencoe, Ill.: Free Press, 1952); Strauss, *Rationalism*, 63–71.

17. Maimonides, *Guide*, II:Introduction:235.

18. Plato, *The Republic and Other Works*, trans. Benjamin Jowett (Garden City, N.Y.: Doubleday Anchor Books, 1973), 389.

19. Charles Taylor, *Sources of the Self: The Making of the Modern Identity* (Cambridge, Mass.: Harvard University Press, 1989).

20. Strauss, *Rationalism*, 6.

21. Ibid., 8.

22. Ibid., 12.

23. Ibid., 16.

24. Ibid., 26.

25. Ibid., 36.

26. Ibid., 38.

27. Leo Strauss, *An Introduction to Political Philosophy*, ed. Hilail Gildin (Detroit, Mich.: Wayne State University Press, 1989), 114.

28. Strauss, *Rationalism*, 16.

29. Leo Strauss, *Natural Right and History* (Chicago: University of Chicago Press, 1953).

30. Cited in Strauss, *Introduction*, 113–14.

31. Strauss, *Rationalism*, 8.

32. Ibid., 142.

33. Ibid., 12.

34. Strauss: *Art*; *Rationalism*, 63–71.

35. Michael Polanyi, *Personal Knowledge: Towards a Post-Critical Philosophy* (Chicago: University of Chicago Press, 1958); *The Tacit Dimension* (Garden City, N.Y.: Doubleday Anchor Books, 1967).

36. Strauss, *Rationalism*, 29.

37. Strauss, *Introduction*, 148.

38. Ibid.

39. Strauss, *Rationalism*, 51.

40. Ibid., 57.

41. Strauss, *Introduction*, 313.
42. Ibid., 152.
43. Ibid., 318.
44. Robert Dahl, *Democracy and Its Critics* (New Haven, Conn.: Yale University Press, 1989).
45. Ibid., parts 4, 5, and 6.
46. From a sheerly logical perspective, a generalized agnosticism is compatible with both participatory democracy in the sense described in Chapter 3 and more conventional forms of liberalism, such as those embraced by Strauss on the right and Dahl on the left. The linkage between a generalized agnosticism and participatory democracy is predicated largely upon rhetorical affinities—such as the duplication of structures of argument discussed in Chapter 3.
47. Strauss, *Introduction*, 319.
48. Strauss's modernism thus corresponds in important respects to the conception of postmodernism I am advancing in this book.

Chapter 7

1. Daniel Yankelovich and William Barrett, *Ego and Instinct: The Psychoanalytic View of Human Nature—Revised* (New York: Vintage Books, 1971), 12–13.
2. Sigmund Freud, *An Outline of Psychoanalysis* (New York: W. W. Norton, 1969), 16.
3. Sigmund Freud, *Civilization and Its Discontents* (New York: W. W. Norton, 1961), 47; see also *Totem and Taboo*, standard ed. (London: Hogarth Press, 1955).
4. Jean-Paul Sartre, *Being and Nothingness*, trans. Hazel Barnes (London: Methuen, 1957).
5. One cannot point to the indictment of civilization in *Civilization and Its Discontents* as a counterexample to what I state in the text, because that indictment is deeply Rousseauistic. While it states that the psychological effects of advancing civilization are insidious, the advance itself is regarded as inevitable.
6. Freud, *Psychoanalysis*, 31–32.
7. Hannah Arendt, *The Human Condition* (Garden City, N.Y.: Doubleday Anchor Books, 1959), 222.
8. Thomas Hobbes, *Leviathan*, ed. Michael Oakeshott (Oxford: Basil Blackwell, 1946), chapter 5. Hobbes is thus a precursor of Freud not only in his mechanism but in his transcendence of mechanism.
9. The term "epic theorists" is famously Sheldon Wolin's.

Chapter 8

1. R. G. Collingwood, *The Idea of History* (London: Oxford University Press, 1963).
2. G.E.M. Anscombe, "On Brute Facts," *Analysis* 18 (1958): 69–72.
3. John R. Searle, *Speech Acts: An Essay in the Philosophy of Language* (Cambridge: Cambridge University Press, 1970), 41.
4. Ludwig Wittgenstein, *Tractatus Logico-Philosophicus*, trans. D. F. Pears and B. F. McGuinness (London: Routledge and Kegan Paul, 1961).
5. Ludwig Wittgenstein, *Philosophical Investigations*, 3d ed., trans. G.E.M. Anscombe (New York: Macmillan, 1969).

246 • Notes to Chapter 8

6. Wittgenstein, *Investigations*, 44, 47, 48, 49, 50, 51.

7. Ibid., 50.

8. This is Wittgenstein's conception—although as I have argued in Chapter 5 it does not actually square with what is going on. In Chapter 5, I analyze Wittgenstein in terms of what I take to be the critical import of his argument—that "philosophy" is attempting to establish its imperium over other language regions. In this chapter, I discuss the incoherencies attendant to taking Wittgenstein at face value—to expose the limitations of the argument taken in its own terms.

9. *The Republic of Plato*, trans. Francis MacDonald Cornford (Oxford: Oxford University Press, 1945), IX. 592.

10. Thomas Hobbes, *Leviathan*, ed. Michael Oakeshott (Oxford: Basil Blackwell, 1946), chapter 7.

11. The monistic epistemology in idealism can only work with—is dependent upon—a dualistic theory of human nature.

12. Are the perplexities that Wittgenstein addresses only generated by philosophers? The philosopher brings the puzzles and paradoxes to self-consciousness—but ordinary men and women generate puzzles and paradoxes anyway just by virtue of going about the daily business of living.

13. See Quentin Skinner, "The Context of Hobbes's Theory of Political Obligation," in *Hobbes and Rousseau*, ed. Maurice Cranston and Richard S. Peters (Garden City, N.Y.: Doubleday Anchor Books, 1972), 109–42; and "Political Thought and Political Action: A Symposium on Quentin Skinner," *Political Theory* 2 (August 1974).

14. Harold Bloom, *The Anxiety of Influence: A Theory of Poetry* (New York: Oxford University Press, 1973). Bloom offers a useful summary of his theory in chapter 1 of *Poetry and Repression: Revisionism from Blake to Stevens* (New Haven, Conn.: Yale University Press, 1976), 1–27.

15. His bitter satirical attacks on ancient modes of philosophizing and their lingering pernicious effects on the universities are strewn throughout *Leviathan*; see especially chapter 46. Specific references to Plato in Hobbes's political writings may be found in *Leviathan*, chapters 15, 25, 31, and 46, and in the epistle dedicatory to *The Elements of Law* (Tonnies ed.; reprint, London: Frank Cass, 1969). Compare Leo Strauss, *Natural Right and History* (Chicago: University of Chicago Press, 1953), 168ff.

16. Strauss, *Right*.

17. Compare Edward Shils, *The Intellectuals and the Powers and Other Essays* (Chicago: University of Chicago Press, 1972), 3; Sheldon Wolin, "Political Theory as a Vocation," in *Machiavelli and the Nature of Political Thought*, ed. Martin Fleisher (New York: Atheneum, 1972), 65–75.

18. This is a psychological twist on the theme of reflexivity.

19. On the centrality of the resoluto-compsite method in Hobbes, see J.W.N. Watkins, *Hobbes's System of Ideas* (London: Hutchinson University Library, 1965), 52–55. The way resoluto-composite method is fused with geometric method in Hobbes's work might be described as follows: The basic elements of man discovered by application of the resoluto part of the resoluto-composite method (which yields the axioms used by geometric method) become the first principles by which human nature is recomposed in pursuance of the composite side of that same method.

20. Hobbes, *Leviathan*, chapter 11.

21. As C. B. Macpherson has classically done in *The Political Theory of Possessive Individualism: Hobbes to Locke* (London: Oxford University Press, 1962), 9–106.

22. It involves the subordination of immediate impulses for the sake of the realization of pleasure and the avoidance of pain over the long run.

23. Hobbes, *Leviathan*, chapter 13.

24. For the role of metaphor generally in Hobbes's political philosophy, see the discussion in Sheldon Wolin, *Hobbes and the Epic Tradition of Political Theory* (William Andrews Clark Memorial Library: University of California, Los Angeles, 1970), 38–39.

25. Compare Leo Strauss, *The Political Philosophy of Hobbes: Its Basis and Its Genesis* (Chicago: University of Chicago Press, 1966), 130ff.

26. Hobbes, *Leviathan*, chapter 13.

27. Compare Strauss, *Right*, 181: "Death takes the place of the *telos*."

28. *The Republic*, trans. A. D. Lindsay (New York: E. P. Dutton, 1957), 303.

29. Ibid., 304.

30. Ibid., 309.

31. Ibid., 320–21.

32. Ibid., 335–36.

33. Ibid., 333.

34. Ibid., 342.

35. Ibid., 340.

36. Since for Hobbes the social contract largely serves as a summary term for a rational reconstruction of the bases of political obligation in civil society—and is not intended to refer to an actual historical event—it is integral to the political consciousness of all those required to obey the edicts of the state, that is, the whole community of citizens.

37. Hobbes, *Leviathan*, chapter 12.

38. Ibid.

39. Ibid.

40. Cited in Max Black, *Models and Metaphors* (Ithaca, N.Y.: Cornell University Press, 1972), 38.

41. Plato, *The Republic*, trans. Cornford, 18.

42. Ibid., 26.

43. Ibid., 356.

44. Hobbes, *Leviathan*, chapter 4.

Chapter 9

1. Jean-François Lyotard, *Peregrinations: Law, Form, Event* (New York: Columbia University Press, 1988).

2. Jean-François Lyotard and Jean-Loup Thébaud, *Just Gaming*, trans. W. Godzich (Minneapolis: University of Minnesota Press, 1985).

3. Terry Eagleton, *The Ideology of the Aesthetic* (Oxford: Basil Blackwell, 1990).

4. Lyotard, *Gaming*, 14–15; cited in Eagleton, *Aesthetic*, 387.

5. Eagleton, *Aesthetic*, 398.

6. Lyotard, *Gaming*, 18; cited in Eagleton, *Aesthetic*, 398.

7. Eagleton, *Aesthetic*, 400.

8. Lyotard, *Peregrinations*, 20–21.

9. Noncognitivism is a cognitivist position in the additional sense that it exceeds the warrant of its own formulation. If noncognitivism were strictly, literally true, one could not formulate one's not knowing (one's inability to know) into a bona fide philosophical position. Not knowing that one knows is already knowing more than one claims not to know.

10. Eagleton, *Aesthetic*, 400.

11. Lyotard, *Peregrinations*, 31–32.

Chapter 10

1. Terry Eagleton, *The Ideology of the Aesthetic* (Oxford: Basil Blackwell, 1990), 373.

2. Ibid.

3. Ibid.

4. Fred Hirsch, *Social Limits to Growth* (Cambridge, Mass.: Harvard University Press, 1976).

5. Robert L. Heilbroner, *An Inquiry into the Human Prospect* (New York: W. W. Norton, 1974), 50–55ff. Throughout this section of the book, "scarcity" is used in a loose way as a shorthand term for diminished economic growth that defies the classic remedies of the right, left, and center to ameliorate—it should not be construed in a literalistic, Club of Rome fashion. I use "scarcity" with the same penumbra of manageable vagueness that people have usually employed with the term "abundance."

6. Hudson Institute, *Synoptic Context One: The Prospects for Mankind and a Year 2000 Ideology* (Croton-on-Hudson, N.Y.: August 1, 1972, HI-1648/4D), 19.

7. Plato, *The Republic*, trans. Francis MacDonald Cornford (Oxford: Oxford University Press, 1945), 427 C–455.

8. Ibid., V. 474 B–480.

9. Ibid., VI. 497 A–502 C; VII. 535 A–541 B.

10. Ibid., III. 412 B–IV. 421 C; IV. 427 C–434 D.

11. Within the Auxiliary class, the spirited elements predominate over the rational elements and the passions, and within the Artisan class the passions predominate over the other two elements.

12. Edward Shils, "The Intellectuals and the Powers," in *The Intellectuals and the Powers and Other Essays* (Chicago: University of Chicago Press, 1972), 3–22. The passage quoted appears on p. 3.

13. Lionel Trilling, *Sincerity and Authenticity* (Cambridge, Mass.: Harvard University Press, 1972).

14. By "traditional" here, I mean specific traditions, those associated with medieval Christian society. Elsewhere in this chapter, I use "tradition" in the more formal sense defined above. The context should make it clear which sense is being referred to. My delineation of the relationship between "sincerity" and "tradition" roughly parallels Calvin Schrag's differentiation of modernity from premodernity in *Life-World and Politics*, ed. Stephen K. White (Notre Dame, Ind.: University of Notre Dame Press, 1989), 81–106.

Chapter 11

1. See my review of Duncan Forbes's *Hume's Philosophical Politics* in *Political Theory* (November 1976): 516–19.

2. Compare C. B. Macpherson, *The Political Theory of Possessive Individualism: Hobbes to Locke* (London: Oxford University Press, 1962).

3. Merrill Jensen, ed., *Tracts of the American Revolution: 1763–1776* (Indianapolis, Ind.: Bobbs-Merrill, 1967), 195.

4. I am indebted to Sheldon Wolin for formulations concerning Locke and American constitutionalism found in the text.

5. Cecelia M. Kenyon, ed., *The Anti-Federalists* (Indianapolis, Ind.: Bobbs-Merrill, 1966), 195.

Chapter 12

1. James David Barber, *The Presidential Character: Predicting Performance in the White House*, 3d ed. (Englewood Cliffs, N.J.: Prentice-Hall, 1985).

2. Ibid., 11–14.

3. Thomas Hobbes, *Leviathan*, ed. Michael Oakeshott (Oxford: Basil Blackwell, 1946), chapter 11.

4. While on a theoretical level the different priorities accorded the notion of self-interest in my two schemata have profound implications, on a practical level the varying status accorded the concept of self-interest issues forth in a difference of degree only. The extent of satisfaction granted particular claims under my first schema will obviously have a very important effect on which claims will be present, clamoring for satisfaction in the future. On a practical level, the distinction between procedure and substance quickly becomes blurred.

5. Hobbes, *Leviathan*, chapter 14.

6. Plato, *The Republic*, trans. Francis MacDonald Cornford (Oxford: Oxford University Press, 1945), 427C–441C; Jean-Jacques Rousseau, *The First and Second Discourses*, trans. Roger D. Masters and Judith R. Masters, ed. Roger D. Masters (New York: St. Martin's Press, 1964), 126–28, 137, 142–44; G. W. F. Hegel, *The Philosophy of Right*, trans. T. M. Knox (New York: Oxford University Press, 1967); Karl Marx, *Economic and Philosophic Manuscripts of 1844*, edited and introduced by Dirk J. Struik, translated by Martin Milligan (New York: International Publishers, 1964); Karl Marx, "On the Jewish Question," in *Writings of the Young Marx on Philosophy and Society*, ed. Lloyd D. Easton and Kurt A. Guddat (Garden City, N.Y.: Doubleday Anchor Books, 1967), 216–48; Karl Marx, *The Holy Family* (Moscow: Foreign Language Publishing House, 1953).

7. For an analytical breakdown of the possibilities confronting parties to the social contract into "state of nature," "lone defiance," and "status quo," see David Lewis, *Convention: A Philosophical Study* (Cambridge, Mass.: Harvard University Press, 1969), 88–96.

8. David Hume, *A Treatise of Human Nature*, 2d ed., edited by L. A. Selby-Bigge and revised by P. H. Nidditch (Oxford: Oxford University Press, 1978), book III, section ii. See also the discussion in John Rawls, *A Theory of Justice* (Cambridge, Mass.: Harvard University Press, 1971), 126–30.

9. Hume is writing in the Hobbesian tradition, with the rules of justice following automatically once the presuppositions of political obligation are clarified.

10. I am assuming throughout that a fully stabilized, resource-deficient world will still be highly advanced technologically. In fact, in order to retard the resource-depletion process, it is plausible to assume, I think, that both government and business will expend large efforts to have technology fill the breach created by a declining resource base. I consider this possibility later in the chapter.

11. There is a contradiction at the heart of social-contract theory that is resolved through the move indicated in the text. If man's natural condition is the inordinately selfish one enshrined in the term "state of nature," how can he ever manage to extricate himself from it and impose upon himself the bonds of political obligation? The classic social-contract theorists answer this question in approximately the same way. Their moral psychology is such, with reason serving in an instrumental capacity to realize the dictates of the passions, that they can point to a "shadow structure" of the self that acts in a more calculating, restrained fashion than the one that seems to predominate in the state of nature. It is the maturation of this other self that psychologically explains the transition from the state of nature to civil society.

12. The postmodernist agility in substituting contradictory sets of background assumptions—for example, what we diagnosed in Chapter 4 as Rousseau's pathbreaking invocation of a realist metaphysics to supplant Hobbesian nominalism, whose political consequences he found unacceptable—coheres very well with the displacement of the Priority of Political Obligation Schema by the Priority of Justice Schema discussed in the text. At the same time, the postmodernist backdrop to the argument—the emphasis that even the most basic assumptions of one's argument originate in human intervention and manipulation—is suggestive of the notion that prospects of human freedom are not being diminished by a shift from the Priority of Political Obligation to the Priority of Justice. The heightening of mass consciousness characteristic of postmodern society serves as a hedge against a glib identification of "political obligation" with liberty and "justice" with authoritarian control. Under a postmodernist political dispensation, there are more moves to the democratic political game than was envisioned in the less fully self-conscious skeptical atmosphere of political and cultural modernism.

13. See, for example, *Work in America: A Report of a Special Task Force to the Secretary of HEW* (Cambridge, Mass.: MIT Press, 1973).

14. See Lester Brown, "Rich Countries and Poor in a Finite-Interdependent World," *Daedalus* 102 (Fall 1973): 153–64; and Willard R. Johnson, "Should the Poor Buy No Growth?" *Daedalus* 102 (Fall 1973): 165–89.

15. Richard J. Barnet and Ronald E. Muller, *Global Reach: The Power of the Multi-National Corporations* (New York: Simon and Schuster, 1975).

16. Hobbes, *Leviathan*, chapter 16.

17. The distinction between the standing-for and acting-for aspects of representation—with the first being late medieval in origin and the second emerging into prominence in the seventeenth century—appears in the *Shorter Oxford English Dictionary*'s account of the word. For a cogent discussion of the nature of modern representation, see Harvey C. Mansfield, Jr., "Modern and Medieval Representation," in *Nomos X: Representation*, ed. J. Roland Pennock and John W. Chapman (New York: Atherton Press, 1968), 55–82, especially 80–82.

18. Hobbes, *Leviathan*, chapter 16.

19. For an excellent conceptual analysis, see Hanna Pitkin, *The Concept of Representation* (Berkeley and Los Angeles: University of California Press, 1967).

20. Hobbes, *Leviathan*, chapter 26.

21. Ibid., chapter 4.

22. Ibid., chapter 13.

23. Ibid.

24. Ibid., chapter 8.

25. Ibid., chapter 3.

26. Ibid., chapter 5.

27. Ibid.; emphasis added.

28. Compare Shirley Robin Letwin's discussion of Hobbes's conception of God, "Hobbes and Christianity," in *Daedalus* 105 (Winter 1976): 1–21.

29. Blaise Pascal, *Pensées*, trans. W. F. Trotter (New York: Dutton, 1958), fragment 206.

30. Hobbes, *Leviathan*, chapter 14.

31. Hobbes thus seeks to substitute the salutary, coordinated distance of civil society for the menacing, uncoordinated distance of the state of nature.

32. Hobbes, *Leviathan*, chapter 15.

33. My argument in defense of a substantive theory of justice has to do with the delineation of an appropriate political rhetoric for a postindustrial civilization—and neither requires nor presupposes epistemological justification in the conventional philosophical sense.

34. Compare Theodore J. Lowi, *The End of Liberalism*, 2d ed. (New York: W. W. Norton, 1979).

35. For a conception of metaphysics as intellectual history—and of the history of philosophy as philosophy—see R. G. Collingwood, *An Essay on Metaphysics* (Oxford: Clarendon Press, 1940), and *An Autobiography* (Oxford: Oxford University Press, 1970).

36. On the emergence of re-charismatized bureaucracies in the former Soviet Union, see Cyril E. Black, "New Soviet Thinking," *New York Times*, November 24, 1978.

37. I owe this phrase to Professor Manfred Halpern of Princeton.

38. In 1937, Roosevelt's plan to "pack" the Supreme Court failed, but in short order the Court shifted its attention away from economic issues. When this occurred, the stage was set for a reorientation of the Court's role as one of the primary guardians of civil liberties in American society.

39. The major period of quiescence occurred during the tenure of the Vinson Court from the late 1940s to the middle 1950s.

40. Two major formulations of the pluralist model are Robert Dahl, *Who Governs?* (New Haven, Conn.: Yale University Press, 1961), and David Truman, *The Governmental Process*, 2d ed. (New York: Alfred A. Knopf, 1961). An important critique of pluralism is found in Peter Bachrach and Morton S. Baratz, *Power and Poverty: Theory and Practice* (New York: Oxford University Press, 1970).

41. Steven Lukes, *Power: A Radical View* (London: Macmillan, 1974).

42. A major purpose of this part of the book has been to overcome the difficulty described in the text by delineating the possibilities of a temporal—as opposed to a spatial—politics.

43. Niccolò Machiavelli, *The Prince*, trans. George Bull (Baltimore, Md.: Penguin Books, 1961), 50–51.

Chapter 13

1. I am indebted to Bruce Jennings for this formulation.

2. Carole Pateman, *Participation and Democratic Theory* (Cambridge: Cambridge University Press, 1970).

3. Compare R. G. Collingwood, *The Idea of History* (Oxford: Oxford University Press, 1946).

Chapter 14

1. Plato, *The Republic*, trans. Francis MacDonald Cornford (Oxford: Oxford University Press, 1945), 18.

2. Ibid., 26.

3. Ibid., 44.

4. Ibid., 31–32.

5. Thomas Hobbes, *Leviathan*, ed. Michael Oakeshott (Oxford: Basil Blackwell, 1946), Introduction.

6. Ibid., A Review and Conclusion.

7. The identification of intellectual work with a secondary, reactive level of classification instead of a primary level of action is in tension with the formulation (see Chapter 13) of "power of rationality," where Hobbes's nominalism is construed as endorsing the view that the allocation of words and their significations remains "arbitrary" and that therefore power becomes the very syntax through which rationality gets expressed. This constitutes another example of how the postmodernist perspective that I am developing in this book leaves us free to invoke alternative sets of presuppositions to the statements that we make and how raw linguistic formulations do not predetermine the sets of presuppositions that are appropriate for them. The enhanced freedom flowing from greater analytical self-awareness is comparable to my argument in Chapter 12 that assigning primacy to the Priority of Justice Schema over the Priority of Political Obligation is still compatible with the preservation of liberal democratic values. This contradictory construal of the metaphysical postulates to adopt as background to Hobbesian nominalism is suggestive of another point, emphasized in Chapters 3 and 7, that from a postmodernist perspective theory devolves into action ("the action is the theory"). Since, as we saw in Chapter 8, "actions" constitute ideal-limits for an unceasing activity of interpretation, the whole process of fixing the content for any statement or action is suggestive of endless deferral—of all the statements and all the actions from the beginning of time existing in a state of suspended animation, awaiting an unraveling that gets transferred to the next statement or action.

Chapter 15

1. Michael Oakeshott, *Rationalism in Politics and Other Essays* (Indianapolis: Liberty Press, 1991), 489–90.

2. Isa. 11:6–7. Trans. Israel W. Slotki (London: Soncino Press, 1949).

3. Ibid., 2:4.

Bibliography

Anscombe, G.E.M. "On Brute Facts." *Analysis* 18 (1958): 69–72.

Arendt, Hannah. *The Human Condition*. Garden City, N.Y.: Doubleday Anchor Books, 1959.

———. *The Origins of Totalitarianism*. New York: Harcourt, Brace, 1951.

Austin, J. L. *How to Do Things with Words*. Oxford: Oxford University Press, 1962.

———. *Philosophical Papers*. Oxford: Oxford University Press, 1961.

Bachrach, Peter, and Morton S. Baratz. *Power and Poverty: Theory and Practice*. New York: Oxford University Press, 1970.

Bachrach, Peter, and Aryeh Botwinick. *Power and Empowerment: A Radical Theory of Participatory Democracy*. Philadelphia: Temple University Press, 1992.

Barber, Benjamin R. "Jihad vs. McWorld." *Atlantic Monthly* 269 (March 1992): 53–65.

Barber, James David. *The Presidential Character: Predicting Performance in the White House*. 3d ed. Englewood Cliffs, N.J.: Prentice-Hall, 1985.

Barnet, Richard J., and Ronald E. Muller. *Global Reach: The Power of the Multi-National Corporations*. New York: Simon and Schuster, 1975.

Benhabib, Seyla. "Lyotard, Democracy, and Difference: Reflections on Rationality, Democracy, and Postmodernism." Paper presented at the 1992 Annual Meeting of the American Political Science Association. Chicago, Illinois, September 3–6, 1992.

Benhabib, Seyla, and Fred Dallmayr, eds. *The Communicative Ethics Controversy*. Cambridge, Mass.: MIT Press, 1990.

Benjamin, Walter. *Illuminations*. Edited by Hannah Arendt. Translated by Harry Zohn. New York: Schocken Books, 1969.

Bernstein, Richard J. "Fred Dallmayr's Critique of Habermas." *Political Theory* 16 (1988): 580–93.

Black, Cyril E. "New Soviet Thinking." *New York Times*, November 24, 1979.

Black, Max. *Models and Metaphors*. Ithaca, N.Y.: Cornell University Press, 1972.

Bloom, Harold. *The Anxiety of Influence: A Theory of Poetry*. New York: Oxford University Press, 1973.

———. *Poetry and Repression: Revisionism from Blake to Stevens*. New Haven, Conn.: Yale University Press, 1976.

Botwinick, Aryeh. *Skepticism and Political Participation*. Philadelphia: Temple University Press, 1990.

Brown, Lester. "Rich Countries and Poor in a Finite-Interdependent World." *Daedalus* 102 (Fall 1973): 153–64.

Cohen, Joshua. "Review of Michael Walzer, *Spheres of Justice*." *Journal of Philosophy* 83 (1986): 457–68.

Collingwood, R. G. *An Autobiography*. Oxford: Oxford University Press, 1970.
———. *An Essay on Metaphysics*. Oxford: Clarendon Press, 1940.
———. *The Idea of History*. Oxford: Oxford University Press, 1946.
Connolly, William E. "Taylor, Foucault, and Otherness." *Political Theory* 13 (1985): 365–76.
Cooper, John M. *Reason and Human Good in Aristotle*. Cambridge, Mass.: Harvard University Press, 1975.
Dahl, Robert. *Democracy and Its Critics*. New Haven, Conn.: Yale University Press, 1989.
———. *Who Governs?* New Haven, Conn.: Yale University Press, 1961.
Dallmayr, Fred. "Habermas and Rationality." *Political Theory* 16 (1988): 553–79.
———. *Margins of Political Discourse*. Albany: State University of New York Press, 1989.
———. "Post-Metaphysics and Democracy." Paper delivered at the 1990 Annual Meeting of the American Political Science Association. San Francisco, August 30–September 2, 1990.
Daniels, Norman. "Wide Reflective Equilibrium and Theory Acceptance in Ethics." *Journal of Philosophy* 76 (1979): 256–82.
Danto, Arthur C. *Analytical Philosophy of History*. Cambridge: Cambridge University Press, 1965.
Davidson, Donald. *Inquiries into Truth and Interpretation*. Oxford: Clarendon Press, 1984.
Derrida, Jacques. "Structure, Sign, and Play in the Discourse of the Human Sciences." In *The Structuralist Controversy*, edited by Richard Macksey and Eugenio Donato, 247–65. Baltimore, Md.: Johns Hopkins University Press, 1972.
———. *Writing and Difference*. Translated by Alan Bass. Chicago: University of Chicago Press, 1978.
Dworkin, Gerald. "Non-neutral Principles." *Journal of Philosophy* 71 (1974): 491–506.
Dworkin, Ronald. *Taking Rights Seriously*. Cambridge, Mass.: Harvard University Press, 1977.
Eagleton, Terry. *The Ideology of the Aesthetic*. Oxford: Basil Blackwell, 1990.
Fish, Stanley. *Self-Consuming Artifacts: The Experience of Seventeenth-Century Literature*. Berkeley: University of California Press, 1972.
Freud, Sigmund. *Civilization and Its Discontents*. New York: W. W. Norton, 1961.
———. *An Outline of Psychoanalysis*. New York: W. W. Norton, 1969.
———. *Totem and Taboo*. Standard ed. London: Hogarth Press, 1955.
Friedman, Thomas L. "As Some Nations Build, the Past Devours Others." *New York Times,* July 12, 1992, 4–1.
Gadamer, Hans-Georg. *Philosophical Hermeneutics*. Translated and edited by David E. Linge. Berkeley: University of California Press, 1976.
Galston, William A. "Moral Personality and Liberal Theory: John Rawls's 'Dewey Lectures.'" *Political Theory* 10 (1982): 492–519.
Habermas, Jürgen. *Communication and the Evolution of Society*. Translated by Thomas McCarthy. Boston: Beacon Press, 1979.
———. *Moral Consciousness and Communicative Action*. Translated by Christian Lenhardt and Shierry Weber Nicholsen. Cambridge, Mass.: MIT Press, 1990.
———. *The Philosophical Discourse of Modernity: Twelve Lectures*. Translated by Frederick Lawrence. Cambridge, Mass.: MIT Press, 1987.
———. "Philosophy as Stand-In and Interpreter." In *After Philosophy: End or Transforma-*

tion? edited by Kenneth Baynes, James Bohman, and Thomas McCarthy, 296–315. Cambridge, Mass.: MIT Press, 1987.

———. "A Review of Gadamer's *Truth and Method.*" In *Understanding and Social Inquiry,* edited by Fred Dallmayr and Thomas McCarthy, 335–63. Notre Dame, Ind.: University of Notre Dame Press, 1977.

———. "Some Distinctions in Universal Pragmatics." *Theory and Society* 3 (1976): 55–67.

———. *The Theory of Communicative Action. Vol. 1, Reason and the Rationalization of Society.* Translated by Thomas McCarthy. Boston: Beacon Press, 1984.

———. *The Theory of Communicative Action. Vol. 2, Lifeworld and System: A Critique of Functionalist Reason.* Translated by Thomas McCarthy. Boston: Beacon Press, 1987.

———. "Toward a Theory of Communicative Competence." In *Recent Sociology* 2, edited by Hans Peter Dreitzel, 114–48. New York: Macmillan, 1970.

———. "Vorbereitende Bemerkungen Zu Einer Theorie der Kommunikativen Kompetenz." In Jürgen Habermas and Niklas Luhmann, *Theorie der Gesellschaft oder Sozialtechnologie—Was Leister die Systemforschung?* 101–41. Frankfurt: Suhrkamp, 1971.

———. "Wahrheitstheorien," in *Wirklichkeit und Reflexion: Walter Schulz zum 60, Geburtstag,* edited by Helmut Fahrenbach. Pfullingen: Neske, 1973.

———. "Was heisst Universalpragmatik?" In *Sprachpragmatik und Philosophie,* edited by Karl-Otto Appel, 174–272. Frankfurt: Suhrkamp, 1976.

Hegel, G.W.F. *The Philosophy of Right.* Translated by T. M. Knox. New York: Oxford University Press, 1967.

Heilbroner, Robert L. *An Inquiry into the Human Prospect.* New York: W. W. Norton, 1974.

Hirsch, Fred. *Social Limits to Growth.* Cambridge, Mass.: Harvard University Press, 1976.

Hobbes, Thomas. *The Elements of Law.* Tonnies ed. Reprint. London: Frank Cass, 1969.

———. *Leviathan.* Edited by Michael Oakeshott. Oxford: Basil Blackwell, 1946.

Hoffmann, Stanley. "Delusions of World Order." *New York Review of Books* 39 (April 9, 1992): 37–43.

Hudson Institute. *Synoptic Context One: The Prospects for Mankind and a Year 2000 Ideology.* Croton-on-Hudson, N.Y.: August 1, 1972.

Hume, David. *Dialogues concerning Natural Religion.* Edited by Norman Kemp Smith. Oxford: Clarendon Press, 1935.

———. *A Treatise of Human Nature.* 2d ed. Edited by L. A. Selby-Bigge and revised by P. H. Nidditch. Oxford: Oxford University Press, 1978.

Isaiah. Translated by Israel W. Slotki. London: Soncino Press, 1949.

Jensen, Merrill, ed. *Tracts of the American Revolution: 1763–1776.* Indianapolis: Bobbs-Merrill, 1967.

Johnson, Willard R. "Should the Poor Buy No Growth?" *Daedalus* 102 (Fall 1973): 165–89.

Kaus, Mickey. "For a New Equality." *New Republic,* May 7, 1990, 18–27.

Kenyon, Cecelia M., ed. *The Anti-Federalists.* Indianapolis, Ind.: Bobbs-Merrill, 1966.

Kripke, Saul. *Wittgenstein on Rules and Private Language.* Oxford: Basil Blackwell, 1982.

Laclau, Ernesto. "Interview." *Strategies* 1 (Fall 1988): 10–28.

Larmore, Charles E. *Patterns of Moral Complexity.* Cambridge: Cambridge University Press, 1987.

Lefort, Claude. *Democracy and Political Theory.* Translated by David Macey. Minneapolis: University of Minnesota Press, 1988.

Letwin, Shirley Robin. "Hobbes and Christianity." *Daedalus* 105 (Winter 1976): 1–21.

Levenson, Joseph R. *Confucian China and Its Modern Fate.* 3 vols. Berkeley: University of California Press, 1958–65.

Lewis, David. *Convention: A Philosophical Study.* Cambridge, Mass.: Harvard University Press, 1969.

Lowi, Theodore J. *The End of Liberalism.* 2d ed. New York: W. W. Norton, 1979.

Lukes, Steven. *Power: A Radical View.* London: Macmillan, 1974.

Lyotard, Jean-François. *Peregrinations: Law, Form, Event.* New York: Columbia University Press, 1988.

———. *The Postmodern Condition: A Report on Knowledge.* Translated by Geoff Bennington and Brian Massumi. Minneapolis: University of Minnesota Press, 1984.

Lyotard, Jean-François, and Jean-Loup Thébaud. *Just Gaming.* Translated by W. Godzich. Minneapolis: University of Minnesota Press, 1985.

MacDonald, Bradley J. "Toward a Redemption of Politics: An Introduction to the Political Theory of Ernesto Laclau." *Strategies* 1 (Fall 1988): 5–9.

Machiavelli, Niccolò. *The Prince.* Translated by George Bull. Baltimore, Md.: Penguin Books, 1961.

MacIntyre, Alasdair. *After Virtue.* 2d ed. Notre Dame, Ind.: University of Notre Dame Press, 1984.

———. *Whose Justice? Which Rationality?* Notre Dame, Ind.: University of Notre Dame Press, 1988.

Macpherson, C. B. *The Political Theory of Possessive Individualism: Hobbes to Locke.* London: Oxford University Press, 1962.

Maimonides, Moses. *Code. Vol. 1, The Book of Knowledge.* Translated by Moses Hyamson. New York: Feldheim Publishers, 1974.

———. *The Guide of the Perplexed.* Translated by Shlomo Pines. Introductory essay by Leo Strauss. Chicago: University of Chicago Press, 1963.

Mansfield, Harvey C. Jr. "Modern and Medieval Representation." in *Nomos X: Representation,* edited by J. Roland Pennock and John W. Chapman, 55–82. New York: Atherton Press, 1968.

Marx, Karl. *Economic and Philosophic Manuscripts of 1844.* Edited and introduced by Dirk J. Struik. Translated by Martin Milligan. New York: International Publishers, 1964.

———. *The Holy Family.* Moscow: Foreign Language Publishing House, 1953.

———. "On the Jewish Question." In *Writings of the Young Marx on Philosophy and Society,* edited by Lloyd D. Easton and Kurt A. Guddat, 216–48. Garden City, N.Y.: Doubleday Anchor Books, 1967.

Mates, Benson. *Skeptical Essays.* Chicago: University of Chicago Press, 1981.

Nagel, Thomas. "Moral Conflicts and Political Legitimacy." *Philosophy and Public Affairs* 16 (1987): 215–40.

———. Review of John Rawls, *A Theory of Justice. Philosophical Review* 82 (1973): 220–34.

———. *The View from Nowhere.* Oxford: Oxford University Press, 1986.

Nietzsche, Friedrich. *On the Advantage and Disadvantage of History for Life.* Translated by Peter Preuss. Indianapolis, Ind.: Hackett, 1980.

Nozick, Robert. *Anarchy, State, and Utopia.* New York: Basic Books, 1974.

Oakeshott, Michael. *Rationalism in Politics and Other Essays.* Indianapolis: Liberty Press, 1991.

Offe, Claus. "Capitalism by Democratic Design? Democratic Theory Facing the Triple Transition in East Central Europe." *Social Research* 58 (1991): 864–92.

Pascal, Blaise. *Pensées*. Translated by W. F. Trotter. New York: Dutton, 1958.

Pateman, Carole. *Participation and Democratic Theory*. Cambridge: Cambridge University Press, 1970.

Pears, David. *Ludwig Wittgenstein*. New York: Viking Press, 1970.

Pfaff, William. "The Absence of Empire." *New Yorker* 68 (August 10, 1992): 59–69.

Pitkin, Hanna. *The Concept of Representation*. Berkeley and Los Angeles: University of California Press, 1967.

Plato. *The Republic*. Translated by Francis Macdonald Cornford. Oxford: Oxford University Press, 1945.

———. *The Republic*. Translated by A. D. Lindsay. New York: E. P. Dutton, 1957.

———. *The Republic and Other Works*. Translated by Benjamin Jowett. Garden City, N.Y.: Doubleday Anchor Books, 1973.

Polanyi, Michael. *Personal Knowledge: Towards a Post-Critical Philosophy*. Chicago: University of Chicago Press, 1958.

———. *The Tacit Dimension*. Garden City, N.Y.: Doubleday Anchor Books, 1967.

"Political Thought and Political Action: A Symposium on Quentin Skinner." *Political Theory* 2 (August 1974).

Quine, W.V.O. *From a Logical Point of View*. New York: Harper Torchbooks, 1961.

———. *Ontological Relativity and Other Essays*. New York: Columbia University Press, 1969.

———. *The Ways of Paradox and Other Essays*. New York: Random House, 1966.

Rawls, John. "The Basic Structure as Subject." In *Values and Morals*, edited by A. I. Goldman and J. Kim, 47–71. Dordrecht: D. Reidel, 1978.

———. "Fairness to Goodness." *Philosophical Review* 84 (1975): 536–54.

———. "On the Idea of Free Public Reason." Paper delivered under the auspices of the Conference for the Study of Political Thought. New York: May 1988.

———. "The Idea of an Overlapping Consensus." *Oxford Journal of Legal Studies* 7 (1987): 1–25.

———. "The Independence of Moral Theory." Presidential address delivered before the Seventy-First Annual Eastern Meeting of the American Philosophical Association, Washington, D.C., December 28, 1974.

———. "Justice as Fairness: Political, not Metaphysical." *Philosophy and Public Affairs* 14 (1985): 223–51.

———. "Kantian Constructivism in Moral Theory." *Journal of Philosophy* 77 (1980): 515–72.

———. "The Priority of Right and Ideas of the Good." *Philosophy and Public Affairs* 17 (1988): 251–76.

———. *A Theory of Justice*. Cambridge, Mass.: Harvard University Press, 1971.

Riley, Patrick. "The Voice of Michael Oakshott in the Conversation of Mankind." *Political Theory* 19 (1991): 334–36.

Rorty, Richard. *Contingency, Irony, and Solidarity*. Cambridge: Cambridge University Press, 1989.

———. "Habermas and Lyotard on Postmodernity." In *Habermas and Modernity*, edited by Richard J. Bernstein, 161–75. Cambridge: Polity Press, 1985.

Rousseau, Jean-Jacques. *Emile; or, On Education*. Translated by Allan Bloom. New York: Basic Books, 1979.

———. *The First and Second Discourses*. Translated by Roger D. Masters and Judith R.

Masters. Edited by Roger D. Masters. New York: St. Martin's Press, 1964.

———. *On the Social Contract.* Translated by Judith R. Masters. Edited by Roger D. Masters. New York: St. Martin's Press, 1978.

Sandel, Michael J. *Liberalism and the Limits of Justice.* Cambridge: Cambridge University Press, 1982.

Sartre, Jean-Paul. *Being and Nothingness.* Translated by Hazel Barnes. London: Methuen, 1957.

Schrag, Calvin. "Rationality between Modernity and Postmodernity." In *Life-World and Politics: Between Modernity and Postmodernity,* edited by Stephen R. White, 81–106. Notre Dame, Ind.: University of Notre Dame Press, 1989.

Schwartz, Adina. "Moral Neutrality and Primary Goods." *Ethics* 83 (July 1973): 294–307.

Searle, John R. *Speech Acts: An Essay in the Philosophy of Language.* Cambridge: Cambridge University Press, 1970.

Shils, Edward. *The Intellectuals and the Powers and Other Essays.* Chicago: University of Chicago Press, 1972.

Skinner, Quentin. "The Context of Hobbes's Theory of Political Obligation." In *Hobbes and Rousseau,* edited by Maurice Cranston and Richard S. Peters, 109–42. Garden City, N.Y.: Doubleday Anchor Books, 1972.

Strauss, Leo. *An Introduction to Political Philosophy.* Edited by Hilail Gildin. Detroit, Mich.: Wayne State University Press, 1989.

———. "The Mutual Influence of Theology and Philosophy." *The Independent Journal of Philosophy/Unabhängige Zeitschrift fur Philosophie* 3 (1979): 111–18.

———. *Natural Right and History.* Chicago: University of Chicago Press, 1953.

———. *Persecution and the Art of Writing.* Glencoe, Ill.: Free Press, 1952.

———. *The Political Philosophy of Hobbes: Its Basis and Its Genesis.* Chicago: University of Chicago Press, 1966.

———. *The Rebirth of Classical Political Rationalism.* Selected and introduced by Thomas L. Pangle. Chicago: University of Chicago Press, 1989.

Strawson, Peter F. *Freedom and Resentment and Other Essays.* London: Methuen, 1974.

Talmon, J. L. *The Origins of Totalitarian Democracy.* London: Secker and Warburg, 1952.

Taylor, Charles. *Human Agency and Language: Philosophical Papers 1.* Cambridge: Cambridge University Press, 1985.

———. *Philosophy and the Human Sciences: Philosophical Papers 2* Cambridge: Cambridge University Press, 1985.

———. *Sources of the Self: The Making of the Modern Identity.* Cambridge, Mass.: Harvard University Press, 1989.

Thompson, John B. "Universal Pragmatics." In *Habermas: Critical Debates,* edited by John B. Thompson and David Held, 116–33. Cambridge, Mass.: MIT Press, 1982.

Trilling, Lionel. *Sincerity and Authenticity.* Cambridge, Mass.: Harvard University Press, 1972.

Truman, David. *The Governmental Process.* 2d ed. New York: Alfred A. Knopf, 1961.

Walzer, Michael. *Interpretation and Social Criticism.* Cambridge, Mass.: Harvard University Press, 1987.

———. *Spheres of Justice.* New York: Basic Books, 1983.

Watkins, J.W.N. *Hobbes's System of Ideas.* London: Hutchinson University Library, 1965.

White, Stephen K. *The Recent Work of Jürgen Habermas: Reason, Justice, and Modernity.* Cambridge: Cambridge University Press, 1988.

Williams, Bernard. "Persons, Character, and Morality." In *The Identities of Persons*, edited by Amelie Oksenberg Rorty, 197–216. Berkeley: University of California Press, 1976.

Wittgenstein, Ludwig. *Philosophical Investigations*. 3d ed. Translated by G.E.M. Anscombe. New York: Macmillan, 1969.

———. *Tractatus Logico-Philosophicus*. Translated by D. F. Pears and B. F. McGuinness. London: Routledge and Kegan Paul, 1961.

Wolin, Sheldon. *Hobbes and the Epic Tradition of Political Theory*. William Andrews Clark Memorial Library: University of California, Los Angeles, 1970.

———. "Political Theory as a Vocation." In *Machiavelli and the Nature of Political Thought*, edited by Martin Fleisher, 23–75. New York: Atheneum, 1972.

Work in America: A Report of a Special Task Force to the Secretary of HEW. Cambridge, Mass.: MIT Press, 1973.

Yankelovich, Daniel, and William Barrett. *Ego and Instinct: The Psychoanalytic View of Human Nature—Revised*. New York: Vintage Books, 1971.

Index